Advance Praise for *The American Dream*

"*The American Dream* by Robert Russell is a consummate account of entrepreneurial financial success obtained through free market capitalism. Russell has assembled a remarkable gallery of seventeen life stories – heroic, tragic, moving – of individuals who achieved financial independence through owning a small business. Based on personal interviews and drawing on his extensive business experience, Russell weaves a factual, thoroughly researched, finely detailed account of each of the individual stories.

"*The American Dream* is a tribute to the spirit of entrepreneurial success and is highly recommended to interested readers."

—**Robert J. Smat, M.S., PhD.**, Organic Research Chemist and Patent Agent E. I. du Pont de Nemours and Co.(retired)

"*The American Dream* by Bob Russell reminds us that the great American success story has been achieved by many North American families. Bob documents the childhood experiences, family life, development of core values, set-backs, and opportunities of his friends and personal acquaintances. Bob's examination explains what happened; however, the question of why is really the central theme of the book.

"Why did these individuals achieve the dream? The book provides many answers including hard work, family values, good fortune, opportunities recognized, a focus on the longer term and unselfish attitudes. In the last section of the book, Bob reflects on whether these same values remain within the American culture and the negative consequences of losing theses ideals.

"The book can be stimulating or distressing. If you be'' cannot regain these values, the book will leave vo· and dwelling on the past. If you see this b·

these values, you will find inspiration. Either way, it is worthwhile to read, as it is a reflection of American culture."

— **Gary W. Rodgers Ph.D**, Professor, Florida Southwestern State
College, Colorado State University-Global Campus

"Bob Russell's book is a resounding endorsement of free market capitalism as told through 17 life stories of entrepreneurs who have achieved significant financial success. These success stories expose and affirm the common thread of a strong work ethic. The stories present excellent testimonies of the amazing potential for financial success when persistent hard work is loosed within an economic system that both encourages and rewards self-motivation.

"Russell's storytelling style reveals many of the personal characteristics and circumstances of these entrepreneurs. Some of the stories even dig deeply into childhood events that helped shape the attitudes that contributed to successful outcomes. This book will no doubt give readers confirmation that free market capitalism, even in the face of strong doses of government red tape and regulation, is the supreme economic system that affords the best possible opportunity for financial success and personal happiness."

— **Professor Tim Allen, Ph.D.**, CCIM, Eminent Scholar and
Alico Chair in Finance, Lutgert College of Business
Florida Gulf Coast University

THE

AMERICAN

DREAM

*Inspiring Life Stories of Entrepreneurs
Who Achieved Financial Success
Through Free Market Capitalism*

Robert J. Russell

Book design and Production by Bookwrights
Cover by Bookwrights
Editing by Natasha Welcher

Printed in the United States of America

Dedication

I'm dedicating this book to my parents, Clarence and Genevieve Russell, for their love and influence on me. Nobody could have had better parents who worked harder to provide a good life for their children. They were always there for me. I'm so proud of them that I've included their life story in this book.

I was also encouraged by my sister, Dorothy French, and her children for what they called inspirational writings to her children. They said I should write a book. I have called on Dorothy numerous times for suggestions on this book.

My sister, Pat Wilock, has been one of my biggest boosters since I was her bratty little brother. I embarrassed her so many times in my youth yet she always had time for me and encouraged me to be the best I could be. She was also a big inspiration for me in writing this book.

I want to thank my friends for allowing me to write their life stories. They spent a lot of time and effort giving me their life histories. They took a chance on me since I had no real writing experience.

Introduction

I wrote this book to celebrate our free market economy and to honor those who have achieved The American Dream through owning a small business. Many books have been written about the great tycoons of past and present who have owned large businesses but not about the unsung entrepreneurs who have owned small businesses. I wanted to write about average people who worked hard and through determination made their dreams come true. Some of these successful entrepreneurs I met during my career as a banker and others I met while playing golf, tennis or bridge during my retirement. I've always been interested in the lives and careers of others and particularly the life stories of entrepreneurs In the Heritage Palms Golf and Country Club community where I live in Fort Myers, Florida, I've come in contact with a lot of successful people, who for the most part, started with nothing and achieved The American Dream. Some of them had little formal education but were smart, talented and dedicated to providing a product or service that was needed. Some of the ways that people achieved financial independence were quite surprising and even astounding. It seems that all successful people have interesting life stories but I've found the life stories of entrepreneurs to be inspirational. Not only have these people achieved great things for themselves and their families but also for their employees, customers and society in general.

When the Pilgrims landed at Plymouth Rock in 1620 they adopted a "communal economic system" in which each family farmed their own plot of land and shared it with the rest of the community. Each family planted and tended their crops through harvest when all the crops were gathered and placed in a central place to be shared by everyone as needed. This didn't work well for obvious reasons. Some farmers worked very hard from sunup to sunset planting, weeding and harvesting their crops. Some others weren't quite as ambitious and started work late in the fields and quit early. Some were downright lazy and produced very little food. The result was near starvation during the first couple of winters.

After the first couple of years, the ambitious families were disappointed that they were producing more but not getting all the fruits of their labor. They had enough of the communal economic system. The ambitious were tired of the lazy and less productive taking advantage of their hard work and enterprise. It was finally decided that each family would be responsible for providing for their own family and would keep the fruits of their labor. The "free enterprise system" was born. Under the free enterprise system, production increased substantially with the ambitious working even harder and the less ambitious and lazy working much harder too. When the less productive had to fend for themselves, they had a much bigger interest in having a productive harvest because there was a direct link between what they produced and how they were able to live. Everyone adopted the farming practices of the more successful. This resulted in a Thanksgiving Day feast to celebrate their bountiful harvest.

This is much like the college professor who gave a lesson in economics to his class. Most of the students believed that in life everyone deserved the same piece of the pie, because not everyone had the same opportunities or capabilities. Most agreed it was fair for the more prosperous states and communities to be taxed more so that extra money could be given to the less prosperous states and communities. The students wanted to see more than equal opportunity—they wanted to see equal outcomes. This has been popular thought for the last half century. Politicians have been elected by promising to tax the successful more in order to give to the less successful. This mentality has led Detroit, Michigan, the most prosperous city in the nation in 1961, to bankruptcy in 2013.

The college professor set out to prove that people are more generous with other peoples' money than they are with their own. The students believed that socialism worked because it was fair with everyone getting an equal share of the pie. To prove the students wrong, the professor agreed to have an experiment. On the next test, all the grades were averaged and everyone got a "B." The students who studied hard were upset and the students who studied little were happy. Knowing that all their grades were going to be averaged together in the future, most of the students didn't bother to study for the next test. The average score on the second test was a "C" so each student received that grade. Each succeeding test resulted in lower test scores and grades and eventually the entire class received a grade of "F." The professor then explained that socialism would also ultimately fail, because when the reward is great, the effort to succeed is great, but when the reward is taken away there is no incentive to work hard. Once incentive is taken away production and achievement decline. I believe all students should be taught about the great success of capitalism and the dismal failures of socialism.

Small businesses are the backbone of our economy and our country and deserve to be applauded for their accomplishments. Starting a small business is very difficult and success requires a lot of hard work and determination. It is also very risky in that usually the owners save money for years and put up everything they have as collateral with a lender to get started. If the business fails they may lose everything including their home and livelihood. So, if the business fails and they lose everything, they must start over without even a job. According to the United States Small Business Administration, more than 50% of businesses fail in the first five years and less than 1/3 survive 10 years.

According to the SBA, two out of every three jobs are created by small business and they employ about 50% of the private sector work force making them vital to the growth and prosperity of our nation. Small business is also vital in reducing costs and efficiencies through competition. That is, in order to succeed a small business must provide a product or service better than someone else. Competition requires that businesses get better and better or new competition will come along and take away their business. It is this competition that keeps companies striving to be better in order to grow and not be driven out of business by others. Some would say that the free market is a cut-throat type of market with everyone trying to outdo the other and take away their business. However, for consumers it is wonderful because it results in better products and services at lower costs.

We can see how competition has improved our lives by some of the inventions and products we buy such as televisions and computers. I remember back in 1951 my parents bought our first television set, a 17 inch Philco black and white table model. I believe they paid about $500 for it and we could only watch three or four channels from Chicago. The TV reception was not very good. Since 1951 the US dollar has lost 89% of its purchasing power, yet you can buy a much better 17 inch color television today for around $100. In today's dollars that television in 1951 cost more than $4,500 or 45 times more than a similar TV today. The same is true of computers. In 1993 a 64-gigabyte computer cost around $3,000 and a much better similar capacity computer today costs around $300. In today's dollars that computer in 1993 cost over $4,800 or 15 times more than the same capacity computer today. Yes, competition drives down costs and improves quality and service. This is the magic of free market capitalism.

The Merriam-Webster dictionary defines Socialism as "any of various economic and political theories advocating collective or governmental ownership and administration of the means of production and distribution of goods." It is amazing sometimes to look around my neighborhood and realize that within five minutes of my home there are several super markets, a Wal-mart, Lowe's Home Improvement, Home Depot, Walgreen's, CVS , several clothing stores and many other stores too numerous to mention. All of these stores are open long hours seven days per week with some open as much as 24 hours per day. Of course, this is not true of government offices. In the old socialist Soviet Union, Union of Soviet Socialist Republic, I understand that people would go to the government market and stand in line for hours only to learn that the store was out of meat and other items. They operated much like our government offices with inconvenient hours and long lines. Why are no government offices open during hours that are convenient to their customers? The answer seems to be that government values its employees more than it values its taxpayers and customers for which it is supposed to serve. Of course, competition would solve this problem.

In our free market economy we have all kinds of competition and the stores almost never run out of what we need. There is incentive up and down the line from the farmer to the supermarket to ensure we have everything we might want. Workers and management up and down the food chain have incentives to make certain the store shelves are full of fresh food products at very competitive prices. Free market capitalism is truly a miracle.

World Bank economist, Branko Milanovic, reported in his book, "The Haves and the Have-Nots" in 2011, that the top 1% of individual incomes in the world make $34,000 annually after income taxes. That is, for a family of four, the top 1% have an income of $136,000 (4 x 34,000). He said that almost 48% of the top 1% of income earners live in the US and that Germany was second with only 7%, followed by France, Italy and the UK with 5% each. He reports that the poorest people in developed countries like the US are wealthy by global standards. He says the poorest 5% of Americans earn about the same as the richest 5% in India. Since the beginning of time, most people have lived under tyranny with little freedom. Yes, we are so lucky to live in the US where free market capitalism has made even its poorest citizens among the richest in the entire world.

This book includes 17 life stories of friends of mine who played by the rules, worked hard and achieved financial independence and The American Dream through free market capitalism. Capitalism is under assault today because it is not understood. If it were not for capitalists like Henry Ford of Ford Motor Company who made automobiles affordable for the average family, our lives would be quite different. He used the concept of mass production on an assembly line to reduce the cost of the automobile to make it affordable for the masses. Ford, Henry Kaiser of Kaiser Industries, Albert Sloan of General Motors and many other industrialists converted their manufacturing facilities to building tanks, airplanes and ships to save our country. With our free enterprise system, we were able to overwhelm Germany and Japan.

In his book, "How Free Enterprise Saved Civilization," Steve Forbes tells about how unprepared we were for World War II and how FDR called on free enterprise and the large capitalists to win the War. In 1939, General George Patton had to order spare parts for his tanks directly from Sears & Roebuck. At the beginning of the War we had the 18th strongest military in the world, about equal to that of the Netherlands, even though we had the largest industrial base. Unfortunately, capitalism is not taught in our public schools so kids today and many adults don't understand that it is the primary reason for our country becoming the greatest and strongest nation the world has ever known. Just imagine what our country would have been like if not for free enterprise. It is hard to overstate that the might of free enterprise saved our country and if not for the miracle of free enterprise we might be speaking German or Japanese today.

If you have an inspirational story of achieving financial independence through free market capitalism, please contact me at: rjr1142@yahoo.com

Contents

Jim Holton

Jim and his wife, Camille, live in a beautiful home over-looking the 10th green of the Sable Golf Course here in Heritage Palms Golf and Country Club. I first met Jim while playing a round of golf and riding in the same golf cart with him. We engaged in conversation and his life story so amazed me that it helped inspire me to write this book about life stories of the entrepreneurs I've known. This is the life story of a man who literally started with nothing and through hard work and determination was able to start a concrete cutting and drilling business and in 36 years turned it into a multi-million dollar business with 25 trucks on the road. During this time, Jim and Camille raised two great children and truly achieved The American Dream.

Jim is a very likeable and handsome man who has a great personality. And he can really pound a golf ball too. Everyone likes Jim. Camille said he was always fair and honest with his employees and they all liked and respected him. These qualities make a great salesman, and they helped Jim get started and succeed in his business. Knocking around from one job to another in his early years gave Jim a background and experience in all facets of construction which added to his success. Working on the family farm in his youth, and running machinery and milking cows by hand helped to form his work ethic. Jim gives a lot of credit to Camille for their success.

Jim's paternal grandparents were born in Iowa. His paternal grandfather was born William Holton in 1876 and his paternal grandmother was born Mary Barnable in 1883. William was a farmer and Mary was a wife and homemaker who raised five children. His maternal grandfather was born Jean Pierre Barthole in 1874 and his maternal grandmother was born Marieanne Kirsch on January 25, 1879. Both were born in Bissen, Luxemburg. Both immigrated to this country and grew up in Iowa. He was a farmer and she was a school teacher. Jim's father was born James Patrick Holton on February 25, 1910 in Iowa and became a dairy farmer but he also raised pigs and chickens. Jim's mother was born Margaret Suzanne Barthole also on February 25, 1910, the exact same day as his father, and was a wife and homemaker. Jim thinks they must have been meant to be together. His parents married in 1931. Jim was born James Nicholas Holton on December 6, 1937, the third child, into an Irish Catholic family of 9 children, with 2 brothers and 6 sisters. His oldest sister, Shirley, was born in 1932 and his youngest sister, Maureen, was born in 1954. Jim believes his father had so many children so he would have plenty of help on the farm for more than two decades.

Jim remembers getting home from school when he was eight or nine years old around 5pm and it was his job to drive the cows from the pasture to the barn for milking. He would take his German Shepherd dog and off they would go to get the cows. They had a Holstein bull in the pasture along with the cows and he weighed around 2,000 pounds. For some reason, bulls are always nasty. Often the bull would hoot, holler and snort and also throw dirt with his hoofs as a prelude to charging. Jim always felt pretty secure because the dog was there to protect him and would always scare the bull away. This particular day, Jim wondered what would happen if the dog chased a rabbit and Jim was left alone to fend for himself. It was a scary thought but that was one of the dangers of living on the farm.

Jim said that life on the farm, in his younger years, was great with plenty of fun things to do like playing ball with his brothers and sisters. It was a rugged life with very cold winters and lots of snow in northwest Iowa. They had no indoor plumbing and no matter the weather you had to go to the outhouse when nature called. Sometimes it would be as cold as -20 degrees and three feet of snow. Jim said on those days and nights you didn't linger in the outhouse. In the winter his mother taught them to play cards and there was always a puzzle on the table to put together. There was always something to do. That changed somewhat when Jim was about 10 years old and he began helping his father with the farm work. They had about 12 cows at the time and Jim started milking cows by hand—he said he would milk one or two cows while his father milked all the others.

Everything in the winter was more difficult. When the temperature got below zero degrees it wasn't unusual for the pipes to freeze in the barn, sometimes requiring that water had to be hand-carried to all the livestock. It was sometimes difficult to start the tractors and other machinery. The silage was sometimes frozen in the silo and everything took longer than in nice weather. During the winter months, working with the livestock was the major farm activity. Besides milking the cows twice each day, once in the morning and again in the evening, it took a lot of time and work to keep all the animals fed and comfortable. When it was very cold the cows stayed in their stanchions all day and night except for a few hours each day while the barn was being cleaned. The manure had to be removed and fresh straw was put under the cows so they would be comfortable lying on the cement floor. The barn had to be thoroughly cleaned and limed to pass inspections of the milk company to whom they sold their milk each day. The milk company inspectors could show up at any time and if the entire barn, milk house, etc. were not spotless they could shut you down until it was brought back up to their standards.

Jim also started working in the fields running a John Deere model B tractor whenever he could. In the spring, summer and fall there was plenty of farm work to do. Besides taking care of the livestock there was a lot of work to do in the fields. During the planting season in April and May there was plowing, disking, dragging and planting the crops. In the summer there was cultivating, weed spraying, baling hay and straw and harvesting the oats, wheat and rye. Jim said it always seemed like baling hay and straw occurred during the hottest days. Once the hay and straw were baled it was loaded onto a hayrack and taken to the barn. There it was stored in the haymow and it was always like an oven up there. When it rained and he thought of goofing off for a while his dad would say they had to fix fence. The farm had a river running through it and when it rained the water current often washed away the fence that crossed the river. In order to keep the cattle from getting away it would have to be repaired. If it wasn't repaired right away you might be awakened in the middle of the night by a neighbor saying your cattle were out; everyone would have to chase the cattle for several hours until they were all located and returned to the pasture. When fixing fence it was usually a hot and muggy day when the mosquitoes and other bugs were at their worst. It was unpleasant work. The job Jim hated worst, though, was cleaning the roosts in the chicken laying house. That was 100% pure manure and it gave off a terrible odor.

In the fall, there was the harvest of the corn and silage. Harvesting corn silage occurred in September and harvesting the corn was done mostly in November. They left the standing corn in the field as late as they dared to let it dry because if you harvested too early the corn would need to be dried or otherwise it would spoil in the corn crib. Jim liked working with equipment and he also enjoyed taking things apart and putting things such as clocks and radios back together again. Jim admits that he was more successful taking them apart than putting them back together again. He was always interested in how things worked and he liked working with his hands. He believes that is why he later got into handling a lot of equipment as an adult.

When he was about 10 years old they got their first television set which was a big event. It was 1947 when his family got a 12 inch black and white Zenith. They could get three channels out of Sioux City, Iowa. He remembers that first night, sitting around the television until midnight until the test pattern came on, and they thought that was the greatest thing in the world. When Jim was about 11 years old he started playing Little League baseball and they played a couple of games per week plus practice. Jim used to ride a bicycle to town, which was about three miles, to the games and practices. Later he played American Legion, and then high school baseball in his freshman and sophomore years. In his junior year his family moved to another farm, about 10 miles away, and he attended a new school where he finished the last two years of high school. The new high school didn't have a baseball team so that was the end of his baseball career. Jim modestly says he wouldn't have gone very far in baseball anyhow.

When Jim graduated from high school in 1955, he said he wasn't college material and didn't know what he wanted to do. He just bounced around from job to job. He worked as a meat-cutter, which was inside work six days per week, and he didn't like it. He felt like he wanted to get outside so he quit. In the summer, he worked for a concrete company, and then an asphalt company, and then a natural gas pipeline company came through town and he got a job with them as a welder's helper. With this company he moved around Iowa and Oklahoma and ended up in Dallas, Texas. But that wasn't for Jim either so he quit and went back home. He then got a job with a telephone company installing telephone lines, so he ended up climbing telephone poles and putting up crossbars, insulators and running the wire. He worked at that for one summer. That job didn't seem like it had any great opportunities for the future so he quit that job. A guy in Sioux City who he knew had an airplane had heard of a job in St. Louis. They flew down to St. Louis in his private airplane and got a job pushing barges down the Mississippi River. He would work two weeks and then get one week off with pay, and they would fly back to Sioux City for the one week they had off. Jim thought it was the greatest job so he worked that one summer and when the fall came he headed back home.

Then he joined the United States Army in 1959. He went to Fort Knox, Kentucky for basic training and then to Germany for 1½ years. While in the Army he met a guy who worked for the airlines and he thought it was a great job. Jim was undecided as to what he would do when he was discharged so he applied for a job with Northwest Airlines and got a job at Midway Airport in Chicago. He worked at the service counter checking people in, issuing tickets, etc.

When O'Hare Field became O'Hare International Airport in 1961, Jim was sent there. He was actually working at the counter there when the very first airplane landed at O'Hare. Jim remembers that the Chicago Sun Times came out and took a picture of him at the counter, sitting with his head in his hands indicating how bored he was because there were no customers. When customers did show up and started asking questions he couldn't answer them because he had no idea where anything was since they had just arrived the previous day. There were three terminal buildings at O'Hare and it was quite a large facility compared to Midway Airport but he soon got the hang of it and learned where everything was located and could accurately answer all the customer questions. He worked there for a while and then one winter they needed help down in Fort Lauderdale, Florida for three or four months because of the influx of people in Florida. Jim thought it would be great to be in a warm climate for the winter so he spent the winter in Fort Lauderdale. Jim said he wasn't making that much money, was living alone and was barely surviving.

When the winter ended Jim met a guy who told him if he ever wanted a good job to give him a call because he had a good job for him in Detroit. So, before heading back to Chicago to his old job at O'Hare Airport, he gave this guy a call and was told to come to Detroit. Jim jumped on an airplane to Detroit. This guy was involved in the manufacture of diamond blades and diamond bits. He told Jim he didn't have a job at that time but he suggested that he go to work for another guy in the air tool business until he had an opening. He told Jim it would be good experience for him. So, Jim went to work for Michigan Air Tool in Detroit.

When Jim was working for Northwest Airlines in Chicago he met a very beautiful young Italian lady named Camille who was working at the insurance counter across the lobby. Jim pursued her and over the next couple years they dated and continued their long distance relationship while Jim spent the winter in Fort Lauderdale. They decided to get married in 1966 and just at that time the guy who had the diamond blade company called and said he had an opening for Jim at his company and wanted him to come aboard. So Jim quit his job at the air tool company and went to Chicago and got married. Jim and Camille went on a one week honeymoon to Las Vegas and then went back to Detroit to start his new job as a salesman for the diamond blade company. Jim said, "It wasn't the greatest job in the world", as he was paid $175 per week with no expenses covered and he had to drive his own car. After about one year they finally gave him a credit card for the purchase of gasoline which was very helpful. In the meantime, Camille became pregnant with their first child and in 1967 their daughter, Christine, was born.

The company for which Jim worked bought its diamond blades from a company in Chicago and private labeled them under its name and sold them. Jim said it was a good product. As stated earlier, Jim was paid $175 per week and in addition they started paying him a bonus of 2% if sales exceeded $30,000 in any one month. In the summer he had the possibility of reaching that number but not so in the winter months. Jim thought his job was not all that lucrative. In early 1968, the company started making its own diamond blades instead of buying from the provider from Chicago. This product was bad and inferior to the product Jim had been selling. Instead of cutting 3,000 feet of concrete with the old blades, Jim's customers were only able to cut about 300 feet with these inferior blades. Jim was losing customers and wasn't making any commissions. One day he visited a customer, Joe Carlo, who told him "Jim, you can come and see me anytime but don't bring me anymore of these blades." Jim went back to the office and dropped the blades on the owner's desk and said, "I can't sell this stuff." Jim said they were all depressed and they acted like he had said something bad about one of their kids. They didn't like the fact that he was critical of their product and so Jim could see the handwriting on the wall and decided it was the beginning of the end. Jim told the sales manager that he was leaving and going back to Chicago where Camille's relatives lived in hopes of finding a better job. With that the sales manager said, "If you're leaving, then I'm also leaving and maybe we can do something together." That sounded good to Jim.

There was a man in Toronto with whom they had done business, Gordon Carpenter, who called himself the "king of diamonds" and who sold the diamond bits to distributors in Canada. Gordon said he would like to get something going in the "States" so he agreed to fund a new business for Jim and his friend for a share of the profits. In October of 1968, they both quit their jobs and started a new company called Cougar Cutting Products. Gordon was funding the business with enough money so they could get their weekly paychecks. They hooked up with a diamond supplier from California which had an excellent product and gave Jim's new company generous terms. They began selling diamond blades and core bits and then they hooked up with a saw manufacturer to sell saw blades. They were just barely getting by.

In December of 1968, Gordon called and said he was having a hard time because he was pumping money into the business but not seeing any returns and he wanted out of the deal. Jim agreed to let him out of the deal and to continue on by himself. Gordon asked for a refund of the money he had put into the business and they would be all square and Jim agreed. Jim went back to Detroit and explained to Camille why there would be no paycheck that week and how Gordon was out of the business and they were on their own. Jim says this was not a good time of year to start any new business but particularly a business selling diamond blades when there was no road work.

They started working out of their basement with Camille doing the books, the statements, invoicing and collecting the money. They made it through the winter because their suppliers were so generous giving Jim's company 90 days and sometimes 120 days to pay their bills. Sometimes their paychecks were a little small and sometimes there was no paycheck at all. As Jim was calling on his customers, he was being told they had no need for diamond blades or core bits because they hired contractors who furnished their own. However, he found that some customers were having trouble getting a contractor to do concrete drilling and sawing and thought they were missing out on some business. Jim had been selling to these types of contractors but had never had a drill or saw in his hand and therefore knew little of that business.

One customer told Jim that he had a job in Port Huron which was about a two hour drive requiring the cutting of 1,000 feet of six inch deep concrete. Jim pondered the idea and called a manufacturer of saws in Chicago and bought a concrete saw for $1,800 on 90 day credit terms. Jim had a friend who was a saw man for a local concrete company and he had a pickup truck and saw trailer. They found a 250 gallon water drum in a vacant yard which they commandeered and put it in his pickup truck, put the saw on his trailer and at 5am they headed to Port Huron to do this job. They sawed all day long and Jim got a chance to use the saw and learn how to operate it. They completed the sawing of 1,000 feet and got home about 9pm. Now Jim was in the concrete sawing business.

Jim's partner was more of a sales guy than working with his hands and wanted nothing to do with the sawing of concrete. Jim decided to try this new business on his own and he set up a new business called Cougar Contracting. During the day he would go out soliciting work and if he picked up a job sawing concrete he would go home, change clothes and do the job. He bought a pickup truck and trailer and he would put a water tank in the pickup and two saws on the trailer and away he would go. He would also saw on weekends if he had to. Little by little they started getting enough work so that he was able to hire a man to do the concrete sawing for him. Then a couple of customers wanted Jim to core drill for them. Jim bought a core drill, a concrete van, some drill bits and started coring holes in floors for plumbers and electricians. One customer wanted him to drill in a wall but Jim didn't know how to hold the drill to do that work. So, he hired another contractor to actually do the work. Jim met him at the job and watched how he anchored the drill to the wall. After learning how it was done Jim had to buy a hammer drill and some bits and he was now in the concrete drilling business.

Things went on and he got a little more work and he finally moved his business out of the basement and into a building. As business grew, they bought another saw and Jim was still doing the work while calling on customers to get new business. As the years went by the workload increased and Jim got more operators and vans that were loaded with everything necessary to be self sufficient on the jobs. They didn't need anyone and just went out and did the work.

They picked up a job in Flint, Michigan at the water treatment plant where they drilled 50 or 60 holes that were 12 inches wide through a huge wall. They drilled those holes, and at the time they thought they were really top notch contractors, but Jim learned years later that 12 inch holes were commonplace. By the time Jim sold the company they were drilling holes as large as 60 inches in diameter through big 12 foot sewer pipe and other things. They drilled huge holes with hydraulic equipment. They did their first job of concrete sawing at a depth of six inches and they thought that was a big deal with a 60horse-power Wisconsin air cooled engine on the saw. Eventually they worked their way up to using 95 and 100 horsepower diesel engines and sawing 24 inch depths in concrete with huge 54 inch diamond blades.

As they went along they started doing some wall sawing in concrete, such as door openings out of poured concrete walls. The machine would attach to the wall and run on a track up, across the wall, and back down. Before that, they used jackhammers to make the openings, but the jackhammers made a mess requiring hours of cleanup when they were done. The saw resulted in clean, simple and perfect openings with no cleanup. The industry has really evolved and Jim eventually had 1,000 gallon water tanks on the trucks and was doing a lot of work on highways cutting patches out and replacing the joints. This work is done with traffic running by at speeds of up to 80 miles per hour, making the work quite dangerous. Fortunately, they didn't have any total disasters, but one time a truck drove through some barricades and crashed into his trailer and truck and hit one of his operators. Fortunately, he came out of it with no permanent damage.

On the drilling side they had a lot of nice jobs like with Ford Motor Company, where they had to drill through a 20 foot wall and come out within two inches on the opposite side. The great part about this business was the bidding of the job by figuring out how the work was to be done and then performing the work in such a way as to make the predicted profit on time and have a satisfied customer. There was a lot of satisfaction in bidding the job and then getting the operators together and determining how the job could best be performed and then actually doing the work. When it all came together correctly it was a beautiful thing but when it didn't it was unpleasant. Jim says his operators were the key to his success in that many were very good and made it work. Some didn't, but that's just like in any business. One matter that was very important to Jim was getting to the job on time and the only possible excuse for being late was because of unusual traffic congestion. All trucks were equipped with two way radios and later with cell phones, allowing them to keep the customers informed in the event of a delay. Also, all trucks were equipped with a GPS device so Jim could keep track of where each truck was at any time. He could even tell if his drivers were speeding. It was very important to get to the job on time but Jim didn't want any traffic tickets.

Jim said he went into his own business so he could have control of the situation, make the decisions and then make it happen. That was the satisfaction that made it all worthwhile. Whether the job was up on the Ambassador Bridge taking out patches or down in a tunnel somewhere sawing whatever, it didn't make any difference. Every job was important and it was very satisfying to look at a job, bid the job and have good people there to perform the work. When the work was done he was able to walk away with everyone being happy with the results.

After 36 years in business, Jim sold his business and retired in 2004 and now spends his retirement between his homes in Michigan and Ft. Myers. Jim still looks in on the business, calls the new owner to see how he is doing, visits job sites with him and gives him any type of help that he needs. The new owner worked for Jim for 25 years so he pretty much knows how to operate the business. He kept it going and kept the name of Cougar Contracting and Jim is proud that it is still ongoing in the Michigan area.

Jim and Camille are especially proud of their two children. Christine, now age 46, attended Pinkney High School, earned a Bachelor's Degree in Communications from Central Michigan University and a Master's Degree in Adult Education from St. Louis University. She formed her own company called, "A Dynamic Speaker" and is now a motivational speaker. She has traveled all over the United States, Canada and Australia giving motivational speeches. She is married with two children, Camille and Donavan. Coincidentally, Camille has the same birthday as her grandmother, Camille, as well as the same first name.

Their son, James Jerome Holton, age 43, wanted absolutely nothing to do with the concrete sawing and drilling business. He attended Pinkney High School and graduated from Central Michigan University with a business degree. His college was located in Mount Pleasant, Michigan which is about 100 miles north of the summer residence of Jim and Camille. In 1995 he renovated the old train depot in Mount Pleasant into a steakhouse called Mountain Town Station where he also brews beer, which is his favorite thing to do. In 2007, he started a micro brewery called Mountain Town Brewery which is now the fifth largest brewery in Michigan. He has distributors throughout Michigan and recently opened up distributors throughout Indiana and Ohio. He is doing well.

In conclusion, Jim said his goal for the business was to make a decent living for his family and be able to control his destiny. He credits his farm background as being responsible for the discipline which helped him to succeed. Jim is naturally proud that he was able to provide jobs for a lot of people over the years and these people were not just his employees but also his friends. Over the years they all made a good living and without those employees Jim said there was no way they would have succeeded like they did. He said the satisfaction of starting with nothing, absolutely nothing, and with the help of suppliers and employees, to be able to stay in business for 36 years is a feat in itself. The fact that they started with absolutely nothing and built it into a multi-million dollar company was great satisfaction for Jim and Camille.

Jim says that after a while Camille no longer did the books but she did what she could, she raised the family, was a great housewife and was Jim's support throughout this entire ordeal. As Jim's friend, I think Jim and Camille have a lot for which to be proud. Not only was their business a great success but importantly they were able to raise two wonderful responsible children, also entrepreneurs, who are also on their way to achieving The American Dream through free market capitalism.

Joe Eaton

Joe and Nancy Eaton

This is the life story of a man who started with nothing except great character and desire and through determination and hard work achieved The American Dream. I have known Joe and his wonderful wife, Nancy, since 1976 when I worked with her. I also knew Nancy's parents who were farmers and her father was one of my mentors when I worked for the Farm Credit System. I am honored to have been Joe's banker and to witness his great story of success both personally and in business. You will see in Joe's life story his great sense of humor and how he credits his father for his determination, discipline and work ethic. His story should be an inspiration to young people looking for a way to achieve The American Dream.

Joe's father was born Harry R. Eaton in Pecatonica, Illinois in 1928 the fourth oldest of five children. Harry's parents and grandparents were farmers. His mother was sort of an early adopter of women's rights. She did not cook or clean their house but paid for these services by training horses for other women. She was an elegant and strong-willed lady and demanded civility and manners even when Joe and his brothers were small children. Joe thinks his father's deep respect for women resulted from this woman. Joe's mother was born Mary P.Tarbert in Pecatonica in 1932 the fifth of six children. Her family lived in Pecatonica—her mother worked at a small assembly shop and her father worked for the public school system.

Joe's father graduated from Pecatonica High School in 1945 and immediately joined the US Army. He was on a troop carrier headed for the war in the Pacific Ocean when the war ended and he became part of the occupying force in Japan. When he returned home he decided his future was not in farming and spent time working at a factory job and as a carpenter for a few years. During this time he married Mary Tarbert in March 1951. Joe was born on February 24, 1952, the oldest of six sons. The first four sons were born at two year intervals while the last two sons were born later. By the time his youngest brother was one year old and in diapers, Joe was 16 years old and had a driver's license. Joe's parents had children in their house for a total of 35 years.

Joe's uncle, his father's brother-in-law, was a lineman for the local gas and electric company. One of Joe's earliest memories was going with his father to see his uncle's lineman's tools. Joe's father was accepted into the line apprenticeship and worked the next 38 years as a lineman, crew leader and supervisor. Joe says his father was a good husband, good father, good provider and a good man. Harry was also a stern man, principled and very independent. Joe jokingly says he thinks his father may have written the Boy Scout Code. The way of the crowd was not his code and he constantly preached to his sons to use their head, make their own decisions and lead their own lives. The trouble came when they made decisions of which he didn't approve.

Harry also believed in work and he was happiest when the boys were all doing something constructive. When they were still young enough to need a step stool to reach the kitchen sink they learned to wash dishes. He would write their names on the calendar requiring each to wash one night, wipe one night and get a night off. It was sort of cast in stone that they would do just that. Joe has memories, although he isn't sure they are fond memories, and he can still hear Harry's words and see his face. On a Saturday in the summer when Joe was 9 or 10 years old he had big plans and was heading out on his bike when his father said, "Hey, where are you going, the lawn needs mowing." Joe immediately started whining and trying to get out of it. He should have known better. Joe's father said, "Come with me" and Joe followed him into the kitchen. He sat Joe down on one side of the table and sat down on the other leaning so far over the table that his face was next to Joe's. He said, "Listen to me and pay attention to what I have to say. This is the most important thing in your life. No one is going to die and leave you money. You're not that good looking and you don't appear to be all that bright. The only way you will ever get by in this life is to work. You need to work as hard as you can, as often as you can and as smart as you can. You can start right now by mowing the lawn with a smile on your face. NOW GET TO IT!" At the time Joe thought it was akin to slave labor but later learned what Harry was trying to instill in him.

Work would become part of life for Joe and his brothers. Harry made sure they were always doing something constructive. A big breakthrough came when they were old enough to work for other people. All of their grandparents lived in town and taking care of their chores was required at no charge, but they were great tippers so it worked out. Other people would pay them to do stuff which they did at home for free or as Harry said "you do it to eat."Harry, never one to miss a teaching moment, explained that if they did a good job, minded their manners and were friendly and helpful, they could make more money and get more jobs. Joe says they sort of learned to milk some of the older people but always did the best job they could. They had the requisite paper route and that made them some money but collecting the money was no fun. Joe was glad to give that job to someone else.

Joe's parents were like Ozzie and Harriet. They truly loved each other and showed it every day of their lives. His mother was a good woman and mother and lived for her family, but she was regularly overwhelmed by them. Sometimes she would start crying, go in the bedroom and close the door. They chalked it up to the frailty of womanhood. She was a great sport and loved a good joke or prank as long as no one was scarred for life. She was a great cook and it was not uncommon for their friends to be there for dinner with all the boys. Later on, as they grew older, it sort of got out of hand—she would cook for hours and they would devour it in 15 or 20 minutes. This of course took a lot of work on her part so the older boys would help her make dinner when they were there. It was a good way to get a little one on one time with her as there was never much of that. She taught Joe to cook, which he still loves to do. Joe says there is something really special about a family dinner with good food and company.

In his mother's early life, she, along with one of her brothers and her two sisters, converted to the Catholic

Church and she was dead serious about it. The boys could get away with murder most of the week but not in church. Acting up in church was a punishable offense. She would get so mad she wouldn't talk to them for a week. Harry supported her but didn't belong to the church. She made it her life's work to change that and he was baptized into the church when Joe was 16. The boys were, of course, brought up in that great Catholic tradition. When he was in high school she and the parish priest thought they could help him hear the call to the priesthood but although Joe listened and listened he says he could never hear the call.

Joe's best church story is how being an altar boy saved his life. The summer he was 16, if he had $10 he could put a little gas in the family car, take his girlfriend to a movie, go out for a pizza and pop and still have enough change left to buy a condom (no wonder he couldn't hear the call to the priesthood). He was very fortunate to go on such an adventure on a beautiful Saturday evening. When he arrived home it was very late, very dark and all was quiet on the home front. He slipped into the house and upstairs to bed. Now he was supposed to be an altar boy at 7am mass and when the alarm rang he gave real consideration to staying in bed and skipping the whole thing. He already knew that if he did, his parents would go to 9am mass, the priest would tell them he shirked his duties and he would get a stern lecture and still have to go to 11am mass. He almost decided it was worth it but then something that could only be the hand of God came over him. He had a moment of clarity and decided he was a man and real men did their duty no matter what. He jumped out of bed, quickly showered and dressed, put on his shinny altar boy shoes and walked out the door to a great summer morning. He walked proudly up the sidewalk, out to the driveway and around to the driver's side of the family sedan that he had taken on his date, the same car his parents were certainly going to drive to 9am mass. Joe was horrified to find that condom stuck to the driver's door and he immediately removed all the evidence. And that's how being an altar boy saved his life.

As a family they invented sibling rivalries. They fought constantly over the smallest things and it got physical. The brother after Joe, Mathew, was bigger than Joe when he was born and they bickered and fought until their parents couldn't stand it. One winter night when they were 14 and 12 they were at each other all night and Harry finally had enough and said, "Go to bed right now and give us some peace." Then, they were in the bathroom and got in a fight about who was going to brush their teeth first. Harry went nuts and grabbed them both by the arms, banged them together like knocking the mud off a pair of boots and threw them out in a snow bank. He slammed the kitchen door so hard he broke all of the glass in the door. Joe and his brother were outside in their underwear and tee shirts, it was in the 20's and snowing but it was a lot safer than in the house. Harry left them out there for what seemed like an eternity and when he came to the door he asked, "Are you guys cooled off yet?" His brother Matt, always the sarcastic one, said "Yea, are you?" As a result they spent the next hour cleaning up glass and taping a piece of cardboard over the windowless door. Not another word was ever said.

Joe says that at some time we all have to learn about life and death. He came to understand his own mortality when he was only 13. The boys were raised in that great Catholic tradition in which being an altar boy was part of the training. During the holidays, Joe served a wedding mass which he said, It was all goodness and light" and he even got a five dollar tip, which was big bucks at the time.

The next summer the groom was killed in a car accident and Joe was again an altar boy for the funeral. He went to the cemetery gravesite for the final rites along with the other altar boys, the priest, and the deceased's family and friends. Seeing all these people under a tent, praying over the casket, Joe realized that even though this guy was dead he still existed.

Joe had a good friend and the two of them were always looking for ways to make money. By this time, they had firearms and were constantly in need of ammo so no job was too large or too small in order to get money. One of their ventures was mowing lawns. The priest had hired them to mow the cemetery on a subcontract basis during the mowing season. The afternoon of the funeral, mentioned above, they mowed the cemetery. It was so different from a few hours earlier because the casket was in the ground, the tent was gone, the dirt was in the hole and the sod had been replaced. Joe mowed over the new grave and it came to him that it was just him, the deceased and the lawn mower,and because there was no stone yet, people wouldn't even know who was in the grave. It made Joe realize, then and there, in his words, "When you die you're dead, game over." This would serve Joe well later because it seemed to him that everything he liked was dangerous.

Joe's father's family had been farmers for generations—two of his brothers farmed, and his dear old dad saw this as a wonderful form of character building for the boys. The boys spent a lot of time at the farms and both of his uncles were great guys. The summer Joe was 14, he went to live with one of his uncles. They taped blocks on the tractor pedals (brakes and clutch) so he could reach them. They milked cows at 5am, had a big breakfast, did the cow chores, cleaned the milking equipment, cleaned the barns and were then on to the business of crops, hay, corn and oats. They had a big dinner at noon then went back to work until 5pm when they had to milk the cows again. They would have a fast supper and there would be enough daylight to go for a horseback ride or maybe even over to see a girlfriend. He would be home by dark, take a quick bath and then was off to bed. This schedule was repeated every day until Sunday when, after morning milking and barn chores, he cleaned up and went to town to mass. After mass he went back to the farm for dinner. After dinner he was free to ride horses, go to the quarry to shoot rifles and shotguns or swim and fish in the river. He had to be back by 5pm to milk the cows for the 14th time that week. Joe was paid $25 per week plus room and board for about 70 hours of work. This is where he really learned to work.

Another thing they learned from Harry was a love of the great outdoors. Harry's brother farmed the family farm which was bounded by the river along with a sand peninsula that was a great place to camp, swim and fish. It was there that Harry and his brothers had a big army tent with rooms. They would set it up in the spring and fall and fish all night. The boys could stay up at the campfire for as long as they wanted and slept in sleeping bags or on a cot. Their grandmother had a cast iron pan so big she couldn't even lift that she used to make great campfire breakfasts after the cows were milked. Later on when they were older they camped by themselves and were shocked to learn their mother hated camping.

Harry also taught the boys to shoot and hunt. Joe says Harry was "serious as a heart attack" about shooting and safety was always the number one priority. Many years later Joe heard a man say, "You can't childproof your guns so you have to gun-proof your child" and he thinks that was Harry's idea all along. Joe got a Daisy BB gun when he was six years old and learned to treat it as the real deal.

If you pointed it at someone or something you shouldn't have, you weren't going to see it for a while. That led to shotguns and rifles and some great times learning firearm safety and shooting with their dad. Joe still has his first shotgun and rifle, but currently have them loaned out to an 11 year old young man whose dad is a Swat Team member on the county sheriff's department. So the kid is in good hands. Joe still enjoys shooting and does it as much as time allows.

Another one of Harry's rules was you had to save your money if you wanted to buy something because borrowing money was forbidden. He was always trying to motivate the boys to work and one time he said "you can buy anything you want if you can pay for it." This would come back to haunt him. The summer Joe was 17 years old, Joe sold his horse and saddle and with that money along with some savings from farm work he planned to buy a motorcycle. Harry flipped out! Joe reminded him that "you said I could buy anything I wanted if I could pay for it." Then Harry got all practical about it and said, "If you can afford a motorcycle then you can buy a car and stop driving mine." Joe explained that he didn't need a car and they went back and forth for a couple of weeks. Finally, Harry gave up and told Joe he could do what he wanted but couldn't drive the family car again if he bought the motorcycle. Joe went ahead and bought a used Honda Super 90 that very day. Joe loved the motorcycle.One of his friends bought one too and they had a blast until the weather turned cold. Harry was a man of his word and Joe rode that motorcycle to work, to school and everywhere that winter. On New Year's Eve, his girlfriend was babysitting about two miles out of town and it was in the 20's with snow flurries. Joe was on his way to see her all bundled up and driving cautiously because the roads were getting slippery. A speeding car passed him and skidded off the road narrowly avoiding Joe which would have resulted in serious injury at best. Joe thought he came very close to death that night and he never forgot it. Joe and Nancy still ride motorcycles today.

Joe was always interested in electricity probably because his father worked in the industry as a lineman for the local utility company. He was also fascinated by the motor drive system in his erector set, did Boy Scout experiments and read books about electricity. He was never afraid to take things apart and did some early electrical work that he says he was fortunate to have survived. When he was a senior in high school, a teacher named Bill Wiley became the principal and expanded the industrial arts program, Joe's area of study, to include more hands-on training with local building contractors. This program gave Joe the incredible opportunity of being hired by an electrical contractor as a helper. Bill Wiley was the first person to help Joe succeed.

His senior year was a great year in Joe's life when on school days he worked for an electrical contractor doing electrical work for money from 7am until noon. He would then go home for lunch, shower and get to class by 1pm. The first hour of class was on "school to work" which was reporting on what he was learning about electrical work. He could skip this class if he was working late. The second hour was an automotive class in which he learned hands-on by fixing or working on teachers' cars or their own cars. The last hour was English class—four years of English was required to graduate but Joe seldom attended this class. The principal, Mr. Wiley, had other things for Joe to do. The school was always understaffed so some days Joe would be assigned to watch the freshman/sophomore study class and other days he stayed longer in his automotive class. He only attended English class if he had to. This was a year of no real studies and he had money in his pocket.

As graduation approached his father told him he wasn't going to learn a trade by working for the local one-horse contractor and it turned out that he was right again. Harry wanted Joe to get an education. So, in the fall of 1970, Joe attended the local community college for a year studying electronics, but his heart wasn't in it. He continued to work for the electrical contractor and the next spring he applied for an electrical apprenticeship in the IBEW/NECA program. At that time, nepotism was the order of the day and he was not accepted. The contractor he was working for bought a snowmobile dealership so Joe spent some time that winter setting up new machines, doing warranty work and electrical service. The owner was badly hurt in a snowmobile accident and when spring came the snowmobile work and electric work both dried up. He laid carpet for a few months and then went to work for the other electrical contractor in town.

Joe moved out of the family home during that winter and was sharing an apartment with another guy. He continued to work at wiring new houses, farms and had some small commercial and industrial projects. He was learning some things, and after a while he was a leader, laying out the work and sort of running it. There were four or five workers depending on the amount of work. The contractor was getting older and liked to manage them without working with the tools. During this time Joe met Nancy L. Clover who would become his wife—they have now been married for 40 years. She worked in the local Farm Credit office and they met when he fixed the light fixture over her desk. They had their first date in January of 1971. They became engaged a year later and were married in September of 1973.

Joe never reapplied for apprenticeship in the union again because he didn't know anyone nor was he related to anyone in the industry. In early 1973, he got a message that Bob Lipart wanted to see him. Bob and his family lived in Pecatonica and he was the branch manager for a large electrical contractor from Chicago which had an office in Rockford. Unknown to Joe, Bob was on the electrical apprenticeship committee and he told Joe he should reapply. He told Joe not to worry about the nepotism and that he should reapply as soon as possible. Joe did as Bob suggested, took the exams, the mechanical aptitude tests and was interviewed. In May, Joe received a letter of acceptance into the program which was one of the best days of his life. This was probably the greatest break of his entire life. Bob Lipart was the second person on the list of people who helped Joe succeed.

In July of 1973 Joe went to work for Blackhawk Electric in Rockford. It was a mid-sized shop which ran about 25 electricians depending on the work, which is always the case with building trades. Joe mistakenly thought that his apprenticeship would be sort of a formality as he already had four years of experience. Joe said, "Wow, was I wrong." After a couple of days the journeyman wireman to whom Joe was assigned said, "Look kid, I don't care what you know or where you learned it because from now on we will do everything my way—got it?" Joe found out that he really had the equivalent of about one year's experience four years in a row. He also found that some of what he knew was wrong. He was humbled yet determined to succeed so as Joe says, "I closed my mouth and kept my head down." He decided the best way forward was to try and build on what he did know and try to learn as much from everyone he could. Things went a lot better with this attitude and while he was no journeyman he was ahead of the guys in his class who didn't have any experience at all. After all, this is where you are supposed to start.

He was determined to use this to his advantage and after a while foremen would ask for him on their jobs. One foreman was Jim Corcoran who was President of the Electrical Workers Union and Joe said he became sort of Jim's dog, Spot. Jim was a very knowledgeable wireman and a controls guru. Joe learned a lot from him including both electrical work and how to work with people. Jim was often away at meetings on union business and would assign work for Joe to perform while he was away. They weren't supposed to do this as Joe was still just an apprentice, but Jim never had him do anything he didn't understand. The knowledge and the experience Joe gained was invaluable to his education. Jim Corcoran was the third person on the list of people who helped Joe succeed.

Jim was the foreman for an industrial customer of Blackhawk Electric and this customer had built a new plant a few years earlier and was in a huge growth mode. This customer always had new equipment to wire, departments to expand and new processes in welding and painting. By the last year of Joe's apprenticeship, it had become Joe's account. He had developed relationships with the company owner as well as the engineering and facilities managers. This is where his real education began. He learned so much about manufacturing, business, human relations and managing people that Joe says he should have paid them to work there. The summer he finished his 8,000 hours of on the job training and graduated to journeyman wireman status, this customer built a large manufacturing plant. Joe became the foreman and ran a crew of six to eight people for most of a year. Again, it was a great opportunity for him to learn and grow.

The year after he graduated to journeyman, Joe was

asked to be an instructor in the apprenticeship program and taught for two years until things changed and he no longer had the time to dedicate to it. He returned to the program later as a contractor and now spends a few weeks each year with the fifth year apprentices discussing how to estimate a job, order materials, manage help and trying to help them see their horizon.

It was now 1978, Nancy and Joe had built their home and he had worked for Blackhawk Electric for five years, the last two for the manufacturing company. One of the founders of Blackhawk Electric had retired a number of years prior and his partner bought him out. The remaining partner then sold some of the company to his son and son-in-law. It turned out to be a very bad idea. Now the owner wanted to retire and turned the operation of the company over to his younger partners and sold them his remaining stock. He handcuffed his son-in-law by only letting him buy 48% of the stock thus giving 52% and control to his son. He did it wrong because the son was a slacker and things went downhill fast. Joe says it was an eye-opening experience to see a previously strong company with a solid reputation decay into a shell of its former self within a few months. Joe assumes the founder took a lot of cash out when he left because at about that same time their paychecks started bouncing. It got so bad that Joe's bank asked him to not deposit the checks anymore. Then the employees would race to the bank the checks were drawn on to cash their checks before there wasn't enough money in the account to honor the checks.

This, of course, was not working and it was apparent to everyone that the company was going to fail unless drastic measures were taken. There was a nuclear power station being built at this time in Byron, Illinois so any wireman could leave his present employer and go to the "big job."

There was a mass exodus from Blackhawk which further damaged their ability to perform work. Joe knew he must make a decision very soon. Joe had a friend, Neil Cuthbertson, with whom he grew up—they are still friends to this day. Neil had attended and graduated from the Woodward Governor Academy but did not like the factory structure. Neil went to work for the second contractor in Pecatonica while Joe was there and they worked together for about a year before Joe left to enter the apprenticeship program. Neil worked about two more years for that contractor and then left to start his own electrical contracting company in Pecatonica doing the same type of work. He worked hard at it for a couple of years and wanted to either grow or get out as he was doing everything himself. They discussed the possibility of Joe buying into Neil's business and trying to start doing the industrial work with which Joe was familiar. It seemed eminent that Blackhawk Electric was going to fail and Joe had always wanted (dreamed is more like it) to be in business so they decided to proceed. He discussed this with his mentors at the manufacturing company and while they believed in Joe they were still loyal to Blackhawk. Although they didn't say so at the time, Joe is sure they had doubts about the future of Joe's new business. It was obvious that Joe would not get their business, at least not at that time.

Just then, there was another huge stroke of luck for Joe in that the customer discovered that the current owners of Blackhawk had been cheating them on the cost of the work. They had a contract for a set markup and Blackhawk was double dipping by invoicing some materials and some labor twice. This led to an in depth review of previous invoices and the discovery that this had been going on since the son had been in charge. Joe attended a meeting with the engineering and facilities managers and they explained exactly what they expected if they gave their business to Joe's new company, including what they would pay and when. Agreement was reached and Joe's company was awarded their work. This was a great start as Joe's company had two to three wiremen in the plant at all times. This was double or more the amount of work Neil was already doing. Joe left Blackhawk and bought into Cuthbertson Electric in the winter of 1979. They signed a contract with the local union and hired a wireman named Glen Gabel. Glen and Joe had been in the same apprenticeship class and Joe liked and respected him. Glen took over some of the load at the manufacturing company and that left some time for Joe to help Neil and attempt to sign other work.

Joe and Neil worked 12 hours a day and most Saturdays for over a year trying to build their company. They grew a little, hired some more help and were able to get a few other industrial accounts, including some from Blackhawk. The issue became that they were running two companies. Neil's work was in the Pecatonica area doing residential and farm work and Joe had already had his fill of that kind of work. Joe was in love with industrial work and believed that was the future of the company and where the money was. Neil didn't want to work in plants and Joe didn't want to work on homes and farms. So, in late spring of 1980, they agreed to go their separate ways. Joe was then a contractor without a company. He had some work but didn't know how to proceed. He was disillusioned at first but after some study he began to believe it could be done.

In the electrical industry, it is said there are four levels of competency. Joe says that level one is unconscious incompetence, level two is conscious incompetence, level three is conscious competence and level four is, of course, unconscious competence. Level one is where you don't even know that you don't know—the point at which you oversimplify everything. You really want to get beyond level one as fast as you can. Level two is where your eyes start to open up and you begin to see the sheer magnitude of the industry and the knowledge and skills you need to learn seem overwhelming. Level three is where you finally start to develop your skills and the classroom and on-the-job training start to come together. You can do the job but it takes all you have. Level four is where things are easier for you, you can do most tasks without thinking about them and can think far enough ahead to be productive and produce quality work, safely and on time. It is generally accepted that this takes about ten years in the trade.

Joe was now at level two in the contracting business. He had seen how fast a well-established and well-run company could fail when wrong decisions were made. He had worked hard for a year and a half, had even made a little money, and yet really didn't have anything to show for it. He had no company and was at square one, although he had some accounts and had watched how successful some companies could be. All of this was going to affect Glen as well. Joe and Glen had learned how well they could work together during the last year and spent much time discussing the possibilities of starting a new company. The discussions included what a new company would look like and what would be the responsibilities of each man. In July of 1980, they agreed to start a new company and named it Special Power, Inc. Their goal was to build and operate a professional electrical contracting company that would deliver the highest level of industrial service and quality finished electrical projects, safely, on time and within budget, thereby adding value and helping their clients succeed. They agreed they would do this completely above board and not get involved in the games, kickbacks and foul play for which the construction industry was known.

They agreed they would dedicate the time and resources required and would not, as Glen said, get caught on a Johnson Silver Minnow. I asked Joe what was meant by that comment and he said, "It is sort of like sitting down to play poker with the guys. If you don't see a fish you're it."

They had big ideas and ideals but no real plan to move forward. They sort of worked it out as they went along. Fortunately they had enough work to keep both of them busy and sort of leaned into the whole contracting thing. They ran the business out of Joe and Nancy's house and Glen figured their first plan and spec bids on Eaton's kitchen table. They built three shelves in the garage to hold all of their materials. They signed a contract with the International Brotherhood of Electrical Workers, IBEW, and the business agent said, "If you two guys want to fool around like a couple of kids with a fruit stand, that's OK. However, if you really want to be contractors go over to the National Electrical Contractors Association and join up." It was very good advice.

Special Power needed to get finances in order, beginning with a new bank. Joe had met me when I worked, for a brief time, with Nancy at Farm Credit. Now I was a loan officer with Illinois National Bank, later known as AM-CORE Bank, in Rockford, and they made an appointment to see me. It was a privilege to work with Joe, who always knew exactly where he was going and how to get there. He asked good questions and was a quick study. My bank was soon able to give Special Power, Inc. a line of credit and other help as was needed. Joe has been very appreciative of the help was able to give him.

They joined NECA and immediately took advantage of their programs for contractors. This was pre-computer times and they had a one-write accounting system that integrated accounting, payroll and job cost. Nancy helped them nights for about six months but she already had a full-time job and they needed to get Special Power out of their house. They rented a small office and shop on Shaw Street in Rockford which had just enough room for a truck, some tools and an office with a couple of desks and a plan table. Glen went to NECA's estimating school and learned that side of the business. They hired a bookkeeper to work nights on accounting and she and Joe did the invoicing. It soon became evident that if they wanted a steady backlog of work they would have to go out and bid it. Their industrial accounts continued to support them but it wasn't always steady. Glen stopped working with the tools and started estimating work full-time. This was a huge increase in overhead and it worried them sick as to whether they could make it work. They engaged a wise old accountant who was as conservative as it gets and they learned how accounting works and what an Income Statement and Balance Sheet really mean. They paid themselves 16 hours of wireman's pay per week for the first year and a half. It took another two years to get up to 40 hours of pay because they had to do this to fund the growth of the company. Joe said, "When you start rolling a snowball with 10 or 12 snowflakes, it takes a while." There was a point where Glen said, "If you could go around the world for a nickel, we couldn't get out of town."

They continued to grow and learn and some of the lessons were hard and expensive. When people don't care what it costs it may be because they don't intend to pay you anyway. Joe said that after a while crooks start to have a smell about them. The really dangerous people are basically honest, but their plan is bad and they are incompetent. They can suck you in and cost you a lot of money when, in Joe's words, "the feces contacts the rotating oscillator." Many other contractors are not honest either with their goal to get you in deep; they delay payments and see if you go broke before you can collect from them. Then they can finish the job with your money and come out ahead. They learned they really had to be careful who they worked for and they learned from their banker not to be bashful about asking how customers intended to pay for this work.

At the end of the fifth year, they finally saw a payoff which allowed them to hire a full-time office manager. Then Joe and Glen didn't have to do accounting at night. They were also able to distribute $5,000 each to themselves. Glen bought a new BMW motorcycle while Nancy and Joe bought a John Deere riding mower. Glen thought they were nuts for being so practical.

After they left Cuthbertson Electric, Neil went back to being a one-person company for another year. He then closed down his company and went to work for another contractor. In about 1987, he joined Special Power as an estimator. A year later Special Power outgrew their rented property on Shaw Street and rented a building on 18th Avenue. They built some offices and moved in. Business was growing and they had acquired a number of new accounts. The company had Glen and Neil estimating and managing work, an office manager who was growing with them and Joe, who had stopped working with the tools. Joe was working as their superintendent, service manager and purchasing agent. They were involved with larger projects and in more engineering of their direct work.

Glen and Joe were no longer working with the tools, but they weren't able to be remote foremen for each and every job. They had hired a couple of good wiremen who were known to them and they were able to rely on them to run the larger jobs. Joe and Glen finally understood that the wage was the same for a wireman if he was an asset or a liability. For the most part, the material costs were the same for all of the contractors. The only thing that set them apart from the competition and made the difference in whether they made money or not was the quality and motivation of the foremen and wiremen who worked for them and their ability to manage them. The ability to provide correct documents from which to build, the timely delivery of correct materials, the right manpower and the availability of quality tools at the right time equals the minimum requirements for them to succeed. Glen said, "You don't trade for Cy Young Award winners, but instead you need to bring them up through your own farm system." They really took that to heart and went on a long-term program that is ongoing to this day to attract the best possible people to join their team. With a dozen notable exceptions, their proving ground was the apprenticeship program.

Coincidentally, at about this time, Joe was on the apprenticeship committee for seven years and interviewed over 1,000 people that applied for acceptance into the program. It was usual to interview 150 to 200 people for 20 jobs in the program. Then Special Power would interview the top people who didn't get accepted in the apprenticeship program for possible jobs with Special Power for warehouse and truck driver positions. Joe would explain the real situation to them by telling them that if they were the right kind of guys and did well working for Special Power it would give them a good chance for acceptance in the apprenticeship program within the next few years. If Special Power did hire them and they didn't work out they would be let go and needn't reapply. This was a long-term commitment to attracting the best people and most of the electricians in their employ today were or are at the top of their class. They are the best in the industry year after year which bears out the adage that a company is only as good as its employees and truly the whole is greater than the sum of the parts. Joe said that this is as close as he will ever come to bragging but they have an available labor pool of over 1,000 wiremen and their company's work force is considered the best of the best.

Neil decided to leave Special Power because estimating work was causing him stress problems and, after all, it wasn't his money with which he was gambling. They decided to change their structure and have the estimator who won the job function as the project manager for that job, as he was the one with the most knowledge about it. Joe had been helping with engineering and budgets for some of their regular clients so he moved over to that seat full-time and they hired a new superintendent. They promoted a seasoned veteran who had worked for one of their competitors for 20 years and got so mad at the owner that he left his office in December and agreed to a job with Special Power wiring a freezer building outdoors. They made him a foreman the first week he was with them. He went on to run other projects and was interested in helping them, so they made him superintendent. This would not be the last key person that left that shop and joined Special Power. This really worked for them and helped them get to the next level.

Special Power had been successful with helping their industrial clients figure out what needed to be done for their projects and decided they could do that with other clients as well. This method is called "design and build" and it allows them to be on the team from the start instead of just another electrical bidder. It has its own pitfalls in that you have to do a lot of free preliminary engineering to help establish a working budget and you assume all of the liability of the engineering company. A lot of electrical contractors shy away from this business because of this. However, Special Power would rather assume that responsibility and leverage that into a few more points at the end of the project, along with an informed and satisfied client that will call them again. Today, a large part of their work is performed on a design and build basis. Joe is still working as an estimator/project manager and the majority of his responsibilities are for design and build work.

By now 10 years had passed and, as was stated earlier, it takes 10 years to be a qualified wireman. Joe thinks it takes about the same amount of time for being a qualified contractor. Special Power was now a solid company financially and otherwise. As Joe says, "We had our feet under us, our head up and our eyes wide open." The only work they were not geared for was the Chrysler plant in Belvidere but otherwise they could bid most any project in the area. With their banker and accountant's help, they had learned how to manage their finances and they got started with a bonding company through the SBA so they could get a performance bond for any project they were qualified to do. They were very conservative financially and learned to do both a best case and worst case scenario before making major decisions and they learned to really check things out before proceeding. Joe said, a wise man once said "Confidence is the feeling you get right before you grasp the full reality of the situation." One time they jumped in on a large project and later found out the general contractor had been getting paid but had not paid Special Power. The general contractor was forging lien waivers in the name of Special Power. This led to a court case and Special Power finally got paid because the owner had to pay twice. The customer's project manager, who was pals with the general contractor, was fired along with some folks in accounting.

Glen said one more good deal like that and Special Power would be out of business.

As technology changed and computers came into both their office and the plant floors, they learned to be integrators in welding equipment and processes together. One of their foreman, Kevin Holder, was a controls genius so they sent him to as many classes and factory schools as he wanted. They began to develop a reputation for being able to perform large, complex, industrial power and control projects on a design and build basis. Their motto became, "The more difficult the project the better we like it." They went on to learn to do high-voltage work as there is much of it in their area. A lot of the industrial plants have class 15,000 volt systems and there were only a few contractors that could perform this work. A couple of them either went out of business or lost the men to retirement who could do this work. Special Power was able to step into that void and again, to this day, they perform most of this type of work in their area. Being able to perform these specialty types of work has helped them gain market share for their other work due to the additional exposure to clients that called them because of the specialty work.

Early on Special Power became very involved with the National Electrical Contractors Association. The local chapter is the Northern Illinois Chapter which is the management counterpart to the electrical workers. These two organizations work together nationally and locally to negotiate contracts, administer the health and welfare programs, local pensions, apprenticeship programs, safety, grievances and disputes, interaction with other trades and contractors and local government. Special Power belongs to the Association in order to have a say in the direction of the local industry, to know and work with their competitors and to take advantage of the many management programs provided by the association. Joe was on many committees and was elected to the Board of Directors. He served on the Board for 18 years, the last six as President. The Association went through some rough labor relations and was able to salvage a better working relationship with the union. However, it left Joe somewhat burned out. He stepped back a little for a few years but the Association came calling again and Joe went back on the Board of Directors again, six years and counting this time. Special Power really can't say enough about the Association; they have learned so much about electrical contracting through the Association which is still leading the electrical construction industry both locally and nationally.

Special Power has been very fortunate to work with a number of very well run companies, both large and small, and enjoy these great relationships. Some names you may recognize are Amerock, AT&T, Aramark, ADT, Alliant Energy, Buckeye Partners, Commonwealth Edison, GE, Contel, Dean Foods, Exelon, Fermi lab, Frontier, GTE, International Paper, Marathon Petroleum, ONEOK, Verizon, Weyerhaeuser, Simplex, Square D, Supplycore, Sundstrand, Kelly Springfield, State of Illinois and State of Wisconsin. In addition they have worked with thousands of companies large and small. At this writing, they just wrote their 23 thousandth job order.

Special Power has been fortunate to be involved with some very interesting projects and people. After the tragedy of 9/11, the Nuclear Regulatory Commission, NRC, took a very hard look at security at nuclear power plants nationwide and discovered they were not really secure at all. They mandated a number of increases at all levels and gave the utilities 24 months to implement or face stiff fines. There must have been some foot-dragging because when Exelon went out for engineering quotes, it was already late. Of course the low bidder for the nuclear plant in Byron, Illinois was a "level one company" and didn't know what was really required to comply and how late it was. All of this was unknown to Special Power when they showed up with a general contractor who does a lot of this work and knew what was up. Special Power had a contract for $36,000 to wire a 1,200 square foot concrete and block building with basic power and light. Joe couldn't go into details about the project because he had to sign a confidentially agreement. However, Joe says you can rest assured the nuclear power plants in this country are now secure.

Next, they came out with some plans to get utilities to this building and wondered if Special Power could do it? Joe said, "Of course we can." Then they asked if Special Power could wire these towers and fences. But before Special Power could answer they told Joe to wait because the plans they were given yesterday were wrong. They gave Joe a new set of plans and asked if Special Power could do the high voltage feeders. Exelon finally came clean and invited Special Power to a meeting with some very high-powered people from the utility company. Their project manager scolded the engineering company and then dismissed them to get to work. He then explained the real scope of the project and gave an impossible deadline to Special Power. He said if this job goes a million dollars over budget, it's no problem, but if it goes one day over schedule he would lose his job. He said, "Do you understand me? Can you do it?" Eight weeks later Special Power passed the NRC inspection with no issues. This $36,000 job had a $1.2 million change order and it turned an average year for Special Power into a good one.

In 2009 Special Power got a call from a company in Chicago that needed some high voltage advice and maybe a quote for a test lab and wondered if they would be interested. Normally Special Power would not have been interested in work in Cook County because of the Cook County labor union. The union requires that you use their workers and can only bring in your own people for supervision. As Glen would say, "Not enough carrot, too much stick." Work was scarce for Special Power at that time and since they wanted to meet on Saturday, Joe thought, "What the heck, all we can lose is a little of our time if they aren't serious." It turned out to be a good move. They were very serious and were talking about a huge project. It was a large, international company that sells, services, repairs and enhances output for the large pump industry. The work was primarily for the pipeline transfer, mining and nuclear industries. They wanted to build a pump test facility that was certified to a number of federal, ANSI and NRC standards. They had bought a building and understood exactly what they needed for a lab from a pump standpoint but were "level two" on the electrical side. There was a 100,000 gallon water tank under the floor and a 50,000 gallon tank overhead in the crane bay. There was a piping manifold that has pipes from 8" to 24" and there was a 5,000 horsepower drive motor that the pumps get connected to for test. When the whole operation runs it consumes five megawatts of electricity. It was very impressive. Joe explained to them that Special Power could help them (Special Power has a lot of lab experience) from plan to run but Special Power would require that they be on the team from the start. Joe wanted an agreed upon markup, an open book and then Special Power would lead the electrical work with the city and the utility. It was an incredible project, very interesting and specialized work. Special Power got the job. They continue to use Special Power for certain tests when the electrical requirements are involved.

After the tsunami in Japan, the NRC got very serious about testing emergency feed water pumps at the nuclear plants. Apparently, the pumps in Japan ran dry before the emergency water supply was on line and some of the pumps failed. The NRC directed Exelon to test a 1,250 horsepower vertical feed water pump. They certified it was within specifications and then tried a number of different scenarios of low pressure, high pressure, no flow and so on. The last test consisted of running water through a five gallon bucket of sea shells to see if it would damage the pump. The NRC staff was sure the shells would damage the pump beyond usefulness but they did not. The test was witnessed by at least 25 people from their industry and it passed all tests. Special Power helped with all of the setup and was on standby in the event of an electrical problem.

In about the year 2000, Kevin Holder and John Larson, both key employees who had worked for Special Power as apprentices and had now been with the company more than 10 years, came to Glen and Joe and asked about their plans for retirement and what they planned to do with the company at that time. They were very interested in buying the company and made it clear they wanted to be a part of the business. Glen and Joe took that to mean they were going to start their own company if they couldn't buy into Special Power. It was a perfect fit as Glen and Joe had discussed this and had decided if they were to sell, it would have to be to someone they trusted to be able to pay for it, and not sell to one of their competitors or close Special Power and take the money. The last two options weren't that appealing because they had invested a good part of their lives in the company and their egos were just big enough that they wanted to see the company succeed them and prosper. They had an attorney draw up an agreement adding the new partners.

Glen had some health issues in about 2006 and he retired in the middle of 2008 when the economy slowed down. The company bought Glen's stock and resold it to Kevin and John. This left Joe with half the company and two new partners. As history shows, the economy tanked and they had, as Joe says, went from fat, happy and no debt to no work and a big debt to Glen. This became a real struggle for a couple of years; salaries were reduced and they cleaned their own offices. Trucks and tool purchases were put on hold. All of their available cash went to pay down the debt to Glen and they paid him off in full by early 2012. That year their work came back some and they were able to make some money and upgrade some of their trucks and tools. By then, John had taken over the administration of the company as well as bidding the majority of the plan and spec work. Kevin had developed the industrial control systems into a division of the company and things were back on track. It was apparent that the profits came from the work of all three of them and Joe didn't deserve one-half of the proceeds so he sold enough of his stock to John and Kevin to make them equal partners.

They have had a good 2013 through the third quarter and have a reasonable backlog of work as they head into 2014. Joe is still working with their regular clients and helping out Kevin and John where he can. Joe will be 62 in early 2014 and he plans to retire in another year or two. He said he is absolutely sure the company they built over the last 33 years is in good hands and will continue to grow and prosper. Joe said he would love to be around for their 50th anniversary.

Joe's family has grown, even though Nancy and he never had children. Some of his brothers took up that slack and now there are many nephews, nieces and grandchildren. They are very close and get together many times during the year for holidays, family picnics and BBQs. It is the same with Nancy's family with her sister, Diane, and husband, Richard, living next door to them. Nancy and Diane bought their other sister out of her share of the family farm and they really enjoy the land and country living. They have lived there since 1977 and plan to live there for the rest of their lives. Diane and Richard had three great sons and so far, three beautiful grandchildren. Their youngest son, Eric, is an apprentice electrician. Joe says, "Go figure."

Joe says it was a great experience and he is very thankful for all of the help he received along the way and the many opportunities that were available to him. He feels indebted to everyone who helped him, from his parents who taught them the right path, to the teachers who helped open the doors, to the very knowledgeable wiremen that taught him the trade and industry, to the businessmen and leaders that showed him the way forward. He wishes he could say thank you to all of them face to face. The most thanks goes to his wife, Nancy, who was always there for him, who always knew what to say and who took the bad times in stride. She never wavered and has always been his rock and reason to keep going. He is looking forward to trying to make up for all of the times he wasn't there and the things she missed in the name of Special Power. She is his everything and they just celebrated their 40th wedding anniversary. He hopes to have many more years with her at his side now that he has achieved The American Dream.

Clarence and Genevieve Russell

This is the life story of my parents, who started with absolutely nothing and got no help from anyone including the government. With little formal education and no money they were able to achieve financial success and a great life. I am so proud of them, not only for their accomplishments, but for being the people they were. They were honest, hard working and respected by all. I thank God almost every day for giving me such wonderful parents. Their success was truly amazing and it shows that anyone in our free market economy can through hard work and determination achieve The American Dream.

My dad, Clarence Russell, was born in 1898 and grew up on a farm in South Dakota as the oldest boy and the third oldest of five children, three girls and two boys. His father was not very ambitious and Dad had to quit school in the fourth grade to help support the family. He lied about his age so he could join the Navy in World War I and sent most of his money home to support his siblings. After the War he lived in Chicago and worked construction including building the new Evanston Township High School which was very hard work and little pay. Eventually one of his relatives helped him get a job with Chicago Motor Coach as a bus and street car driver where he worked for several years.

My mother, Genevieve McCanny Russell, was born in 1900 as the third oldest of four girls and one boy. Her mother died when she was only six years old and her father was not able to care for and support all these children so he shipped the girls off to relatives but kept the boy to live with him. The relatives sent all these orphans to a Catholic boarding school in Adrian, Michigan until my mother graduated from eighth grade. Mom was somewhat disabled in that she suffered from scoliosis, a curvature of the spine. This was a very painful condition and there was no cure for it at that time. Doctors tried all kinds of remedies including requiring her to sleep on a wood mattress and wearing a back brace for many years. She suffered with this condition her entire life.

After graduating from eighth grade in 2013, Mom went to live with two aunts in Evanston, Illinois and worked in a local five and ten cent store while attending high school. After a few months she had to quit school because her back made it difficult to both work and attend school. This was very disappointing for her because she was a good student and looked forward to school each day. However, she had to pay room and board to her aunts so she couldn't afford to give up her job. She eventually made her living as a seamstress for a very exclusive dress store in Evanston where they copied dresses from Paris, France. Mom worked her way up and eventually was one of the best dressmakers in Evanston. This was excellent work and it allowed my mother to sit while working which was much easier on her bad back.

Mom and dad met at a party in 1922 and were married in 1925. My father continued with his job at Chicago Motor Coach and my mother continued work as a seamstress and between them they were able to save some money. One day my father got aggravated by one of the passengers on the bus he was driving and he pulled over to the side of the road, parked the bus and never returned to his job. They say, "You can take the boy out of the farm but you can't take the farm out of the boy." After Dad quit his job with Chicago Motor Coach they took their life savings and in 1931 moved to a farm near Dundee, Illinois just west of Chicago. During the first year on the farm, Mom stayed in Evanston working as a seamstress, which provided much needed working capital and returned to the farm on weekends.

As tenant farmers they moved around a lot and lived in abject poverty during the Great Depression. They burned corn for fuel and were able to survive by the meat and milk provided by their livestock. The next year,1932, they moved to a farm near Capron, Illinois where my brother, George, was born. Then they moved to a farm near Harvard, Illinois where my oldest sister, Dorothy, was born in 1935. They moved again the next year back to a farm northwest of Capron, known as the Johnson place, where my other sister, Patricia, was born in 1936. In 1939 they moved again just a couple miles away to a farm known as the Conyes farm. Each time they moved it was to a better farm so they could improve their living standards.

They never had electricity or indoor plumbing until a couple years after moving to Capron, Illinois in 1941. In 1941, my parents bought a 180 acre farm located four miles south of Capron for a price of $15,500 or $86 per acre and took possession in March, 1942. They had to sell most of their livestock in order to come up with the $2,000 down payment. However, things got much better for the entire family in 1942 when the "light of their life" was born. Yes, I was born that year. Now there were four children, George, Dorothy, Patricia and Robert.

The farm was in very poor shape with many acres too wet to farm and the buildings, including our house, were in terrible shape. Since my mother and father had almost no money they did the best they could with what they had. Farm commodity prices were good during World War II so

Dad was able to scrape together enough money to do some remodeling to the buildings and buy some good livestock. Dad, with the help of a carpenter, removed the old wood stanchions and wood floors in the dairy barn and replaced them with modern metal stanchions with waterers and a cement floor. He also built a new milk house, renovated the rest of the barn and poured concrete in the cattle yard so he could qualify for selling Grade A milk. To qualify for selling Grade A milk everything had to be neat, clean and well kept. This paid off handsomely and he made good money during World War II.

All the work in the fields had been done with horses until 1943 when Dad bought our first tractor, an International Model "M". Until then, Dad plowed with a "one bottom plow" which only plowed about 16 inches but with the new tractor he could use a "three bottom plow" which would plow 48 inches at a time and with so much less physical labor on Dad's part. He must have felt like he died and went to Heaven. During this time, Dad remodeled all the farm buildings. With the help of a carpenter he built a large corn crib which was storage for 2,500 bushel of ear corn on both sides of an alley way used for machinery storage. He also built a large machine shed and a large chicken laying house in his spare time. Dad loved to work and he was very talented. He also had built a new 50' x 16' silo to store corn silage. He then hired someone to tile the wet fields so all the land could become productive. With all these improvements and good farming practices Dad was able to pay off the farm debt in full in 1949.

He almost built a new house that year but a contractor convinced him to remodel the existing home instead on a "time and material" basis. This was the worst decision Dad ever made because, as he told me years later, "Time and material contracts make a crook out of the most honest man." Dad said the remodeling ended up costing more than what a new home would have cost.

Through a lot of hard work and determination life got much better for our family. Dad worked long hard hours doing physical work that was unimaginable. He was up at 4am each day to milk the cows by hand at first and later with milking machines. Life as a dairy farmer required milking the cows twice each day at around 5am and again around 5pm. He also had the pigs and chickens which were all labor intensive. In 1952, Dad sold all the dairy cows and set the buildings up to feed beef cattle. This required remodeling the barn again and enlarging the concrete cattle yard. He also built a new cattle shed for the beef cattle and a large concrete cattle yard which allowed us to handle 150 head of beef cattle. Dad would usually buy about 150 head of steers or heifers calves weighing about 400# in the fall each year and feed them to a weight of 1,000# to1,200# which took nearly 12 months.

My father did all the farm work and my mother took care of the house and her chickens. She worked very hard also and with her bad back it must have been incredibly hard work. Each spring she bought 500 white leghorn pullets, day-old chicks. She carried five gallon pails of water and feed, a distance of about 200 feet, to the "brooder house" where the young chicks were kept. As the chicks got older, they had the run of the farm all summer long but stayed close to the feed. In late September, we would move the chickens into the "laying house." It was quite a job to catch and move the chickens to the laying house. My parents, my two sisters, my brother and I would spend many evenings catching the chickens. We would catch most of them in our orchard and other trees by shining a flashlight into their eyes, which seemed to freeze them in place, and snagging their legs with a long wire, pulling them down and carrying them to the laying house. Then the real work would begin.

Once the chickens were in the laying house my father, my brother or I fed and watered them. Usually one of us kids would gather the eggs from the laying house and take them to our basement where my mother got them ready for sale. Mom was responsible for gathering, cleaning, weighing and packing the eggs which numbered about 200 or more each day. Sometimes she would contract the eggs with a wholesaler and other times she would take the eggs directly to a retailer, whichever resulted in the best price. The money my mother got from the eggs was her budget to run the household. It was a big job for her especially with her bad back.

My mother didn't have any modern conveniences. She had a "wringer clothes washer" with a gas engine which required a lot of work although it was probably a little better than beating the clothes with stones like the Indians did. This required that she put each article of clothing through the wringer by hand twice, once to wash and another to rinse. She would then hang the clothes outside on a clothes line if weather allowed or in our basement during inclement weather. My sisters and I laugh sometimes that we hardly remember seeing my mother without clothes pins in her mouth from hanging clothes on the clothes line. It was especially difficult for my mother with her bad back. She made sure that all of us kids had clean and ironed clothes each day for school so there was a lot of laundry to do. She also cooked lavish meals three times per day and we ate like kings. She had a vegetable garden and canned tomatoes, pears, apples and other items. She made pies or cakes almost every day. I don't know how she did all this. She used to say, "A man works from sun to sun but a woman's work is never done."However, she may have been better off than a lot of farm women as many of them also worked with the livestock in the barn and in the fields which she did not.

My father was a rather stern man who didn't show his emotions very often. He was usually very serious because his responsibilities and workload were a great weight on his mind. Working 14 to 16 hour days on a regular basis year after year required a person of great character and singleness of purpose. He had little time for small talk and joking with the children. However, his great love for his children was displayed when my sister, Pat, fell out of the haymow onto a concrete floor resulting in her losing consciousness. In those days, you didn't run to the doctor with every minor injury. My father held her on his lap and rocked her all night long after having worked his regular 16 hour day. When morning came and Pat awoke he put her in her bed and went outside to resume his farm work without any sleep. There were other occasions when he showed similar love for his children but he was not inclined to tell us how much he loved us. However, he showed it often in how he took care of us and provided for us. I guess you could call him the strong silent type.

My mother was completely different from my dad. She was emotional, I suppose like most women, and showed her love for us by both word and deed on a daily basis. My mother was someone who was very approachable and we went to her with our small problems and forsympathy and support. She always had time for us. If we went to her for a problem too big for her to handle she would call in our father to solve it.

My dad was someone that all the other farmers in the area came to when there was a difficult or dangerous job to be done. Dad was absolutely fearless—he was afraid of nothing. Everyone who knew him marveled at the risks he was willing to take to get the job done. He could do anything and did and was well known in the area for his climbing ability and his fearlessness. I've seen him working high up in our barn above a cement floor with almost nothing to hang on to and get the job done. On a few occasions we would be up high in the barn on a horizontal beam, that was no more than eight inches wide, and he would do a little dance, to show off his fearlessness, with a cement floor about twenty five feet below. We were always afraid he would fall and would beg him to stop. Many farmers came to him rather than tackle their own dangerous jobs.

Dad was a very successful farmer. Although he lacked much formal education, he was very well-read and knew everything he had to know to be a success. He read *The Farm Journal, The Prairie Farmer, Saturday Evening Post, Collier's Magazine, American Legion, Chicago Daily News, Capron Courier, Belvidere Daily Republican* and others in his spare time. He was a real American patriot and was active in the local American Legion Post. He attended meetings regularly and always worked at the Capron carnival selling raffle tickets on a new car. He was also active in the Democratic Party and held political office as the Democrat Precinct Committeeman. He seemed to be aware of everything through his readings. Through his readings and other study he kept up with the latest trends in farming including soil conservation through contour farming, strip cropping and crop rotation to reduce soil erosion. He was one of the first farmers to use fertilizers, insecticides and herbicides which greatly improved productivity. These advanced farming practices contributed greatly to the profitability of the farm.

Dad was such a hard worker that it probably dissuaded me from becoming a farmer. For my dad there was always work to be done. On rainy days when we couldn't work in the fields, many farmers would jump in their pickup trucks and go off to town to visit their friends and talk with their suppliers and machinery dealers. I looked forward to rainy days in the hope that we might do what the other farmers did. However, usually my dad would say, "This is a good day to fix fence" or "Let's wash all the tractors" or "Let's change the oil in all the tractors." When my dad was finished with a farm implement for the season he would always wash it, oil and grease the appropriate parts and house it so that when it was time to use it again it would be ready. When it was time to plant corn or whatever the job, his equipment was in perfect running condition. He was always planning ahead. With my dad there was little time for fun as there was always work to be done. He was the hardest working and most honest and caring man I've ever known.

My mother was from the city so all this physical work was new to her and it was a very lonely life. Though she had only completed the eighth grade, she was a great homemaker. Because of her experience as a seamstress, she made many of the clothes for my sisters when they were young including prom dresses. In her spare time, she was continually taking in and letting out our trousers and lengthening and shortening my sisters' dresses.

In 1956 Dad bought another farm consisting of 140 acres a couple miles from the home farm which was intended for my older brother to reside and to run. The land was good but there was a lot to do to bring this farm up to the standards of my father. To bring the new farm up to his high standards we first had to remove all the fences so our farm equipment would not be impeded which resulted in just one big field. We also had to remove all trees, bushes, brush and rocks that were in the fence lines. There was a modern hog house but the trees, brush and fences around the buildings had to be removed for efficiency and beauty. This meant cutting down some of the trees and then digging out the roots and sawing up the wood. In order to make the barn ready for feeder cattle, we had to remove all the dairy cow stanchions and remove the numerous support beams so our tractor could move about unimpeded when necessary. We then had to put in new support beams. Then we used a jackhammer to remove all the different levels of cement and pour new cement so we had a smooth surface enabling our tractor and end loader to have easy access for removal of manure and other functions. My father and I spent the entire first summer after buying this farm to do this work. It was quite an undertaking.

He then hired a contractor to build another adjacent 30' x 50' cattle shed, a large cement yard, a 50' x 16' silo and silo shed. Dad and I then built several feed bunks from which the cattle would eat. It was a big job but my father was very confident and was never afraid to tackle difficult projects. My father and I worked together seven days per week that first year to get all the work done and he was nearly sixty years old. When the facilities were completed, Dad bought 150 head of steers and/or heifers for this farm as he did on the home farm.

After a couple years my brother decided not to be a farmer and moved back to town. Dad then hired a couple to reside on the new farm and work with us taking care of the hogs, cattle and field work. When I graduated from high school and went off to college in 1960 Dad realized I didn't want to take over the farms. This was a big disappointment to him and I know now how much that really hurt him. He had worked so hard to build up a wonderful operation and then his sons were not interested in taking over for him. The next year, at age 63, he sold the home farm as well as all the livestock and farm equipment and retired to a lake home in Chetek, Wisconsin which was about a five hour trip, 300 miles, by car. Dad bought a beautiful pleasure boat and a fishing boat and lived the "life of Riley." The children and grandchildren loved visiting Mom and Dad and it was a great life. Dad went fishing each day and took care of a couple rental properties they owned. Mom, for the first time, had an automatic clothes washer and dryer and they were living the life for which they had always dreamed. They had achieved The American Dream.

After a few years of this easy life, Dad got tired of fishing every day and Mom missed the children and grandchildren so they moved back down to where they had spent most of their lives on the farm and bought a beautiful four-bedroom brick home in Capron, Illinois, population 500. My parents had a great retirement in Capron and were visited almost every day by their children and grandchildren. I was always very close to my dad and he helped me a lot with my apartment buildings in the late 1960s and early 1970s. In retirement they had lots of free time and were fun to be around. They loved playing card games like Pinochle, 500 and Hearts and a board game called Wahoo. They bought a travel trailer and spent their winters traveling throughout Florida and Arizona visiting relatives and friends. After about 20 years of retirement my dad had his first heart attack and then didn't feel up to traveling anymore. From then on they stayed close to home but still enjoyed life to the fullest with their children and grandchildren. My father died in 1986 at age 88 of a heart attack. My mother then moved to a nursing home and died of old age in 1991 at age 91.

As I look back on growing up on our farm in the 1940s

and 1950s, I'm amazed at how hard my parents worked and the struggle they endured. Although my parents worked very hard they didn't require my siblings or me to do as much work as most of our peers who lived on farms. Life was very hard on the farm but my parents could solve any problem—we felt very safe and secure. My siblings and I have had many conversations about my parents and we think we were so lucky to have parents who were so dedicated to our health, happiness and future. We feel truly blessed to have had such great parents. We really miss them.

Finally, I think my parents were most proud of their children. My brother, George, was the oldest and was a really good athlete. He was captain of both the basketball and football teams in high school and played first base on the baseball team. He went on to become a welder in the Plumbers and Pipefitters Union until he retired. He died of cancer in 1998 at age 66.

My sister, Dorothy, was the real achiever and "brain" of the family. She got straight A's in high school and was the class valedictorian. She was also the Prom Queen. She went on to become a nurse and earned a Bachelor's Degree in Nursing from DePaul University and eventually earned a Master's Degree in Nursing from Northern Illinois University. Later in life she became an entrepreneur and owned and operated a KOA campground in Utah with her son. After selling the campground she retired to a country club community in Fort Myers, Florida. She is in great health and still plays tennis at least three times per week and does a lot of traveling.

My sister, Pat, was liked by everyone. She was a cheerleader in grade school and high school and the Homecoming Queen in high school. She is best known for being the Harvard Milk Day Queen in Harvard, Illinois which is known as the "milk center of the world." This was a big deal in that only one other person from North Boone High School, before or since, has ever won that contest. Pat attended Mundelin College and worked as an Executive Secretary in downtown Chicago until her marriage. She and her husband retired to Belvidere, Illinois.

Rick Diamond

I've known Rick for many years and have enjoyed playing tennis and bridge with him. Rick and his wife, Nancy, reside in a beautiful home overlooking the Caloosahatchee River at The Landings Golf, Yacht and Tennis Club which is a gated community in Fort Myers, Florida. Rick and Nancy are both "master" bridge players. Rick had a phenomenal career in the printing and newspaper businesses and has been a very civic-minded citizen. He is a very smart and accomplished man with a great personality. Everyone likes him. Rick truly did achieve The American Dream through free market capitalism and I'm very proud to call him my friend.

Rick spent 40 years in the newspaper business and owned the *Trumbull Times* an award-winning newspaper and the Trumbull Printing Company. Beginning in 1968, he wrote a weekly column called The Connecticut Spotlight which was syndicated in one-half of the newspapers in Connecticut. His column broke some important stories and made an impact in state politics. After selling his businesses to the *Milwaukee Journal* in 1979, Rick and Nancy retired to Florida. However, soon thereafter, Rick was persuaded to go to work for the Scripps News Service where he spent the next nine years commuting back and forth between Connecticut and Fort Myers.

Richard M. Diamond was born in Newark, New Jersey on March 24, 1927. It was his mother's 25th birthday. At age two he received the nickname Ricky from his sister Leila who was 20 months older and had trouble saying Richard. All Rick's grandparents were born in Europe but, as children, their parents brought them to the United States around 1880 and they all settled in Newark. From 1880 to 1910 over two million Jews immigrated to this country from Eastern Europe with most settling in New York City and the overflow going to cities like Boston, Newark and Philadelphia.

Rick's mother, Molly, was born in Newark in 1902 and attended Southside High School where she was voted "beauty queen" and was always able to retain her good looks throughout her life. At age 20, by chance, when visiting a friend in the hospital, she met her future husband, Herbert "Dick" Diamond, then 25, who was recovering from an appendectomy operation. Rick's father was known in Newark as "Diamond Dick" because of his baseball ability. He attended Barringer High School where he was quarterback of the football team and third baseman and captain of the baseball team. He graduated from high school in 1915, turning 19 on July 17, when he was already playing on a professional baseball team. Two years later he joined the Navy in 1917. According to his admirers, Dick should have made the big leagues but the loss of two years in the Navy and his marriage to Molly on February 23, 1923, cut his baseball career short. He spent the rest of his life in the insurance business.

Rick's earliest recollections were in 1930 when he had just turned three and the family moved to 37 Hansbury Avenue in the Weequahic section of Newark which was predominantly Jewish. The family lived there for the next seven and a half years. By depression standards they were fairly well off.

While the Weequahic section was a very safe neighborhood the depression was never far away. Several times people, obviously in poor straights, would ask if they could pick dandelions from their yard which apparently made a good salad. Once in a while, they would drive by the Newark Airport and see Hooverville, a shanty town of tin and cardboard shacks, home to 30,000 people.

From kindergarten on, Rick and Leila walked to Maple Avenue School. It was at least a half-hour walk—over a mile. He finished fifth grade at Maple Avenue School and loved every moment of it. At age seven, Rick was given a stamp book and started collecting stamps. He also loved geography and by age ten he knew almost all the countries in the world. Geography and history were, and still are, his favorite subjects.

In the summer of 1937, there was a very slight improvement in the economy and they moved to South Orange, a mostly upscale suburb, and this ended his days in Newark. It was a rude awakening for Rick when they moved to South Orange, a suburb of Newark. There he ran into anti-Semitism and bullying. His father had the answer for that problem. For one year Rick took boxing lessons from Solly Castelan, a former ranking welterweight contender. One day Rick stood up to one of the bullies and did well enough that bullies never picked on him again.

Rick had always liked school, especially the three years, from seventh to ninth grade of junior high school. However, high school was not a happy experience. All his friends had grown tall but he entered tenth grade at 5'2" and 105 pounds. He was miserable. He never dated, was too small to play sports, and was not a particularly motivated student. His one passion was keeping track of all the war news and getting into the war and showing people that he could be someone. After finishing the eleventh grade, Rick's father sent him to a farm in Vermont to work for the summer. From the first day Rick loved it. He liked the farmer, his dairy cows, the dog who rounded up the cows for milking, pitching hay, milking cows, tending the garden and picking the vegetables and fruits. Most of all he liked Vermont, including the people, the beautiful countryside, the square dances and the trip every two weeks for shopping in Rutland which was 14 miles away. He could not wait to return the next summer after graduating from high school.

When he returned home from Vermont he had shot up four inches during the summer and entered his senior year at 5'10" and he forgot all about the farm in Vermont. Rick couldn't wait to graduate and get into the war before it was over. He turned 17 in March 1944 expecting to join the Navy after graduation from Columbia High School in June, as his father did in 1917. His parents had different ideas. They said that since he loved Vermont so much, how about a compromise? They asked him to spend July and August in Vermont on the farm and if he still wanted they would sign for him in September, since parental approval was needed at age 17.

It was the best summer of his life. The Vermont countryside was so removed from the war, unlike New Jersey, which had many military bases and, in 1942 and 1943, had German submarines sinking over 100 ships just off the shore. Except for waiting for the mail, which contained the Rutland Herald and the war news, Vermont seemed untouched. That summer he met 16 year old Mary Ann Pratt, his very first girlfriend. Rick said that if Nancy, his beautiful and loving wife of 56 years, hears that name one more time, she threatens to tell him about her former beaus.

Upon returning home to South Orange around Labor Day, he enlisted in the Navy but had to wait several weeks before being called up on September 17, 1944. Rick was sent to boot camp on Lake Geneva in New York State and then to Quartermaster—Signalman School in Bainbridge,

Maryland. For some reason, his excellent eyesight enabled him to read Morse Code, sent at a fast rate by someone operating a shutter on a lantern which was how ships communicated in those days from over a mile away.

Upon graduation from Quartermaster school, Rick was sent to the Brooklyn Navy Yard, assigned to a brand new 2,250 ton destroyer named the U.S.S. Steinaker, DD 863, after a sailor who had been killed earlier in the war. Two days after the devastating death of President Franklin Delano Roosevelt, on April 12, 1945, Rick was on his way to New York. The rest of April included the commissioning ceremonies and some final repairs. The ship was nearly 300 feet long and its crew included 300 men and officers. Rick was designated as a quartermaster in training, whose duties included assisting the officers on the bridge with visual bearings including ship positions by starlight, keeping the log and acting as helmsman during refueling and entering or leaving a port.

However, on a small ship he also served as a signalman. In the shipyard was a tower with a signalman who practiced sending messages, by light, to other ships. A petty officer first class, with 20 years of service, was in charge of the eight member Quartermaster—Signalman division. On the third day on board, a routine message from the tower was sent to his ship at a rapid speed to test the division's ability. As was the practice, the signalman first class read the message as the rest of them stood behind him. At least four times he passed the shutter down twice—making a dot, dot to repeat the word. Each time Rick called out the word, thinking he was helping. When the message was finished, he turned around and his face was a fiery red and he bellowed, "As long as I am on this ship, you will never again be allowed on the bridge." At an early age Rick learned an important lesson; just because you know something there is a time and a place to show how smart you are.

For the next four months, until the first class signal-man was transferred, Rick had the daily job of seeing to it that all 32 clocks, all over the ship, were set to the exact same time, Greenwich Meridian Time (GMT). He clearly remembers knocking on the captain's cabin saying, "It is I, seaman Diamond, to set your clock." It was not a difficult assignment and he was able to make friends all over the ship, from the engine room to the captain's quarters. It was not until the end of April that the Steinaker ventured out into the Atlantic, headed to Newport, Rhode Island. Seven days later the war with Germany ended. They arrived in Newport Harbor just in time to see an American crew aboard a German submarine bringing it into port. It was a sinister looking vessel and Rick wondered how it had survived because all submarines had been cleared from the east coast since 1944.

Finally, near the end of July, 1945, the Steinaker, all loaded up with supplies, shells and torpedoes, headed for the Pacific. They were halfway to Hawaii when they got the message, on August 14, that the Japanese had surrendered. Rick felt the war had passed him by. To his great disappointment Rick's ship was ordered back to the naval base at Norfolk, Virginia. One month later, following the surrender of the Japanese to General MacArthur aboard the USS Missouri, the victorious Third Fleet under the command of Admiral "Bull" Halsey, left for a victory parade up the Hudson River in New York City.

When the fleet passed Norwalk it requested two destroyers to lead the process and Rick's destroyer was first in line and was chosen to follow him. When they finally reached the NYC outside harbor, their Commander gave Rick the honor of being at the helm. Four million people lined both banks of the Hudson River, fireboats shot off streams of water and tugboats tooted their horns as over 125 ships wound their way up the Hudson, about 10 miles, to the George Washington Bridge where their ship anchored. It was the most exciting day of his life but he said he felt like such an imposter because Rick felt he hadn't really participated in the war.

From December of 1945 until his discharge in July 1946, Rick's destroyer traveled to the Arctic Circle, Iceland and then to South American ports including Rio and Trinidad. Finally, it is was back to the Brooklyn Navy Yard and to Long Island for his discharge. With accumulated leave time he was given credit for two years of service and the rank of Quartermaster Third Class. Years later, after graduation from college, Rick would receive a commission in the US Navy.

Rick had never given much thought to what college he wanted to attend. He was accepted at the University of Wisconsin and Rutgers but ended up going to Cornell University where he found housing in a fraternity that had room and board for about 16 non-fraternity members to help defray their costs. Rick's roommate was Marvin Josephson from Atlantic City who was determined to hit the big time and he did. The next semester Rick and Marv found a room in a private home and they both joined the Pi Lam Fraternity where they took their meals. Their second year they rented a basement apartment in a residential section of Ithaca. They were young and veterans, but that cut little ice with the 800 female students, who were outnumbered 8-1 by male students. To ask them out on a date for the same night was an insult as they were booked for at least 10 days in advance. Rick and Marv solved that problem by buying a two-seat coupe and it enabled them to visit at least half a dozen girls' colleges in the area.

Rick moved into the Phi Lam house in his junior year as the incoming treasurer. He was elected president of Phi Lam for his senior year. One of his proudest moments was when Phi Lam was chosen as the most outstanding fraternity in 1950, the year Rick was president. There were 56 fraternities on campus, including eight other Jewish fraternities so it was quite an honor. Phi Lam finished fifth in academics, second in intramural sports, third in important positions on campus and second in community service. The number two ranking in sports was due to their first place finish in basketball and their third place finish in baseball.

Following college graduation in June 1950, at age 23, Rick's goal was to own a newspaper and give himself a platform to express his views. He says now that it probably was more of a dream or an ego trip, because he had no writing experience, no money and no idea how to proceed. Rick looked into various opportunities for the next one and a half years but nothing really materialized. Then at his mother's urging he went into the insurance business with his father. He hated it from day one but with his business acumen finally showing, he correctly advised his father to concentrate on life insurance and to turn his casualty insurance business over to his friend who had a large agency for a fifty-fifty split. The casualty business consumed 70% of his time with claims but produced only 20% of his income. In life insurance there is only one claim.

Rick decided to pursue his goal of owning a newspaper in the Miami area of Florida. First he got a job, with the now defunct Miami Daily News, selling advertising to restaurants and bars, mainly on a commission basis. Then in 1956 he went back to New Jersey and became business manager of the Paterson Sunday News. The owner's main business was a weekly newspaper for the liquor industry and he promised Rick a free hand. The "free hand" never materialized and Rick became disillusioned and left the paper after a short time.

Rick then took a job as district manager in circulation for the Newark Star Ledger. It was rare for a college graduate to be a district manager and his first assignment was a completely black district to see how long he would last. He was up to the challenge. In those years it was boys mainly who both delivered and collected for the newspapers and he quickly recruited boys from the local parochial school because he knew there would be more parental support. He did not mind getting up at five in the morning and loved the work. Each district had about 25 boys, including occasionally a few girls, who were responsible for both delivering and collecting over 2,000 newspapers. Within a year he was a zone manager in charge of eight districts and the following year was promoted to city manager in charge of 24 districts. While the work honed his organizational skills, he finally realized there was no future in the family run Newhouse chain of newspapers and the pay was not high enough to save much money.

Rick quit this job and looked at his situation. He was 29 years old with no job, very little money and, while most of his friends were married, and he was still single. He moved home for the first time since he was 17 and though his parents said nothing, he knew they were worried about him. Next Rick went to work for the Winnipeg Sun which had recently raised its price and was in danger of losing its circulation lead to the competing Winnipeg Free-Press. Rick moved to Winnipeg, Canada in November 1957 and received a small salary plus a four dollar commission for each new subscription. Rick found a low rent apartment and spent very little money. He did a very successful promotion and by the end of April, 1957, one month after his

30th birthday, Rick had obtained 5,000 new orders and had actually saved $20,000 during that six month period. That was quite a large sum in 1957.

Rick started his search to purchase a newspaper. When he realized he was starting to live on his savings he approached Joe Youngblood, his former circulation manager at the Newark Star Ledger, and asked him if he could run a district. Rick told him that the newspapers would always be delivered but that he would be done for the day by 8am. He consented, but over the next four months he gave Rick two of the most messed up districts to straighten out. However, Rick got $120 a week so he no longer was living on his savings.

When Rick was in West Hartford looking for a newspaper to buy he saw an old friend, Peter Savin, who had married a lovely girl named, Elaine. She gave Rick a list of six young women to call who were living in New York City. At the bottom of the list was a young lady named Nancy Schatz. Rick called Nancy in early July and they were married four months later. Rick says he always kidded Nan, a nickname he uses, that she was the only one who would go out with him. Elaine Savin explained it differently, "I never thought you two would hit it off." Just prior to their wedding on November 17, 1957 in West Hartford, Rick told Peter that he had finally found a weekly newspaper in Stratford, Connecticut for $17,500 and he would take over as owner of The Stratford News as soon as they returned from their honeymoon. Peter offered to put in $20,000 for working capital in exchange for a 50% ownership in the newspaper. Rick mentioned that to Nan and she mentioned it to her father, Julie Schatz, who said, "No way." He marched Rick down to his bank and co-signed a $20,000 loan. It took Rick nearly three years to pay off the loan but Rick said it was the best thing anyone had ever done for him. He liked his in-laws to be, Madeline and Julius Schatz, especially his father-in-law, a highly regarded litigation attorney.

When they returned from their honeymoon in St. Thomas, Rick immediately sensed that he had purchased the wrong newspaper. Prior to leaving for their honeymoon, he mailed 2,000 subscription renewals from a promotion the former owner had run the previous year. To Rick's dismay there were only 400 renewals for the newspaper. To make matters worse, the editor that he had hired turned out to be over the hill and Rick had to let him go after only one month. Rick also received a luke-warm reception from the eight merchants in Stratford Center who seemed to be waiting for him to fail.

Rick was determined to make the best of a bad situation and caught a break. He met a couple who lived locally—the husband was a public relations executive at Avco Lycoming, a major industrial firm, and a former newspaper editor while his wife was a former editor. The wife, with assistance at night from her husband, solved his editorial problems. Rick fired a young reporter he had hired and hired a woman to sell advertising. She prepared ads for different types of stores and did quite well. Rick saved money by switching his printing to Guilford, 40 miles away, even though it meant lugging the newspapers to the Bridgeport Post Office at 3am every Thursday morning.

Rick had come to the realization that Stratford would never be a good weekly town. It was too close to Bridgeport both geographically, and employment-wise, to have its citizens reading a weekly newspaper that concentrated on local news. His concern was how to sell without losing his purchase price, save some of his diminishing working capital, and pay off his $20,000 loan.

Rick and Nan still had to live. They had rented a three

bedroom, one bath home, in the lovely Lordship section of Stratford for $130 a month. They were three blocks from Long Sound and the beaches. They had two daughters, Lisa and Julie, in their first two years of marriage. They lived in that house, with the rent unchanged, for six years.

It was almost six months to the day as publisher, when in June, 1952, Rick received the biggest break of his business career. Rick says that everyone needs at least one break to succeed and this one was huge. Grand Union, a popular food market in the northeast, had been constructing two side by side buildings in the middle of Stratford for over a year. Two days before it opened, Rick received four pages of advertising, two for the food store, and two for the adjacent Grand Way, a clothing and supply store. Rick says, to be honest it was not quite four pages, sometimes there was room for some editorial copy on the top or side of a page. It never averaged less than three and one half pages for one year and there was no quibbling about their advertising rate.

That day it not only rained, it poured. Under the door of their office, by special delivery, was a full page ad from the A&P.

Then he had a call from the printer in Guilford telling him that he could save one-third of his printing bill if he printed on Thursday. Food markets insisted that their ads always run on Thursdays so weeklies had to print on Wednesdays to get the newspapers in the mail that night. Since Rick was Guilford's last customer, sometimes The Stratford News did not get on the press until four in the morning, for a 20 minutes press run, and a 5:30am post office deadline. With all his circulation experience, it took only weeks to set up a boy delivery system and save on his printing bill. His cup was running over but, from the experience of other weekly publishers, when food markets open a new store, they promote in weeklies for exactly one year and then stop. Rick figured he had one year, with money flowing in, to plan his future.

Rick decided to take an evening course in a Dale Carnegie Speech and Memory class. It was very helpful but, in addition, he became friendly with two classmates from the neighboring town of Trumbull, Nick Gengrasso, a lawyer, and Joe Sciortino, a builder and police commissioner. Over the weeks they both continued to urge Rick to start a weekly newspaper in Trumbull. While Bridgeport bordered Trumbull on the north, the east-west Merritt Parkway separated 90% of the town from Bridgeport.

Parts of Trumbull, at that time, were still rural with more than a half dozen large operating farms. However, post-war developments, with an influx of Bridgeporters, had jumped its population to 15,000 in 1958. There was still no high school and students had to be transported to Bridgeport and a tax re-evaluation the previous year had most Trumbull residents up in arms. For the first time since the Civil War era a Democratic Administration had been voted into office. That election was really a wild one with both parties publishing their own tabloid newspapers, slanted their own way, while the regional daily Bridgeport Post, which relied on two local part-time reporters, did not adequately cover the town. Rick took the time to visit a number of town officials and some local stores and there seemed to be genuine interest in a town newspaper. Trumbull appeared to be the correct choice for him, but the question was how to proceed and still keep The Stratford News going until he could find a buyer.

It was already December, 1958, and the food markets rents would stop in June so Rick knew he had to launch the Trumbull newspaper by then. Over the next few months, he rented a second floor office in a Main Street office building across from the Trumbull Town Hall. He reached an agreement with a reporter he admired from the Post to be his editor, and his wife to be his assistant and feature writer, a part-timer to do sports, and a young man to do advertising.

On June 1st the plan went into operation and the team had 18 days to turn out its first newspaper. This time the printing was to be done by the Milford Citizen about ten miles away. The editorial team was on schedule for the Thursday, June 18, 1959 first issue. Again reverting to Rick's experience at the Newark Star, he had a promotion piece inserted into every issue. It was a raffle for an Eastern Airline trip, and hotel stay. He says it was the best $500 he ever spent on a promotion. There were 6,500 households in Trumbull and they ended up with 4,000 subscribers at four dollars each. That was an amazing 62% return, due in large part to the excellent newspaper the editorial team put together.

A few months later Rick sold the Stratford News for $13,500. With money in his pocket and the Stratford News off his back, it was time to see what could be done in Trumbull. He was never really happy with printing in Milford. The composing room foreman was a grumpy old timer named Sam Rittenhouse and the *Trumbull Times* were billed extra for every little thing. Rick promised himself that he would never nickel and dine his customers if he was ever in that position. Rick held true to his promise in the years to come, because when he later got into the printing business he instead evaluated each customer annually. Those that were always late, or turned in sloppy copy, for example, received a higher annual increase.

After one year, Rick was approached by Stan Smith, the assistant composing room foreman, who told him that if he could find adequate space in Trumbull for used equipment, a linotype, Ludlow headline machine, and a mat roller, he could do the composing with one linotype operator. Rick liked and trusted Stan and started looking. Rick found and rented a two story professional building in Trumbull Center with a basement, whose entry in the back was down four steps into a two door entrance. The only basement tenant was a dentist's office.

In six weeks they were in business—they moved to a second floor office, and their linotype, which he purchased in Boston, was placed in the basement furnace room. It was a heavy lopsided piece of equipment that took three strong men to get down the steps and into place. The other side of the basement corridor space was turned into a composing room, and in the corridor they placed the mat roller. For the $10,000 capital investment they could now do their own typography. Each completed page was placed on the mat roller, and a soft cardboard mat was placed on top of the page. Then they turned on the mat roller and with great pressure, it left an impression on the mat. On press day, these mats were sent down to Milford and cast into metal pages that went on the press. They were to use Milford for another two years.

The *Trumbull Times* evolved into a solid newspaper, featuring detailed accounts of town meetings, along with solid, in-depth reporting in every issue, which were read intensely by the readership, and searched for evidence of bias by the local politicians. In 1963 the Connecticut National Bank's new building created 3,000 feet of empty space on the lower level with room for parking. At the same time the Rockwell-Goss Company, one of the biggest manufacturers of printing presses, came out with a small 3-unit Community offset press, capable of printing 12 standard or 24 tabloid pages at a time at a speed of 25,000 copies an hour. After being assured that its seven foot, two inch web would pass safely under their 7'6" ceiling, Rick took the plunge. The press was only the fourth sold by the company and the first one sold in Connecticut. Early that year they moved their offices and composing room into the building. They built a beautiful entrance, with a large bay window, and a sign in blue reading the *Trumbull Times*. When shoppers entered the center from Daniels Road they now had wonderful exposure.

Alongside the entrance they placed an overhead door so 1,000# rolls of newsprint could be placed inside. With an offset press they used special typewriters to produce column wide stories that could be pasted down on a page and then the completed page photographed. The negative then burned into a thin aluminum plate and when all the plates were loaded onto the press, it was time to print. Trumbull Printing Company had just been launched.

Since the Trumbull Printing Company was the first in Connecticut familiar with this process, some upstart computer companies used them as a guinea pig. Within five years, a reporter was able to electronically send a story to the copy editor who, after corrections, would send the story to a processing machine which prints columns to paste on a page. Out went the linotype, and all hot metal equipment, in came their own dark room and new customers both in composing and printing. By 1969 they had outgrown their space so the next year they built a 10,000 square foot building on 50 acres Rick had purchased on Spring Hill Road in the town's industrial section, bordering the town of Monroe.

Within less than two years they had outgrown that space and, since the old space in the bank was still available, they moved the *Trumbull Times* back there, along with their business office and Trumbull Printing occupied the entire 10,000 square feet. In 1975 Rick added another

10,000 square feet and the 24/7 activity was too much for him so he turned his big office over to his general manager, Stan Smith, and moved back to the *Trumbull Times*. Finally in early 1978 Trumbull Printing expanded to 30,000 square feet and purchased a Goss Suburban press with three folders. With the three folders they were now capable of running a 16 page newspaper or three different products at the same time.

A huge break for Rick was when Arnold Bernhard, the owner of the *Value Line Advisory Service*, wanted to move his printing out of New York City. The publisher of the *Westport News*, Rick's print customer, once worked for him and Bernhard, asked if he could recommend a printer. He recommended Trumbull Printing. Rick met with Mr. Bernhard at his 24 acre estate in Westport, Connecticut to discuss the matter. His *Value Line Advisory Service* was a 96p age magazine, listing the top stocks that were mailed weekly to over 100,000 subscribers. The magazine required a three-ring punch in order to be saved in a binder. There was much more printing to be done, including a four page tabloid promoting the stock of the week.

Rick told him that some specialized equipment was needed and Bernhard agreed to buy everything that was needed, and place it on the floor of Trumbull Printing. The cost of the equipment was over $500,000. All *Value Line* printing was done on Mondays and the agreement was for Rick to maintain the equipment and then Trumbull Printing could use it the other six days for its other customers. Within a year they had enough business to keep the equipment busy 24/7.

Another big break came on a trip Rick took to Israel in 1972. On that trip Rick met a lot of very important people in Israel as well as from the United States. 'Stop and Shop' was the biggest food market in New England but Rick could not even submit a bid on its circular work. The chain's owner and Rick were on the same Jewish Federation trip to Israel and got along well. When Rick returned home, he wrote and told him that he did not like to bring up business following their wonderful trip but he would like the opportunity to submit a printing bid. In three days, Rick received a print order and, apparently, they did such a good job that Trumbull Printing soon did all their circular business. Every three weeks Trumbull Printing printed 500,000 color circulars. By using two of their folders they could print 50,000 circulars an hour and finish the job in 10 hours. Years later the advertising manager told Rick that they were the only vendor that ever worked out.

Another big customer was "Faith," a 7x10 inch magazine that was mailed to 600,000 subscribers every month. On one of Rick's folders they had a parallel folder which allowed the newspaper to be folded over and then printed lengthwise. Trumbull Printing then fed the newspaper into one of their two Mueller five knife trimmers and staplers, courtesy of *Value Line*, and out emerged, at 50,000 an hour, trimmed and stapled magazines.

In 1978 Rick took stock in his situation. Ninety percent of their gross income was in Trumbull Printing Company that in a few more years would probably reach $10 million annually. However, Rick was no closer to his goal of owning a daily newspaper. They had 120 full time employees and 20 part-timers in Trumbull Printing but only 18 employees in the *Trumbull Times*. It was time to sell the printing company which he did later that year to the Milwaukee Journal. The Journal required that Rick also sell them the *Trumbull Times* in the deal. The Journal was as a big company that, in addition to printing a morning and an afternoon newspaper, also owned TV stations and a number of printing companies. Rick agreed to stay on for one year, 1979, to help with the transition of the *Trumbull Times* while Stan Smith would continue with Trumbull Printing.

June 18, 1979 was the 20th Anniversary of the *Trumbull Times* and when Rick told the story 34 years later at age 86, he said he could recall almost everything. There were many ups and just a few downs. In 1963 they finally had enough money to buy a small house in Trumbull and Rick, Nan and their two daughters moved there that summer. His daughters, Lisa and Julie, would eventually graduate from Trumbull High School. In 1966, their son Michael was born and shortly thereafter they built a larger home. In the summer of 1979, Nan and Rick, along with Michael, attended Cornell Alumni University for 10 days where Michael took photography and Nan and Rick took a business course. It was the first time Rick had money to invest and he thought he might get some guidance. The director, however, took the easy way out and each day had a person in some aspect of business—real estate, retail, manufacturing, etc., lecture their class.

One day a man named Keith Trowbridge, dressed in sandals, ragged pants, and a shark-tooth necklace around his shirt, lectured them about his success with time-share units in Sanibel, Florida. At Christmas vacation time that year, Rick and his family spent two weeks on Sanibel. While he resisted the sales pitch to buy a time share, the husband of one of the salesladies talked him into building two four-unit apartment buildings with him. After several visits to check on the progress of the buildings, Rick convinced Nan to move to Sanibel temporarily, along with Michael, then 14, until he decided his future.

Rick first purchased 100 acres of farmland land in east Lee County, near the Caloosahatchee River with the intention of building a house on the river. However it was too remote and when he heard that The Landings was the top tennis community in Fort Myers they bought there on the river after their first year. They are still at The Landings going on 34 years, the first 11 years part time and the last 23 years full time. However for the first 20 years, Rick did raise cattle, with a partner, on the farmland.

Looking back, 1965 was a big year for the *Trumbull Times*. The then 5,000subscriber newspaper won first place for General Excellence in the National Newspaper Association's annual contest for a weekly in its size category.

During his 20 years with the *Trumbull Times*, they won more than a dozen different awards for excellence, but Rick says awards do not tell the whole story. While his newspaper's appearance was often excellent, out-of-town judges cannot tell how well they covered their community. Rick believes they were at their best in the later years. They had matured and their self-critical team approach got a half-dozen minds probing and analyzing every week.

Lastly, he had more time on his hands and, thanks to Lem McCollum the best copy editor he had ever known, Rick learned how to write. In 1968 he wrote his first column, and with Lem's editing it was passable. Lem was completely apolitical but he could tighten up a column, cut unnecessary verbiage, and deliver columns that read well. By 1970 his column, "The Connecticut Spotlight," ran in 27, or half, of the state's newspapers, which included eight dailies and 19 weeklies. With the time spent on research, interviews and trips to Hartford, his cost was well over the four dollars he billed each newspaper for his column.

Rick did, however, achieve one of his goals; a platform from which to express his views. Over the column's 10 year existence, his lawyer, Arthur Friedman, won his case in the Connecticut Supreme Court, which then allowed all newspapers, even individuals, access to the police log.

Previously they only had access to the arrest log and many offenders, with connections, were never arrested. A 5'4" governor, at an annual publishers' meeting, threatened to punch Rick in the nose for accusing, correctly, some of his cronies of benefiting from inside information.

Rick's columns all had to be sent out early on Tuesday morning and, being a procrastinator, he says there were times he did not finish his column until one in the morning. He would awaken Nan, an English major, to edit his column. She never turned him down. Rick admits that being in the limelight for ten years, with a number of coups and interviews with candidates for top state positions, was a big boost to his ego and the highlight of his newspaper career.

In the 1970s, Rick got to know Edward W. Scripps III, the owner of the very large Scripps newspaper chain. Mr. Scripps became fond of Rick and would call him at least three times a year to chat. He was the grandson of the founder of the Scripps newspaper chain and owned over 30 small and medium-sized daily newspapers all over the country. In 1979 Rick told him he had sold his newspaper and printing company and was staying on to the end of the year. Later, Rick received a call from Mr. Scripps saying he and his wife were visiting their New England newspapers and wanted to stop by for lunch the next day. Ed Scripps was about 73 at the time, and his wife about 15 years younger, and Rick thinks she wanted to see if he would be a suitable partner. He made Rick a very tempting offer of running his two newspapers in Hawaii. He promised Rick a 25% stake if he would take over the operation. Nan and Rick finally decided it was just too distant—all their parents were still alive, their two daughters were in college, and Michael was only 13. He told Ed that he would be interested if anything opened up in New England.

That year Rick also found a trustworthy newspaper

broker to see what daily newspapers were for sale in the northeast. His timing was bad as the price for newspapers had gone through the ceiling. The chains that were publicly traded saw their stocks skyrocket. It was no time to buy a newspaper so during their "temporary" stay in Fort Myers, Rick was trying to decide whether to hire a head hunter to pursue his thought of running a large daily or to concentrate on business investments. It was at that time that he had a call from Ed Scripps. He said that his Manchester newspaper was starting to lose money. This was due in large part to a new competing tabloid newspaper that was run by a woman whose husband was the biggest home builder in the area. In fact, the newspaper had run Rick's "Connecticut Spotlight" column and had a top-notch editor. Scripps told Rick he had never folded a newspaper and if he could turn it around he would give him a 50% interest. Rick accepted as long as he could report only to Ed Scripps. Ed agreed.

Rick left Nan and Michael for four months and made every effort to revive the *Manchester Daily News* but it was to no avail. He called Scripps and told him he could stop the bleeding but it would never be a profitable newspaper. Rick told him that he was going back to Florida. Ed then asked if Rick would also run his other two newspapers in New England, the *Haverhill (MA) Gazette* and the *Newport (VT) Daily News*, along with a handsome salary. Rick agreed as long as he could spend some time in Florida and, again, report only to him. He replied that he did not care where he lived as long as Rick was in full charge.

Rick and Nan enjoyed the nine years they spent part-time in Manchester working for Scripps. They purchased a lovely two story condo in Manchester with a back porch overlooking the surrounding maintains. The 60-unit community had lovely stone walls and looked down on a swimming pool and tennis court. They shared their time between Manchester and Fort Myers.

Their son, Michael, was then at Taft, a private school in Watertown, Connecticut. By 1990, Rick realized that newspapers were facing an unstoppable decline. He, therefore, decided to retire full-time to Fort Myers. That year he became a Habitat for Humanity volunteer. From 1992 to 1995 he served as president of the Lee County Habitat for Humanity affiliate and helped celebrate the building of the 100th home.

He had made some investments in both Connecticut and Florida when his time was split between Connecticut and Florida. Rick said he did not know enough about real estate and when Nan suggested that he buy on water, or on Route 41, Rick said it was too expensive. His investments did better in the 1990's, but Nan said if he invested in one more restaurant (two had failed) she was leaving him! Rick gave great credit to Nan and said she has been supportive of everything he did and he doesn't know what he would do without her at his side.

In 1994 Rick was on the committee that drew up the Lee County Home Charter that was passed by voters in 1996. In 2000 he was one of 15 individuals appointed by county commissioners to serve on the first Charter Review Committee and was elected its chairman. In 2004 he again served as chairman of the Charter Review Committee. In 1998 he started to write op-ed guest opinion columns in the Fort Myers News-Press and for 14 years never missed having a column in the newspaper every month. He averaged 15-16 columns a year and has written over 220 guest columns. Seventy-five percent of his columns were about local issues while the rest dealt with state or national issues.

In 2013, he finally decided to stop writing his columns on a regular basis and has only written six columns. As a

WWII veteran, he became a volunteer at Edison State College, to work with some of its 500 veterans who come into the office with questions or needed help on applying for veteran benefits, which occurs mainly at registration time. One of his functions was to search online for grant money and he came up with several promising possibilities. However he is frustrated by his inability to contact veterans because federal law prevents the college from having an email list of veterans. Since the college has no record as to who is a veteran, and there is no college newspaper, Rick is about to search for some other volunteer possibilities.

Rick and Nancy have five grandchildren, ranging from Max Stein (26) and his sister Sophie (21), Allie Diamond (20), Vickie Diamond (18), and Nick Diamond, (11). His daughter, Lisa, lives in Fort Myers; his daughter, Julie, splits her time between Portland and Yachts, both in Oregon; and his son, Michael, lives in Naples. Nan and Rick are both in reasonably good health and they look forward to some weddings and, in two years, Nick's Bar Mitzvah.

Rick's sister, Leila, who never married, passed away 14 years ago at age 73 She was a well-known cancer researcher—first at Sloan-Kettering in NYC and then at Wistar Institute in Philadelphia. She was the first woman to head a committee at the then 15,000 member National Association of Cancer. At her memorial service, seven or eight women said Leila opened doors for them that previously had been unavailable for women.

One of my favorite times was when Rick and I started a men's bridge club on Tuesday mornings at The Landings. We had a group of about 20 people that we invited who were all friends, and I played golf and tennis with most of them. Rick was a Master Bridge Player so he ran the "duplicate bridge" games. Before each session, Rick would give a 15–30 minute bridge lesson and covered mistakes that he noticed in our play from previous sessions. It was really helpful because in a short time the players with less experience became much more competitive.

I am saddened to report that Rick passed away on December 24, 2013. I had spoken with Rick on December 23, as he wanted to be sure that I had all the necessary information to complete his life story. I attended his funeral which was held on December 26 at Temple Beth El in Fort Myers. At the funeral, Rick and Nancy's three children, their son-in-law and their grandchildren spoke of what a great husband, father, grandfather, friend and mentor he had been to everyone. They spoke of his selflessness, community activeness and how he loved Nancy above everything else. He will certainly be missed by a lot of people.

I miss him, too, as do all his friends with whom he played tennis and bridge. His best friend, Jim Holly, told me that he misses the daily telephone calls from Rick, which always served to brighten his day. Rick and I had many interesting discussions together. Although I would consider Rick's political philosophy a little left of center, he was always willing to hear the other side with an understanding tone. He made me feel that although he didn't agree with me on many issues he was always respectful of my comments. We had great discussions and I certainly learned a lot from him. There will never be another Rick Diamond and I'm so pleased to have known him.

Tom Guzik

This is the life story of my friend Tom Guzik who I have known for several years as a teammate on my tennis team and also as one of my regular tennis partners. He and I have even competed in a few tennis tournaments together. Tom and his lovely wife, Pam, live on the 7th hole of the Sable Golf Course in a beautiful three-bedroom home here in Heritage Palms Golf and Country Club. Tom's story is one of having a loving and devoted extended family who gave him a great childhood and upbringing. Tom was able to use his experience in the hotel industry to succeed in buying and operating his own motels and achieving The American Dream and retiring at age 52.

Tom's grandfather, Bruno Guzik, emigrated from Poland to this country in 1905 and landed on Ellis Island. He first worked in the coal mines of western Pennsylvania. After a while, he realized the future in coal mining didn't offer The American Dream. He thought about other opportunities available to him. The Polish people along with all the other new immigrant nationalities stuck together because of language and other differences. He decided to move to a Polish community in Detroit where he and his wife bought a neighborhood grocery store. In those days neighborhood grocery stores were quite common because transportation wasn't as easy. He and his wife lived above the grocery store which became a model investment for his future. He would buy existing neighborhood grocery stores and renovate the stores and living quarters above the stores and when the business was running smoothly he would sell the property. They did this with approximately 15 properties.

Tom's father was born Stanley Guzik in 1924 and he helped his father in the grocery stores while growing up. He joined the Army right after the bombing of Pearl Harbor at 17 years of age and served in the infantry in Germany. Stanley was wounded several times and won both the Bronze Star and Silver Star for bravery. He was discharged after the War as a Sergeant. When Stanley returned from the War he continued to work with his father in the grocery business. In 1946 Stanley married Wanda, Tom's mother, and they both worked for Tom's grandfather in the grocery store business and lived above the grocery store with Tom's grandparents.

The year 1950 was an eventful one for Stan and Wanda, both personally and professionally. They bought their first business, a grocery store, and renamed it S&W Market. The store served the needs of the Polish community along Michigan Avenue in Detroit. Their building also housed an independent bakery and meat market. Later that year they had their first child, their son, Tom. In 1954, their daughter, Laurel, was born. Stan, Wanda, Tom and Laurel lived with Tom's grandparents at 6898 Edward Street, about a mile from the grocery store.

In 1955, Tom's parents bought their first home in suburban Farmington Hills. After Bruno's death in 1957, Tom's grandmother sold her home on Edward Street and moved in with Stan and Wanda to help raise Tom and Laurel. She continued to live there for the rest of her life. In 1960, Tom's parents sold their S&W Market to Stan's sister. With the proceeds they bought a wholesale costume jewelry business named Alure Jewelry located in downtown Detroit. They kept that business for over 30 years until their retirement. Stan is now deceased and Wanda, now

89 years old, still lives in her home. Wanda has dementia and Laurel has moved back home to care for her mother.

Tom was an excellent student and athlete. He had what I would describe as the perfect childhood. He lived in a lower middle class neighborhood, was very happy and wanted for nothing. He played sports every free moment while growing up. He had many cousins who would sleepover at his house or he would sleepover at their homes. Tom said his parents rarely disciplined him and pretty much let him do as he pleased. That was probably because Tom knew the boundaries and always stayed within them. There were always plenty of aunts and uncles around and everyone knew the correct behavior. Tom's uncle Ed, who had five daughters but no sons nicknamed him "the greatest" and he always instilled confidence in Tom that he could accomplish whatever he desired. Tom's parents were also very supportive of all Tom's activities.

During the summer, each Sunday, the entire family of aunts, uncles, grandparents, cousins and parents would picnic at Sugden Lake, which was located in Commerce Township, Michigan. They usually had about 60 relatives who would spend the entire day at the lake playing games and swimming. These were some of Tom's fondest childhood memories.

Also during the summer, every Wednesday, and sometimes other days, Tom would ride downtown with his father to the jewelry store along with his mother, grandmother and sister, and sometimes his cousins, where they would spend the day going to movies and ending the day with a steak dinner at Flaming Embers restaurant. Often Tom and his baseball and hockey buddies would travel by bus downtown to Detroit Tiger baseball games, Detroit Red Wing hockey games and to see the sights. Tom said his parents set very few rules and he was for the most part free to do as he wanted. That was probably because Tom never got into any trouble and was always dependable. He used good judgment and was very mature for his age.

He played Little League, Pony League and Colt League baseball and was an All Star in all three leagues. When Tom was in Little League during ages 10-12 he played for the Red Sox at second base, third base and shortstop. His Little League All Star team did very well and one year they won the regional finals. Tom was a good hitter who had a high batting average, but he hit mostly singles, as at the time he was short and slim. He played in Pony League during ages 13-15 and the Colt League during ages 16-18. After their games they would usually stop by a drug store for ice cream or coke and rehash the game. He also played hockey and was the captain of his team. Tom was on a traveling team which traveled into Canada and even played in Olympia Stadium which was then the home of the Detroit Red Wings. Tom was a good skater and shooter. He really enjoyed the competition and hanging out with the various teams. It was always lots of fun. Tom said he lost some of his interest in hockey when in one game he had a tooth knocked out by a hockey stick.

Tom excelled at economics and competed in a school competition in which he won. His first job was as a baby sitter for younger neighborhood children and Tom made a game out of making money. He would write on a calendar the amount he was paid and the date and keep it for future reference. As soon as Tom was old enough, age 12, he became a caddy at the local country club. He was paid around $10 for 18 holes. He got to caddy for local celebrities such as Dick LeBeau, the defensive coordinator for the Pittsburgh Steelers and Detroit Lion football players, Gail Gogdill and Roger Brown. He did this for a couple years until he was old enough to work in the locker room at age 14.

In the locker room he shined shoes and rented lockers. He usually got a $1 for each pair of shoes he shined and 25 cents for each locker rented. He was so busy that at times he hired an assistant to keep up with upwards of 100 pairs of shoes. He usually earned about $100 per day. Later he also worked on banquets and other special events. Tom remembers the adult entertainment the men had at the country club including adult movies and strip shows. He became aware of adult life as an observer. His country club work was his start of becoming a capitalist.

While working at the country club, a side benefit was playing in several pro- ams with the club's pros, Stan and Cass Jawor. Tom got to play a lot of golf and at the age of 17 he got his handicap down to 12. Tom did very well in some of the golf tournaments and won many gift certificates for as much as $100 or more. The best score he ever shot in a tournament was 74 at age 17. He still plays a little golf and enjoys an occasional afternoon of nine holes of golf.

As I said, Tom was a very good student and after his high school graduation he was accepted at General Motors Institute. GMI is a great school in which you attend classes and also work in the factory in alternating six week intervals. Tom was accepted into this program because of his mathematics acumen. Tom excelled in mathematics which included calculus in high school. At the end of one year in this program, Tom decided he did not have the ability to visualize conceptually the engineering drawings and decided he was more inclined toward a business degree. He had an acquaintance who was attending the University of Hawaii and since Tom liked the beach and ocean he decided to go to school there. He lived with this friend and his three roommates on Waikiki Beach. It ended up that there were two girls and three guys living there and all but Tom were hippies. They all slept on their own mattresses that they just threw on the floor. They lived a very liberal lifestyle except for Tom who retained his conservative philosophy and morals. Tom said it wasn't unusual to wake up to the others smoking "pot."

While attending college Tom spent a lot of time on the beach and hotels on the beach and was infatuated with that lifestyle. He lived only a 20-minute walk from the university and usually arranged his classes for just three days per week, which allowed him plenty of free time. School was easy for Tom so the other four days per week Tom would spend on the Waikiki Beach where he would surf and just lie on the beach. Tom attended lots of evening hotel beach shows listening to the music while sitting in the sand with his back resting on an outrigger canoe. He spent a lot of time in the hotels and the fine restaurants even though he was very frugal with his money. He said there was a new crop of girls every week who wanted to have a good time on the beach and Tom was gracious enough to give them what they wanted. Hawaii was where he developed an interest in hotels and motels.

Tom majored in Business Administration and graduated from the University of Hawaii in just three years at the age of 20. His first job after graduation was with BASF Wyandotte which was a very large chemical company. After a couple years, Tom decided that type of work was not for him and he landed a job with Westin Hotels. They first sent Tom on a first class tour of their finest properties around the United States like the Century Plaza in Los Angeles and the Saint Francis Hotel in San Francisco. For a young man just out of college he thought that was the life for him. They picked him up in limos and took him to these various hotels where Tom got to see the finer things in life. This really keened his interest in the hotel business.

His job with Westin was as sales manager for Michigan Inn, a 400-unit hotel located in Southfield, Michigan which is a suburb of Detroit. This was a very upscale hotel with a fine dining restaurant and bar, indoor pool and tennis courts. His responsibilities included booking state and national associations at this hotel. He worked with general managers of various sports teams in the National Hockey League and college basketball. His job was to "wine and dine" prospective customers to get them to house their teams on their visits to Detroit at his hotel. He often held parties for prospective customers and brought in various high profile speakers as a draw. These speakers included Al Kaline the great player with the Detroit Tigers and Buzz Aldrin, the astronaut. Mr. Aldrin told Tom that "although Neil Armstrong was the first man to walk on the moon that he was the first to pee on the moon."

After doing this for about four years and booking hundreds of thousands of dollars of business into this hotel, Tom felt he was making the company lots of money but not sharing in the wealth. He was working on salary with no commission and that is when he decided to go into business for himself and become an entrepreneur.

He was fortunate to meet a motel broker, Barrett Broad, who served as his mentor in the motel business. He taught Tom one important lesson about buying motels. He suggested when Tom was first starting out that profit was more important than prestige of a property in evaluating a business. This was an important lesson for Tom. He would really take this to heart and was very particular about the kind of motels he would eventually own.

At age 20, after graduating from college, Tom purchased a condo in Farmington Hills, Michigan with the money he made and saved from babysitting, as a caddy and working at the country club. Tom was never one to flaunt his success and never bought the toys that so many young men desire. He has never financed a car in his life but instead has always paid cash. This concept of delayed gratification is the secret to a successful capitalist as it provided the seed money to buy a business. This frugalness allowed Tom the money he needed to buy his first motel at age 26.

Tom says that all successful businessmen need a lot of luck as well as the ability to recognize an opportunity and the guts to put their money on the line when buying a business. In 1977, after several months of searching, as far away as Florida, Tom thought he had found the right property. He looked the property over very carefully including the building and financial statements. It was a 21-unit property built in 1960 known as the Imperial Motel. It was located in East Detroit, now known as Eastpoint, and owned by a man and woman partnership. The man was having an affair and the wife found out about it and forced him to sell. Tom made an offer to purchase, on a land contract, contingent on inspection and approval of the condition of all rooms. After the seller accepted the contract he changed his mind and tried to rescind the deal. Initially he offered Tom $5,000 to get out of the deal and when Tom refused the seller kept raising his offer. It was then that Tom realized what a great deal he had negotiated and forced him to follow through with the sale. They closed on the deal and the seller left without giving Tom any assistance on how to run this property. In order to make the required down payment, Tom sold his condo in Michigan and his realtor even loaned Tom his commission so he could make the deal.

For six months, Tom lived at the motel and learned the operation of the business and how much the books of the business had understated the income. Tom was on duty 24 hours per day so when someone called in the middle of the night needing a towel it was Tom who had to take the call and deliver the towel. Often someone would arrive late at night and Tom would have to clean a room that was vacated earlier in the evening. Tom said he was glad to do it because every dollar counted. He rarely got a full night's sleep but Tom felt he had to do it to learn the business and to save money.

After six months, he felt the business could sustain a husband/wife team to run the motel. That is generally how he ran each of his properties. He would hire a husband/wife team to live on each property to run the operation.

Obviously there are two ways to increase profits in a motel. One way is to increase income and the other is to decrease or at least control expenses. One of the problems Tom had to contend with was the zone control valves located in each unit. The motel had a boiler and the rooms were heated by hot water circulating through the water pipes in each unit. The circulation of hot water is controlled by zone control valves which often get stuck because of lime in the water. It is a great heating system except for this one problem. Tom sometimes found that, when the zone control valves got stuck, occupants would open the windows to cool off the units in the middle of winter. This can really increase the cost of operation if it isn't corrected.

There was no room to expand this motel because all the land was needed for parking. Tom decided that he could reduce the size of the laundry room and storage areas in order to build three additional motel rooms and increased the total rooms from 21 to 24. Increasing the size of the motel immediately increased his income and profits by more than 14%, which obviously also increased the value of the motel by the same amount. Another way to increase income was through re-rents which is renting to more than one tenant in the same day. That is, often people will only stay for a few hours and check out. This gives the owner an opportunity to make extra money by having the managers clean the room at odd hours so the room can be re-rented. One of the problems with that is many managers keep the money for themselves. Tom had a bonus system in which he shared this extra income and he also kept the managers honest by keeping a tab on the linen used compared to the rooms actually rented. Tom would pay bonuses only at the end of each year so this encouraged managers to not leave voluntarily before completing their one year contract.

About two years after buying his first motel, he started looking for his second property. His parents saw the success of his first property and they wanted to get involved. Tom and his parents decided to form a partnership and in 1979 they bought a small "adult motel," the Bali Motel located in Detroit. Business was good but extremely adventurous. There was a drug gang known as Young Boys, Inc. which caused a lot of trouble in the area. One night the police were chasing gang members, resulting in gunfire. One of Tom's air conditioners was hit, resulting in an explosion which caused a lot of damage. Once they found a dead body in the dumpster. Often a man would call down to the lobby and say a woman had stolen his money and clothes and he was in the bathroom and pleading for help. Many times they would rent rooms for a four-hour period, called "short stays," for prostitutes and their clients, men and women committing adultery or young lovers needing a place for a couple hours. This allowed them to sometimes rent a room for two or even three times in one day. They sold this motel in 1986 after owning it for seven years.

In 1982, Tom and his parents knew some family friends who owned a large Best Western property in Mackinaw City who were ready to retire. Tom and his parents bought the motel which was a seasonal property open between

May 1 and October 15. This property had a lot of different needs and a much better clientele—it was an upscale property. At the time, this was the only franchise motel in the area and they often had more requests for reservations than they had rooms. It worked out really well until other motels obtained franchises and competition became keener. The clients stayed there to have access to Mackinaw Island which was only reachable by boat. They once had a fire in this motel which destroyed 15 rooms. Tom and his parents were fully insured so they were able to rebuild the rooms and buy new furniture with the insurance proceeds. They also had business interruption insurance so they came out very well on this disaster. Tom recalled one time when a married man died in one of the rooms while accompanied by his girlfriend. They sold this motel in 1993 because Best Western was continually demanding more and more improvements as they kept trying to upgrade the requirements for all their franchise motels.

In 1987, one of Tom's tennis buddies saw the success of his operation and asked Tom to go into business with him and two other partners. They formed a partnership with Tom owning 2/5ths and the others owning 1/5th interest each. They bought a 40-unit property called the Surf Motel on the water in Mackinaw. After a couple years the tennis buddy had learned the business and no longer needed Tom's help in the operation of the motel. His buddy was getting married and wanted to increase his income from 1/5th of the profits to 3/5ths and bought out Tom's interest in 1989.

Tom's stockbroker suggested to him that he consider a limited partnership in hotels. Limited partnerships are appealing because there is no time or effort needed by the investor—it is just like an investment in the stock market. Tom decided to purchase a limited partnership involved in a Ramada Hotel in Southfield, Michigan. The investment didn't work out that well and after a couple of years he sold this investment. Tom felt that without his personal management the deal had limited success. He decided at that point not to invest in properties unless he had a say in the management of the property. Later this hotel was sold and the hotel demolished because it was felt that the highest and best use for the land was not as a hotel.

Tom's 6th and last motel, was a 40-unit property in Dearborn, Michigan, known as Mercury Motor Inn, which he bought in 1985. This was another property where luck played a big part in the success of the business. Motels usually sell for a multiple of gross earnings. After he bought the motel he landed a contract with a Japanese firm which rented half of the motel on a long-term contract. Tom recognized that this additional volume made the value of the property much larger and he sold this property in 1987. On the actual sale of the motel, he said he got lucky again. The buyer was from the "old school" and he wanted to make a large down payment on a land contract instead of the standard 20%. Simultaneously, the man from whom Tom had bought the motel, also on a land contract, was retiring from his manufacturing business and offered Tom a substantial discount if Tom would pay off the original land contract. Tom used the excess cash the new buyer was giving him and paid off his land contract.

Tom sold his first property, the Imperial Motel in 2002, and retired at age 52. This was the first motel he owned and the last one he sold. All of the motels were bought on a land contract with the standard 20% down and were sold the same way. Tom has always been very conservative with his liquid cash by putting the greatest share in annuities and municipal bonds. Tom also invests in the stock market but said he was always less invested in the stock market than the usual model of investing 100% minus your age. Tom is a very knowledgeable investor who does some day trading but is very cautious and conservative in his investments.

In summary, Tom said the key to his success was adhering to the concept of delayed gratification. He put making money ahead of prestige which gave him the money to take advantage of opportunities when they were recognized. That is, the financial return on a prestigious property is usually less so Tom concentrated on the types of properties that, though not prestigious, were real money makers. It is important to keep your eyes open and continually look for opportunities. Sometimes, like in Tom's first property, the income on the books is understated and can result in a much better deal than appears on the surface. In addition, it is necessary to have the cash available in order to take advantage of these opportunities through delayed gratification. Finally, it takes a lot of luck.

James W. Drury

Jim & Greta Drury and their family

I was so pleased when Jim consented to allow me to tell his life story. I've known Jim for nearly 14 years and met him playing golf and tennis at The Landings, where I once lived and we played on the same tennis team. This is the story of a very successful man who spent his career as owner and operator of grocery stores. Later he began investing in apartment buildings and commercial property. In 1993 with his profit margin declining because of competition and Wal-Mart moving in as more competition, Jim sold his grocery business. He has continued to expand his real estate holdings and has started a new bank, of which he is a director that now has over $800 million in assets. Yet, Jim says his greatest success is his nearly 50 years of marriage and his three children and six grandchildren.

Jim was born on August 3, 1940 in Hopkinsville, Kentucky at Jennie Stuart Hospital. His parents were George Embry Drury and Eldon Carnahan Drury. Both of his parents are now deceased. He has two sisters, Donna Ingram, who is two years older than Jim, and lives in Huntsville, Alabama and Debbie Gould, who is 13 years younger than Jim, and lives in Memphis, Tennessee. Jim, his older sister, Donna, and their parents lived on Virginia Street until their parents bought a home around the corner at 106 Mooreland Drive in 1943. Jim and his sisters lived in this home until they went off to college and started their own lives. Jim's parents lived in this home until they both passed away.

Jim's father, George Drury was born in Hopkinsville on May 9, 1913 on a small farm in Christian County. George was next to the youngest child in a family of seven brothers and three sisters. He told Jim many times that life was very hard and they all had to work long hours but they didn't know any other way of life. He said that even though life was hard, they always had plenty to eat because they grew or raised everything on the farm. Money was so scarce that George's mother moved to town and opened a boarding house and took in boarders on a daily or weekly basis. George's youngest brother was named Jimmy, and he was George's favorite sibling. Jimmy was born with a heart defect and George, since he was next to the youngest, was responsible for looking after Jimmy and would pull him around the farm in a little wagon. George loved Jimmy so much that he named his only son, Jim, after his favorite brother.

Since the farm was too small to support all the children, when his dad turned 16, he left the farm and went to work at the local A&P grocery store. He became a butcher for A&P and was moved around to several locations until he found himself in Murfreesboro, Tennessee as a head butcher at the local A&P. Jim says his dad was making around $12 per week, was a nice looking young man, and owned a Model T Ford. There was a college in Murfreesboro, Middle Tennessee State College where there were many beautiful young female students. Jim jokes that his dad thought he was a big man around campus with money in his pockets and a nice car to drive the girls around town. He met a beautiful young lady named Eldon and fell in love immediately. They dated for about one year and then they were married.

Jim's mother, Eldon, was born in Moss, Tennessee on March 20, 1916. His mom grew up in this small town and was the daughter of a Church of Christ minister and school teacher/principal. She had one brother who incidentally worked for many years for A&P Grocery in management. After his mom graduated from high school, she attended college at Middle Tennessee State College which is now Middle Tennessee University. When she attended college in Murfreesboro, her dad moved the family there. He continued to teach and preach there. She graduated from college with majors in English and Math. After she married, she never worked outside of the home and used her education to help teach her three children. She also used her ability in teaching children for many years in Sunday school.

After their marriage, George was offered a manager's position at an A&P store in Nashville, Tennessee. All of his associates at A&P warned him not to take this job at this particular store because the managers were fired on a regular basis. His dad wanted a manager's position so badly that he took a chance and accepted the promotion. George and Eldon moved to Nashville and he worked night and day to make this store successful. The store was located in a bad section of Nashville and inventory control was very difficult because of pilferage. After a couple of years, like all the managers who preceded him, he was fired.

Jim says that besides meeting his mother, this was the best event in his father's life because it was a turning point that totally changed his entire life. After being fired and not knowing what he was going to do for a living, George and Eldon moved back to Hopkinsville. He turned to the only thing that he really knew, running a grocery store, and bought a small building on 7th Street in Hopkinsville. He raised the money to purchase this building by selling his Model T Ford, George's father sold his small farm and George's brother sold a small herd of pigs. George, three of his brothers and their dad, pooled their money and went into the grocery business together as "Drury Brothers" and opened their doors in December of 1937. They built their own shelves and talked a Nashville wholesaler, CB Ragland Company, into selling them their first grocery order on credit. CB Ragland was so supportive of George that he never bought from another wholesaler the entire 58 years they were in business. They operated at this location for several years until they outgrew this small store.

They opened four other small stores in Hopkinsville and Pembroke, Kentucky. George and his brother, Coleman, sold all these small stores and moved to their next location in December of 1948, along with their dad, who was called "Pa" by all their customers. The other two brothers, who originally went into business with them, decided they didn't like the grocery business and left the business.

Jim's grandfather and his wife divorced and Pa Drury, the only name Jim ever heard anyone call him, moved into the family home on Mooreland Drive and lived there until he passed away several years later. Jim was very close to his grandfather and loved him very much. Jim says, that as long as he can remember, his grandfather would rise around 5:30am and as he went to the kitchen to prepare his breakfast he could hear him whistling as he walked down the hall. There was an African American man named Solomon who had worked for his grandfather on his small farm. When he sold the farm to help put Jim's father in business, Solomon went to work for Jim's dad in the grocery business and continued to work for them for 55 years. When Jim's sister and Jim were young and going to grade school and high school, Solomon would come by their house and pick up his grandfather, his sister and Jim in their Studebaker delivery truck and take them to school. They would then continue on to the grocery store and open up for the day's business.

When Jim's dad opened their new store on Ninth Street in Hopkinsville, it was one of the largest stores in Hopkinsville competing with A&P and Kroger. This store was built when Jim was around eight years old in 1948. During the summer and also on Saturdays when Jim was in school, his dad started taking him to the store to learn how to stock shelves and sack groceries. His parents believed in teaching their children at an early age that learning how to work was a very important lesson to succeed in life.

His dad continued to expand his business in Hopkinsville and in January, 1954, built a store that was approximately 10,000 square feet, the largest grocery store in Hopkinsville at that time. Their business grew rapidly in this location and after about four years his dad added around 3,000 square feet of additional space to this building. When his dad was in the process of building this new store a very tragic event occurred. His dad had many customers who had loyally shopped with him since he had started his business and his dad was very loyal to them also. One of his customers, Ide Bouldin, a local electrician, was hired to do all the electrical work in this new store. His dad also hired a plumber who happened to belong to the local plumbers union. The union leaders came to his dad and asked him to fire his friend because he wasn't a union member and hire a union electrician. His dad, being loyal to his friend, instead replaced the union plumber. After he made this change, they were awakened one night by a call from the police telling his dad that the back wall of his new building had been blown up by a bomb. The FBI was called in, but no one was ever arrested for this bombing. His dad still stuck by his friend and rebuilt the damaged part of the building and they never had further trouble.

Jim says he had a wonderful childhood growing up on Mooreland Drive because there were many young boys and girls to have as friends. His dad and mom were very instrumental in giving him tremendous work ethics and moral values as he grew up. He worked around the house and also at the grocery stores. Jim worked on a regular basis during his summer vacations but his dad was very good about letting him enjoy his summers and would let him take off at times to learn how to play golf and water ski at Kentucky Lake. His mother, whose dad was a Church of Christ minister, was very adamant about them going to church. They were there every Sunday, both morning and night, and also on Wednesday night. When he was 13 years old, his mother and dad had another daughter, Debbie. His mother was around 40 years old and someone becoming pregnant at that age was almost unheard of at that time. Needless to say, when she was born, everyone spoiled her to death.

Jim and his older sister attended grade school at Virginia Street School, which was about two blocks from their house. When the weather was nice they would walk to school with all their friends instead of riding in the Studebaker delivery truck. While he was in grade school he played football, baseball and basketball on the little league teams. Jim says he was very fortunate to have participated on the very first little league teams in each of these sports.

Bud Hudson, the local Postmaster, was instrumental in starting all three of these programs. When Jim's son was in grade school he helped coach him in Little League Football and Bud Hudson was still involved every day.

Jim attended Hopkinsville High School on Walnut Street in the eighth grade through the twelfth grade. While he was in high school he played coronet in the band in the eighth through the tenth grades. His mother talked him into trying this and he didn't like it very much and was not very good at playing the coronet and was very happy when he could quit the band. He played on the football and golf teams the entire time he was in high school. They only had 27 boys on their football team but during his junior and senior years they were ranked in the top 10 in Kentucky and several weeks in his senior year they made it to number two in the State.

Jim graduated from high school in the spring of 1958. He went to David Lipscomb University in Nashville, Tennessee his freshman year and then transferred to the University of Kentucky his sophomore year. He pledged the Delta Tao Delta fraternity when he went to the University of Kentucky. He says he would like a do-over of his four years of college. He didn't work hard enough and after attending four years he quit and joined the Army Reserves. He served six months active duty at Fort Knox and six years in the reserves in Hopkinsville.

After college and after completing his six months of active duty in the Army Reserves, Jim went home in 1963 and joined his dad in the grocery business. He bought his Uncle Coleman's interest in the business and became a partner with his dad. After being home for around one year, in 1964, Jim married a wonderful girl from Paducah, Kentucky named Greta Woodall. He had met her in college and dated her for several years. Greta and Jim were married on December 27, 1964 at the Broadway Methodist Church in Paducah and her parents, Dalton and Charlotte Woodall, had a beautiful wedding reception for them at the Paducah Country Club.

They drove to New Orleans the next day and spent several days at the French Quarter including going to the Sugar Bowl. They then traveled to Miami and boarded a ship to Nassau. They were on a ship named the Yarmouth Castle and several years later it sunk in a terrible storm. Jim says he is glad it waited until they were off the ship. They spent several days there and then flew back to Miami. They drove up the east coast and visited Savanna and Hilton Head Island. They were stopped twice on their honeymoon by the police and given speeding tickets. They told the officers that they were on their honeymoon but to no avail. Heartless! They returned home and began their wonderful life together.

After they had been married about three years, in 1967, they decided to build their dream home. Jim's dad told them that they were crazy to go into so much debt so early in their marriage. After they moved into their home at 402 Deepwood Drive his dad changed his mind and said that it was the wisest thing they could have done. Right after they moved into their house, prices on home building started a rapid rise. Their oldest daughter, Charlotte, was four years old when they moved into their new home and Greta was pregnant with twins, Spencer and Lucinda. Jim says they have lived in their dream home ever since and plan to live there until they are carried out. Jim and Greta will be married 50 years on December 29, 2014.

The grocery business continued to grow and a group of businessmen opened up a strip center called Indian Hills Shopping Center on another side of town. They talked to Jim and his dad about opening up a grocery store in this center. They were very excited about being included in this new development and opened up this new store sometime in 1964.They continued to grow and opened up their third store on North Main Street in Hopkinsville in the early 70's. They were the first grocery in Hopkinsville to offer scanning, the first to have a complete deli including outside catering and first to remain open 24/7.

They had around 175 employees after opening the third store. They had a wonderful catering business which would cater weddings, parties and dinners as large as 700 people events to areas within a 60 mile radius of Hopkinsville. They tried to offer their employees as many benefits as they could possibly afford. They paid their full-time employees full family health benefits, and had both a profit sharing and pension plan for their full-time employees. They also gave their employees a Christmas bonus. They were so surprised when their employees wanted to have a union election in their small grocery operation. They had to hire lawyers and try to convince their employees that this would be a bad thing for them. They had an election and the union was defeated.

Unfortunately his dad had been with management with A&P and had dealt with the union when he was with the grocery chain. He also remembered the store bombing back in the forties when George refused to hire union contractors. After the election, Jim's dad said that he just couldn't go through this again because of his age. He knew that they would probably be facing a union election every year so he wanted Jim to buy him out so he could retire. Jim agreed with this, but the only way that he could afford to purchase the business from his dad was to sell two of their stores. They also thought that downsizing would make the union less interested in organizing their business.

After they sold two of their stores and consolidated into one grocery location, their customers were so loyal that Jim did almost the same volume of business in the remaining store as they were doing in all three stores. It was a wonderful situation but put a real strain on this store and was the reason they went to a 24/7 operation.

While they were in the grocery business, they decided to branch out into real estate. They had the opportunity to purchase a six-unit apartment building, Cardinal Apartments, around 1973. It was one of the nicer apartment buildings in town. It contained four units of 1,900 square feet each and two smaller one bedroom units. They purchased two-four unit apartment buildings, the Circle Drive Apartments, around 1983, that were located a short distance up the street from the Cardinal Apartments. They kept their eyes open for other opportunities and around 1985 they purchased a 48-unit, nine-building complex, Thornton Court Apartments. This complex was built in an historical residential section of Hopkinsville in the mid-1950s. They were all brick with hardwood floors but needed a great deal of updating. They immediately renovated this property by putting in central heating and air, new appliances and all new cabinets. They added a one bedroom unit to one of the existing buildings at Thornton Court. They also had an empty lot at the Thornton Apartment complex, so sometime around 1996 they built a 12-unit apartment complex, Thornton Terrace Apartments. Jim was managing these 75 units from their grocery store on North Main Street. Needless to say, this kept Jim very busy.

After Jim's maternal grandfather retired, he moved to

Hopkinsville where his first wife died at an early age of a sudden stroke. When he moved to Hopkinsville, Jim's dad let him work in the grocery store on 7th street alongside Jim's paternal grandfather, Pa. They became wonderful friends and when Pa was around 75 years old he asked Jim's maternal grandfather to baptize him. They went to the small church which Jim's parents attended by themselves and his mother's dad baptized his father's dad. Jim always thought that was a special event.

The saddest thing that happened in his mom's life was when she was around 70 years of age, when she experienced a Transient Ischemic Attack (TIA), or mini-stroke. Jim's dad tried to take care of her but died of lung cancer when he was 73 years old, while he was trying to assist her. Her TIA scared her mainly because her mother had died very young of a stroke. Jim says she seemed to totally give up and stayed in bed most of the time. Jim prodded and argued with her to get up and get off all the medicine that she was convinced she needed but she wouldn't listen. She just gave up but lived another 23 years mostly in bed. She was such a beautiful and intelligent person, but this fear totally took over her life. She spent the last four years in a nursing home. They took her off all the medicine except for one pill but her inactivity had already taken its toll. Jim used to visit her many times at meal time and she would smile and wait until he would pick up a spoon and feed her. When he would leave she would wave and smile. Many times when he left her one of her nurses would follow him and laughingly tell him that when he wasn't there that his mom would feed herself.

There was a local bank named Planters Bank and Trust which was formed in the late 1800's. It grew and became the largest local bank in Hopkinsville. Around 1969 Jim had the honor of being asked to be on the board of directors at Planters Bank. He served on this board until he resigned in 1995. Planters Bank had some large investors located in Nashville, Tennessee and they merged Planters Bank with a bank in Williamson County, Tennessee. Shortly after this it merged with Commerce Union Bank in Nashville, Tennessee. It then merged with a larger bank and became Sovran Bank. It then merged and became C&S/Sovran, then Nations Bank and finally a merger with Bank of America. Jim resigned in 1995 before the merger with Bank of America.

There were several reasons for his resignation from this bank board. Corporate decided to force retirement of the local personnel director who had worked for the local bank for over 20 years. He only had two years left before retirement. They then closed the local trust department and moved that operation to Nashville. They fired all the employees in that department. The people who ran that trust department had a combined 60 years of service to the bank. They didn't try to relocate them to another area of the bank. A local bank immediately hired these two people and put them to work in their trust department. Jim's bank lost over 70 million dollars in assets to this bank in the next two months. At the next board meeting Jim asked the Nashville representatives to explain how they could justify these decisions. They brought charts and put on their dog and pony show and said that if they could cut certain expenses and only lose a percentage of business that was their objective.

They then fired the vice president who had been brought in from Nashville several years before all of these mergers. He had over 15 years with the bank. Jim wrote a resignation letter and presented it to the board. He explained that he didn't want to be involved with an organization which treated employees in this manner. He told them that he was just a small town man but he was convinced that this was not the way to grow a strong company. He stated that their lack of interest in small businesses and small customers was foreign to him. He always felt that you treated everyone the same, not only because that was what his dad had always stressed to him but because you never knew when a small business might grow into a large customer.

When Jim resigned, the local president, Mike Fels, called him into his office and closed the door. He said that he was also depressed about the events that were happening in their local bank. He was almost in tears while telling Jim that he was the one who had to fire these wonderful employees. He then went on to confide to Jim that if he could get a group of investors together and start a local community bank that he would resign and help run this bank. Jim was shocked and felt that this was an endeavor that he didn't want to tackle. He went home and after much thought and discussion with his wife he decided to contact several of the local businessmen and women around the community to discuss the idea of forming a new bank.

He approached many people in the community including three previous board members of this bank. They finally had five people who wanted to pursue this challenge. The five organizers were Jim, Ben Fletcher, a local lawyer, Bill Williams, a local farmer and developer, Randy Arnold, a local farmer and gasoline distributor and Kathryn Flynn, a local clothing manufacture who was the largest local employer in Hopkinsville.

They met with lawyers in Louisville and Nashville who helped them obtain a bank charter. This group worked diligently and after a year and a half of hard work they obtained the bank charter. This was just the beginning of their challenge to get this bank off the ground. They had to find a location that would make a statement, they had to think of a name for this bank, they had to hire the best people they could find to be successful, and so many more things too numerous to list. One night Jim and Greta, his wife, were trying to think of a dynamic name and he said wouldn't it be fantastic if they could name the bank Planters Bank, after the original bank that he had served on the board in Hopkinsville. He met with the other organizers and told them about his idea on the name. They all agreed that it would be fantastic. They applied to Frankfort, Kentucky for this name. Bank of America immediately objected but they found out very quickly that when they bought the original Planters Bank that they had forgotten to reserve the name. The bank organizers were so excited that they could use this name and the community was also appreciative.

They then started looking for their first location. After much thought and consideration they chose a location that was one of the oldest buildings in Hopkinsville. It was built in the mid-1800s by a local farmer for his home in town. He loved steamboats and he designed this house in the shape of a steamboat. He moved his daughters to town and lived there with his family. During the Civil War the house was occupied by the Confederate Army and then by the Union Army for their hospital. Many years later the home became the location of a very popular antique store named Gordon Cayce. Customers from all over the United States came to shop at this wonderful store. After Gordon Cayce died, this location was occupied by several more antique owners but none could seem to keep the same mystique as the original store. The building was finally sold to an out-of-town accountant from Mayfield, Kentucky who tried to break into the local market but finally closed the business. The building sat vacant for several years and was deteriorating badly. Bill Williams and Jim met with the owners in Mayfield and after much deliberation they purchased the building for their first location. The community was very excited about them saving this historical site.

They had an original offering of the bank common stock in Hopkinsville and sold seven million dollars of stock at $20 a share to start their operation. They opened the doors in September 1996 with seven employees. They worked very hard to build business in Hopkinsville. Mike Fels was the original president and after about three years the bank had grown to about $50 million in assets. One morning, Mike Fels walked out of his shower and had a massive heart attack. All of a sudden, they were not only devastated by his death, but were left without a president. The bank had only been in operation for three years, and they searched for a new CEO and president for another year. They finally hired a young lady, Elizabeth McCoy, for the job. She was president of a local US Bank operation. She graduated from the University of Kentucky with a major in accounting and has attended many banking schools throughout her career. After taking the helm she started surrounding herself with an amazing group of employees. She hired the best commercial and consumer lenders in the market. She has led their bank to heights beyond their wildest expectations.

After a short time with Ms. McCoy at the helm, they decided to branch out into the Clarksville, Tennessee market. Clarksville is one of the fastest growing towns in Tennessee and they felt this was a great market for them. They opened a loan production office in Clarksville after hiring Paul Shauff from another bank. He was a tremendous local commercial lender and had a great following in Clarksville. They chose some outstanding Clarksville business leaders to be on their Clarksville advisory board. They purchased their first location from Regions Bank, which had decided to leave the Clarksville market. They operated out of this branch while they built the main operations building in downtown Clarksville. They now have five banking offices plus a mortgage office in Clarksville, Tennessee.

They recently purchased five branches in Western Kentucky from Northern Trust out of Evansville, Indiana. They have three locations in Hopkinsville and a six-building downtown campus around their original location. These buildings have all been remolded and contain their IT operations, trust department, commercial lending, operations, main banking and entertainment-board room. They have improved the downtown area by buying and improving these various locations. Planters Bank now has close to 180 employees and is continuing to look for areas to grow. Ms. McCoy, the board of directors and their dedicated and talented employees have grown this bank far beyond their wildest dreams.

The bank now has close to $800 million in assets with very small losses. They never had any subprime loans and never took any TARP money from the government. The bank stock was recently appraised by outside professionals and has a current value of $90 per share. Jim says this has all been accomplished by a great board of directors, a truly diligent CEO and president and an outstanding group of employees. He says it has truly been a dream come true and the most fun of any endeavor of which he has ever been involved. Ms. McCoy has not only been a tremendous CEO but is also totally involved in their community. She served on the local hospital board for several years, served on the local sewerage and water commission, is president of the local economic development committee and is involved in many other community projects. She has also been named president of the Kentucky Chamber of Commerce for 2014.

Jim was in the grocery business until the spring of 1993. He still had a good business but it was becoming harder to make a fair return on investment with Kroger building a new large store and with the addition of a Wal-Mart in their community. An out-of-town realtor contacted Jim and told him she had a client who wanted to buy 25 acres. She looked at a parcel that Jim owned but instead of Jim's land they chose a parcel on the other side of town. During one of their conversations she let it slip that her client was a Wal-Mart Super Center which wanted to locate in Hopkinsville. Jim knew he could stay in business and compete against them with their extensive deli operation but the profit margin would continue to slide. He contacted a firm that had around 100 stores and sold out to them in June of 1993. He hated to get out of his life's endeavor that his dad had started but he figured that it was a good time to move on at 53 years of age.

In 2001, Jim and two other men, Bill Williams, with whom he served on the Planters Bank board of directors, and Bobby Cumbee, a local builder, formed a partnership. They built two commercial buildings which Jim helped manage for this partnership. The first building was built and leased to the FDIC and the second was built and rented to Atmos Energy which is the local natural gas provider for Hopkinsville. These entities are still renting these buildings. They probably would have continued to build commercial buildings but sadly he lost both partners at very young ages, one to a heart attack and the other to cancer. Jim still manages these properties for himself and his previous partners trust accounts. Jim says he misses these friends very much.

After he sold the grocery business he continued to manage his apartment business. In 2007, Jim and a friend, Hal McCoy, formed a partnership named Drury-McCoy LLC. Hal is the husband of Planters Bank CEO and president. Hal had a 30 acre piece of property on the new bypass around Hopkinsville. There are many new businesses, a new YMCA and hospital offices on this bypass. They decided that Hopkinsville needed some upscale apartments and so they started designing and planning this new development. They started land preparation in 2009 and built their first two apartment buildings and opened them in October 2010. These buildings consisted of 16 units per building and the complex was named Griffin Gate Apartments. They were well accepted and filled up immediately. They started construction on the next phase and completed another building in February 2012 which contained 16 units and it also filled up immediately. They started construction on the fourth building right away and finished construction on this building in June of 2013. They stay 100% occupied and are now trying to decide when to finish the final construction. They have room for two more buildings which would add 32 more units making Griffin Gate Apartments total 96 units. They added a swimming pool in 2012. They have more room on another section of this property and they think that duplex homes would be great but this is in the future.

After they completed the first two buildings in Griffin Gate, Jim started analyzing his 75 older apartments around Hopkinsville. They were all fully rented and he had always kept them in first-rate condition but as they grew older and the section of town in which they were located was starting to decline. Jim, along with his maintenance man, Hermon Goodwin, who has worked for Jim for over 30 years, totally managed these 75 units for all these years. They would take all the calls, show the units, repair all the units and solve all the complaints. Jim analyzed the property and decided it was time to sell. He located a buyer and finally sold all 75 units in June 2012. Jim says he had many disappointed tenants because Hermon and Jim really prided themselves on great service and attention to the tenant needs. Jim still gets calls from these tenants telling him that it is not the same at these apartments since he sold them. Some of these tenants have moved into Griffin Gate Apartments.

Greta and Jim now spend around four months in Fort Myers, Florida. They love to play tennis and golf in Florida. They live in a gated community called The Landings Golf, Tennis and Yacht Club and have met a group of new friends from all over the United States and Canada. They are both on two tennis teams which play different clubs around Fort Myers. They enjoy the beach on Sanibel and love to ride their bikes. Jim says that God has blessed his entire life and has been an important part of the lives of his entire family. He feels like a very blessed man and he attributes their success to the hard work and great values that their parents taught and instilled in them. They taught Jim the value of hard work, the importance of friends and that family is the most important thing in life. Jim says some people might consider him successful because of what he has accomplished in business, but he has a totally different idea of success. He says that he and Greta will have been married 50 years on December 29, 2014. They have been in love from the day they met until now and he considers this their greatest success. In addition, they have raised three children who they tried to teach the same values of hard work, honesty and total loyalty and dedication to family and friends. Jim considers his children to be their second greatest success.

When their children were three and six years of age, they bought an old 54 foot Seagoing steel hull houseboat. They docked this boat at the Barley Lake Marina which is near Cadiz, Kentucky. They remodeled this boat and spent many fun-filled weekends with their kids. They had a small ski boat and the kids would ski from early morning until almost dark. All of their kids could ski before they were six years old. The kids brought their friends on many occasions and Jim taught them to ski. Jim says he probably taught over 50 kids to ski over the years. After skiing all day, they would buy worms and crickets and fish for sun perch, catfish and bass until late into the night. Sometimes they would pile into a car with other friends on the dock and go frog gigging in nearby ponds. Many times they would have dock parties and cook all the fish that they had caught.

They had this Seagoing Houseboat for about five years and then traded in for a new 52 foot Gibson Houseboat. This boat was beautiful and they took many trips up and down Cumberland River which was dammed up to form Barley Lake. Jim says their family memories of time spent on the houseboats on Barley Lake are some of their most wonderful times together. When their kids began to drive a car, they weren't as interested in going to the lake. One winter night, sometime in the early 1980's they were sitting at home and received a call from one of their boating friends who informed them that the marina where their boat was docked was on fire. They drove down to Barkley Marina in a snowstorm and watched their boat burn and sink. There were 16 of their friends who also lost their houseboats along with many other types of fishing and ski boats. After that, they didn't get back into boating for several years.

Greta and Jim have three beautiful children and six wonderful grandchildren. Their oldest daughter, Charlotte, lives in Hopkinsville and has three children. She is married to an outstanding man, Jason Powell. They met in Nashville Tennessee and have been married around 20 years. Jason works for Mizuho OSI, a Japanese company that sells technical operating tables. Charlotte, while raising their very busy children, is on the children's ministry team at the First United Methodist Church in Hopkinsville and also manages Trifecta Solutions which sells all types of promotional material and advertising ideas.

Their children are Gretchen, 17, Mary Glenn, 14 and James Spencer, 8. They are outstanding children and are all active in scholastic and athletic events at their schools. Gretchen is a senior at University Heights Academy, is president of the National Honor Society, has played the violin for 14 years, is a cheerleader for the high school and plays on the high school tennis team. She just won the local Distinguished Young Woman contest in Hopkinsville and competed in the state contest in January 2014. She is a member of the Christian Athletes Club and has attended many youth missions in different cities with her youth group at church. Mary Glenn is in the ninth grade at Hopkinsville High School, is an outstanding student, and is on the varsity soccer team and on the varsity tennis team. She would love to try out for the golf team but it conflicts with the soccer season. She also has attended several summer youth missions with her youth group at church. Spencer is in the third grade and is a very good student. He loves to play the guitar and is a professional WI player. Jim says he won't even attempt to play him. He also likes to play tennis.

James Spencer and Lucinda are their youngest children

and are twins. They both live in Duluth, Georgia. Lucinda is married to a wonderful man, Charles Burts. Charles is from Columbia, South Carolina and is a communications specialist. He and Lucinda met while they were both working at Accenture, a large consulting company. He was a partner at Accenture and worked there well over 15 years. He recently resigned and went to work for Amdocs OSS, a network and telecom solutions provider. Lucinda worked for Accenture as a project analyst. She resigned when she started her family because she wanted to be home with her children. She loves tennis and has played on several winning Alta tennis teams in Atlanta. She loves to play golf but doesn't have much time to participate. She is very active in her church and is on several committees at the church. She has recently gone to work at Greater Atlanta Christian School where both her children have started attending. She is program planner at Greater Atlanta Christian.

She and Charles have two beautiful children, Charlotte and Dalton. Charlotte is 11 years old and a very good student and made the honor roll. Her favorite sport is riding horses and she has attended a horse camp for two years in the summer. She is also a very good tennis player and loves to play the violin. She was recently in the wonderful school play "Annie." Dalton is also a great student and recently made the honor roll at school. He is an all-around athlete who plays golf, tennis and basketball. He plays golf at the Atlanta Athletic Club and has won several youth golf tournaments.

Jim's son, Spencer, also lives in Duluth and is married to a wonderful lady, Mary, who is from Columbia, South Carolina. Spencer works for Atlantix Global Systems which buys and sells IT hardware all over the world where he is a sales manager. He has been with this company for over 10 years and has been very successful. Spencer is very active in his church—he sings in the choir, is a member of a men's early Morning Prayer group and is on many committees at the church. Spencer is a two handicap golfer at his club and also on their Atlanta Alta tennis team. He is a great father and devotes as much time as he can to be with his only son, Wyndall Benjamin, who is five years old. He is a wonderful grandson who already loves golf. Maybe the next Tiger Woods? Mary is a stay at home mom watching after their active son. She plays on their club's Alta tennis team and has been on two winning Atlanta Alta tennis teams.

Greta and Jim were fortunate to go on many wonderful trips together with family and friends. When their kids were in school they started vacationing in Florida ever school spring break with many families from Hopkinsville. They would go to Panama, Destin or Daytona Beach, Florida and spend a fun-filled week swimming in the ocean, building hundreds of sand castles, eating at wonderful seafood restaurants and getting sunburned. They even decided to take on an educational trip to Washington, D.C. one spring break when they were teenagers. When they look back on this trip they have wonderful memories, but at the time Jim thinks their children were sort of bored.

They also vacationed in Cancun, Mexico on one school break and it was a disaster. When they look back on it they laugh their heads off. First, the airline lost Greta's luggage and it wasn't returned until they returned home. The weather was cold almost the entire trip. They went scuba diving one day and, as his son jumped in, his air tank hit him in the head and slightly cut his head, which started bleeding. Their daughters and Jim were already about 30 feet in the water and wondered why he wasn't following them. Spencer had climbed back into the boat and the Mexican divers, who couldn't speak very good English, said that he was okay and back into the water he went. They were down for about 30 minutes and luckily no sharks were attracted by his bleeding head. Jim didn't know this had happened to him until they surfaced.

During the time they were underwater, the ocean was rocking and rolling up above and Greta, who decided not to dive, was in the boat and everyone around her was getting seasick. Thank goodness they made it back to shore safely. The final blow was that Charlotte, their oldest, and Spencer caught the Montezuma Revenge. They finally got back to Hopkinsville but they have never returned to Cancun. They also went on several ski trips with their kids to Vail, Aspen, Beaver Creek and Snowmass, Colorado. They had a ball on all these trips.

Jim says the reason he worked hard was so he could help his family to be able to have the same opportunities that his father provided for him. He probably could have been more financially successful but it was more important to him to be at all the functions in which his children participated and to focus on spending as much time in family events as possible. His children now have families and seem to have the same focus on the importance of family over anything else. Jim and Greta are now enjoying many of the events in which their grandchildren are involved. Jim says that life is so very short and they have learned to try and live each day as if it were their last. They certainly have achieved The American Dream.

Adrian Stevens

I've known Adrian for many years here in Heritage Palms where we play tennis together. Adrian and his wife, Cindy, live in a beautiful home here in The Enclave which is a gated community within our gated club. This is the story of one of the most ambitious men I've ever known. He credits his parents for giving him the drive, ambition and training needed to be so successful. He is very religious and gives credit to God for his great life. His life story is one of starting with nothing and retiring at age 44 after having achieved The American Dream.

Adrian was born in 1959 to Lester and Nell Stevens, the fifth of eight children, six girls and two boys, in Monmouth County, New Jersey. His parents were working poor. They lived their lives quietly, working hard every day and trying to give their children a better life than they had. His father was born in the 1930s and lived most of his life in New Jersey. He grew up in extreme poverty in Tinton Falls area and lived in a house with a dirt floor.

Adrian says his paternal grandfather was a mean alcoholic who had lost a leg in a car accident and relied on odd jobs to make a living. He was a local "tinker" who could fix most things but made little money. His paternal grandmother was a cleaning lady and did whatever work she could find during the Great Depression. He never met either of his paternal grandparents.

Adrian's father was an excellent baseball player and during his sophomore year of high school he was spotted by a baseball scout for the Carolina leagues and was asked to pitch for them in the southern leagues of the day. He left school and played baseball, learned auto mechanics and body work to pay his bills in the off season. About four years later he met his future wife, whose brother married his dad's only sister. Within a year his parents were married.

His mother was born in a small town in the mountains of Kentucky during the Great Depression of the 1930s. She was one of 16 children and only finished the eighth grade. At age 13, she moved to Chicago to live with her brother and his wife to escape the poverty she grew up with and make a better life for herself. She came from a home that was abusive and harsh. Her father was a part-time farmer, coal miner, preacher, moonshiner and a violent alcoholic. Adrian never met him, but did meet and know his maternal grandmother, Louise, who they called "Lewdee."Adrian says she was a character, smoked a corncob pipe and kept her hair in a bun. When she took her hair down it reached almost to the floor. She died at age 86.

Every year Adrian's parents and siblings would visit his maternal grandmother and her family in Gannon Hallow, Kentucky the last two weeks of August. All 10 of them would drive the 17 hour trip in a station wagon. It was a poor area with no indoor plumbing and a very simple lifestyle. Some of his memories were playing with cousins who had a funny accent, bathing in a wooden tub and the smell and taste of his Aunt Maczeen's corn bread. The woods were filled with rattlesnakes. His aunt and uncle would warn them not to wander too far into the woods so as to be shot by the moonshiners if they got too close to the stills. Adrian remembers on the very long ride home from Kentucky and thinking "and I thought we were poor."

Most of his growing up, from six to twelve years old,

was on a 70 acre horse farm in Ocean Township, New Jersey, which his parents rented since there were few places that could house eight kids. The farm was known locally as Greendale Farms and remained a farm until 1973 when it was sold to be developed as an apartment complex. The farm was also a means of additional income for his parents, who leased horse stalls and hosted 4-H horse shows where they ran the concession stand. They grew hay in summer months and sold it in the winter. His mother babysat other kids for extra money, his sisters did stall work for renters and tended to their horses in exchange for money and use of their horses. In the summer months, they would grow and harvest hay and store it in the main hayloft for winter use. Adrian says that's where he learned that working 12 hours a day simply meant you only worked half a day so he should stop complaining. His parents started their day at 5am and ended it sometime around midnight six days a week. Adrian says that Sunday was a day of leisure so they only worked from 8am to midnight.

His mom ran the household like an Army drill sergeant who gave orders and took no lip. You were expected to do your chores without being told. When the kids got home from school they completed their homework and after a 10 minute snack they did their chores until called for supper. Adrian says it didn't matter whether it was 100 degrees or below zero outside. The only time they were allowed back into the house before mealtime was to report a near fatal event. When his mother called them at mealtime she expected them to come running and it wasn't healthy to be a straggler as you might incur her wrath or that of his father. His parents weren't big on corporal punishment but on the rare occasion that it was inflicted it was memorable. Adrian said his dad's hands were like concrete from years of hard work. They were hard-working people who took the job of raising their kids very seriously. The kids were expected to be clean, respectful of authority and they had to work for everything they got—there was no freeloading or handouts.

When Adrian was 10 years old he got his first job working at a local sweet shop, which doubled as a restaurant. Adrian and a friend would ride their bikes, two miles to the restaurant and work from 5am until 10am on Saturday and Sunday for five dollars each plus a butter roll and a hot chocolate. Adrian worked that job until a regular Saturday customer, Sid Levine, who owned the dry cleaners in the same strip mall, offered him a better job. Mr. Levine came into the restaurant for coffee and a bagel every Saturday and admired Adrian's hard work. He offered him a job for two hours per day after school and six hours on Saturday to clean the dry cleaner and the other equipment. Adrian says his mother's boot camp training was about to pay off. He was paid $1.35 an hour and he thought he had hit the jackpot. His parents required him to save half of his earnings and he was allowed to spend the other half. Adrian says that lesson in thriftiness and frugality it one he still lives by today and was one of the personal lessons that allowed him to retire financially independent at age 44.

His dad worked for a truck and car tire dealer in Red Bank, New Jersey for 18 years, starting as a mechanic and later becoming the general manager. He and his mom had been promised by the owner of the business that they could buy the business from him. Then in the summer of 1972, after returning from his August vacation, he was told the business had been sold and the new owner was no longer in need of his services. Adrian says his mom was devastated but his father did what real men do—he picked himself up and decided at the age of 41 to try to start his own truck tire business. Adrian's parents had just purchased an old farmhouse and were in the process of fixing it up; Adrian's older sister was getting married; and they were out of money.

In the new business, his father used the family station wagon as a service truck to call on former customers from 5am to 5pm asking to fix their truck tires. He then pumped gas from 6-10pm, six days per week. Sunday was the only day the family really saw their father. He spent his day off renovating their home so they could sell it and use the money to grow the business. When the work was completed, the home was sold and the money was used to buy a closed-up gas station in Ocean Township, New Jersey and open his first real service truck business. It was now 1974 and Adrian was entering his freshman year in high school. There were five children still at home ranging in age from eight to eighteen.

Adrian worked for Sid and Sylvia Levine for about two years.He says that they treated him like a son and as Adrian proved himself they gave him more responsibilities. Adrian really appreciated that and worked even harder to please them. When Adrian went to work for his dad at the Mobil gas station in 1974, he was 14 years old. He worked after school until 9pm, weekends and 50-60 hours per week during the summer for two dollars an hour without overtime pay. There he learned to pump gas, fix car and truck tires, do some light mechanical work and learn how a business actually worked. It was long hours and hard work. He watched the economic lessons he was being taught by Mr. Leftsky, his high school economic teacher, being applied in the real world. He discussed with his father the lessons from class and compared the theory to actual practice and why he made certain decisions in the business. It was the beginning of his understanding of how the theories in the academic world differed from how a business and the free market work. Theories were one thing but the practical application was often very different.

The bulk of his father's business was his commercial truck tire repair that was 24/7. When they would get an after hour's service call, his father would come into the bedroom of Adrian and his brother and ask who wanted to go with him. Adrian would go, half asleep; his father drove and they would talk. Those father and son talks ranged from how to drive on icy and wet roads, to anything related to girls to the importance of a good education. He told Adrian that some of the smartest men he would ever meet are farmers. He told Adrian to "talk and listen to everyone you meet because every person you will meet is like a book you need to read. If what they are saying or showing you is something you already know, look at it as a review of information you already know for the next test life gives you. If it is new to you, add it to your library of books and try never to forget it." Adrian says that his father understood that education is the key to freedom.

Over the next four years, those late-night service calls, working with him after school and over the summers, began the preparation for the difficult times that were to come. Adrian says that God was preparing him for something that he would need to be ready for and not until later in life would he really understand. It was five years later at the age of 47 that his father died suddenly of a heart attack in his sleep. His father left a 44 year-old wife and five children ranging in age from 13 to 22 years. Adrian was the oldest male in the family then and suddenly everyone turned to him for leadership.

Adrian remembers well the day that changed his life forever. It was Sunday July 2, 1978, at 10am when he got to the family home to celebrate the high school graduation of his brother, Keith, and his sister Liz's 16th birthday party and found his father dead in his bed.Adrian had just lost the best friend he had ever known. He says his dad gave him his intellect, his work ethic and his compassion and drive. He taught Adrian that you can be both a strong and compassionate man at the same time. Through his life he demonstrated that real men of power demonstrate their power not through the use of that power but the restraint of its use. That night he stayed at his parent's house in his old bedroom. He remembers vividly when he put his head on his pillow thinking that his life was about to change and would never be the same. He cried himself to sleep, a scared teenager and awoke a scared new head of a family of five. His life did change forever.

Adrian believes he owes his success to his incredible parents and early family life where he learned his values and principles of hard work, frugality, the importance of education, right from wrong, respect for authority, independence, the adage that "your word is your bond," honesty and love of country and family. His educational experiences from kindergarten to high school prepared him for his adult life by teaching him to think for himself and how to problem solve. He was an average student and as a typical boy struggled early on. It was his fourth grade teacher, Mrs. White, who changed the direction of his education. She took the time and effort to turn him around and taught him how to learn and why it was so important for his future. Adrian says he will forever be grateful to her. There were also many other teachers including his economics, history, math, physical science, biology, English, German, chemistry and physics teachers who were instrumental in his success. He graduated in the upper 10% of his class, a four year Spartan Scholar, National Honor Society member, a multi-year letterman in wrestling, track and field and co-captain of the varsity football team.

Adrian, as co-captain of his high school football team

His business journey began at 10 years of age working at the "Sweet Shop." He was mainly driven into business for two reasons, the first was the death of his father which required that he work to support his family and the second reason was to escape the embarrassment of being poor while growing up. He was driven to experience the freedom from want that came from not being poor.

His father's illness and subsequent death had taken a toll on the small family tire business. It was in disarray and the seven employees as well as the customers were concerned as to the direction of the business. Adrian's mother was basically the bookkeeper with no ability to perform the day to day tasks of running the tire business, and employees were leaving for more secure jobs elsewhere. The customers did not really know who Adrian was and they began leaving too. By September 1978, only two months after his father's death, the business was down to four employees in addition to Adrian and his mother. Adrian was still trying to figure out how his father had priced his services and how the fleet programs really worked. He was also trying to understand accounting and the financial statements.

By January 1979, they had lost all but two of his father's original staff as they were experiencing employee turnover on what seemed like a weekly basis. Their competitors, who all knew and respected his father and who had cried at his funeral, had turned on him. Adrian says they began to take his customer base apart piece by piece like vultures over a dead carcass and they weren't even dead yet. It was a painful process to experience at the ripe old age of 19. The business was dying because they had already lost 30% of their commercial accounts which represented 70% of their business. His mom was understandably distraught and fearful of losing everything with each passing day. Adrian says her fear paralyzed her from acting to change what she and his dad had always done. Adrian says they either had to change or the business would die.

About six months after his dad's death, Adrian began to understand what he was doing. His idea of fleet maintenance for truck tires as it applied to truck fleets was nothing new to the national fleets; however, it was basically non-existent for non-national fleet companies. There were basically two parts to the maintenance his company performed. The first part was to check the fleet on a weekly basis and perform weekly maintenance on the tires. The weekly maintenance included everything from the most important thing of correct air pressure, which causes 85% of most fleet problems and drives costs up, to catching worn out or damaged tires from getting on the road during the work week. The larger fleets did this work daily before the fleets would roll out in the morning. It was preventative maintenance not unlike changing oil before the old oil failed and damaged the engine. Today this seems like just good common sense but at that time most didn't do it at all and if they did, it wasn't consistent or reliable.

The second part was to provide the best road service 24/7 so when a truck went down, costing the company a lot of money, Adrian's company would respond to the call within an hour. Their company logo was, "We Sell Service!" They were one of the few companies that serviced 24/7. His father's color theme on the trucks was a unique scheme of red, white and blue (he was very patriotic) which no other company had and the trucks stood out on the road.

Adrian would discount their tire products to the customer provided they did the service too. His dad would never discount the service charge but would reduce the rubber costs so he could be more competitive with the larger dealers in the area who buy in larger quantities allowing them to sell for less. Adrian often got the service work because they were good at it but lost the big ticket sale of the tires to the bigger dealers. They were a small dealer in a big dealer world.

The challenge for him was he didn't really understand it and was not experienced enough in the technical side of the tire business to make informed decisions. And at the same time, their competitors were tearing them up. Customers were leaving and they had a bank note due in six months for which they did not have the money to pay. Adrian had a college prep high school education that had nothing to do with the tire business and the employees were leaving as fast as he could replace them. His mom would not take any action that required the expenditure of capital or was not how "your father did it." They were an authorized dealer of Kelly Springfield, Michelin and Yokohama tires. Most of all their sales were Kelly tires. Michelin was a very expensive purchase initially although it was the lowest cost per mile of any tire on the market in the long run. Michelin only made a radial tire which in the seventies was not in much use in car, truck and off the road uses. Yokohama was a relative unknown at the time.

The young Michelin representative, Chuck Lotocki, was newly assigned to Adrian's territory shortly before his dad's death. He was a person who really helped Adrian in his business career. Most tire dealers were not big fans of Michelin Tire in the 60s and 70s because of their marketing model. They would set up dealers, who were reluctant to sell a tire that would last four times longer than non-radial tires and require fewer repairs due to its radial design and steel belts. A 10 x 20 inch Kelly bias tire sold for $150, would last about 15,000 miles before it had to be replaced and experience at least three flat repairs during that life cycle. The Michelin radial truck tire would cost more at $275 per tire but would go twice as many miles before needing replacement and may experience one flat repair during its life cycle. Naturally, dealers would make much more money selling Kelly than Michelin so they pushed Kelly tires.

As result of this reality, Michelin had its representatives selling the advantages of the Michelin products directly to the end user. Michelin was taking the newest technology and driving the demand from the user end since the dealers were not doing it. The marketing strategy was working as customers were now asking for Michelin tires which was angering and isolating their older dealer network. Many dealers felt that Michelin was "stealing" their customers by switching them from the more profitable bias (non-radial) tire to Michelin's radial steel belted tires. This provided an opportunity for Adrian to get into the game where the bigger dealers did not want to play.

Also, unlike the other dealers, Adrian was far more accepting of Chuck's efforts to put more Michelin tires on the street. At this point he was willing to put anything on the street that would give him an edge in the marketplace and Chuck was quite happy to work with a dealer who was willing to push his product.

Chuck made arrangements for Adrian to attend a Michelin Tire Dealer's training program for a week in their corporate headquarters in Lake Success, New York. In that one week, Adrian learned more about the technical side of tires than most dealers in the business at the time. He was also exposed to some of the best salespeople in the business. Tires may last six months, 12 months or as long as five years depending on the number of miles driven. Adrian took what he learned at the Michelin Training center on how to use mileage projections charts and graphs, repair and operating expenses, and fuel savings to validate the products lowest cost per mile claim. Chuck and Adrian were making sales calls one day and were discussing how with Michelin tires and their service programs that they would easily double, triple, even quadruple the mileage over any bias truck tire on the market. Adrian decided he would offer a guarantee that any Michelin tire that "Stevens Tire" sold and on which they also did the maintenance on the fleet or truck, that the Michelin tire would double the mileage over the bias tire on the same vehicle. When Adrian told his mother of his "guarantee plan" she gave an "absolutely no" but Adrian did it anyway.

Adrian started with refining his father's concepts of fleet maintenance and 24/7 service, using the Michelin product with the "double mileage" guarantee offered only by Stevens Tire. He presented his plan to one of their last remaining large fleets, a Pepsi-Cola bottler which had a very large and diverse fleet and put on huge amounts of mileage each year. Tires were a large operating expense for them and when a delivery truck went down on the road it was a big deal for them. Stevens Tire did all the afterhours and weekend service work for them but got very little of the new or recapped tire business which were the big ticket items. Pepsi was able to buy at National Account Pricing which was only given to larger dealers. Adrian pitched their fleet maintenance concept to Pepsi including providing all the tires at a discounted price (over his mother's loud objections) with Michelin being the lead product when it was applicable. If the program performed, Pepsi's fleet manager would give a written recommendation of their program and their company. Due to the high mileage of the fleet, Adrian was able to project out the tires' performance expectations, not unlike computer models do today, and their program and Michelin products worked, as he knew they would.

Adrian took those results and used them as his foot into a lot of fleets in their area. Also, part of the problem of his father's existing customer base was that it was seasonal and industry lopsided. Most of the customer base was in construction, building, roadwork and summer related businesses. They were busy in the summer and nice weather but very slow in the colder months. Adrian began to go after winter businesses like fuel oil companies and year-round businesses like newspaper companies and transport fleets, moving companies, etc. This allowed Stevens Tire to grow sales volume without adding additional equipment and manpower costs to the operational expense of the business. Also, extending the fleet program and tire discount program to a number of high volume users like Pepsi, it allowed him to buy tires from the manufactures at deeper discounts. This improved their margins on the high volume users and even more on their regular customers. It also allowed him to be competitive when he needed to be on many deals. This was a game changer for them.

The experience from when his father died through the years of being in the tire business was only the beginning of his business life. It prepared him for what was to come. Adrian gives his mother most of the credit for preparing him in those years for what was to come. His dad gave him the desire to learn, educate himself and his intellect. He taught Adrian his respect for women and how to be powerful yet always measure the use of his strength against its outcome for good and not evil. His mother gave him his drive, toughness and that killer instinct. Adrian says his father died too early so he learned those tough survival skills from his mom. He says that "she was one loving and tough woman." It was that "toughness lesson" that was much needed in his future business endeavors.

In Adrian's third year of running the company they had expanded to a second location and were thinking of a third location. Adrian went from surviving the death and disruption the death of his father caused the family and business to looking forward to the future. Only after a discussion with his mom on how and where he fit in as it pertained to the company and its future did he realize that in her mind Adrian was simply one of eight children. He would be given no consideration different from the others; he was simply an employee who got paid what he was worth. Adrian says it was a harsh and tough conversation which gave him two choices. He could stay and be an overworked, underpaid family employee with no consideration given to what he had accomplished over the last several years. Or, he could leave knowing that the business would not survive. He knew that if he started his own tire business the demise of the family business would be in a matter of months, not years. He didn't know what to do.

Adrian looked at his situation. He was 23 years old and had built a million dollar business from a damaged mom and pop tire business. He still had a sister in college and a mother who would not budge on her position on equitable allocation of the family business ownership. He was lost. He knew it would be difficult to get any executive management or high salary sales employment for several reasons but mainly due to his age and lack of a college degree. The business he knew was the tire business but staying in that field would destroy the Stevens Tire Company, which his mother and other dependent siblings were dependent upon for their survival. Adrian thought what happened next was a chance meeting, a lucky break, an incredible coincidence but later in life he came to understand that there are no such things as coincidences. Adrian says that "coincidences are God's way of brushing up against you and steering you in the direction He wants for you." It was not until he got saved, when he was 40 years old, that his eyes were opened and he could see for the first time in his life the presence of God in every day of his life. God was always there beside him, in his worst and best of times even though Adrian was blind and deaf to His presence. Adrian says that "his fallen and arrogant human nature blinded him."

At that time, Adrian and his wife had a 10 acre farm with horses where they lived in Ocean Township, New Jersey. She was into buying and selling horses, giving riding lessons and competing in horse shows. She mentioned to him that a woman named Carol, to whom she was giving riding lessons, had a boyfriend (Carol later married and is stilled married to Cory), whom Adrian should meet. She said that Carol's boyfriend worked all kinds of crazy hours for a restaurant owner and was looking to start his own restaurant. One day, Carol brought her boyfriend out to

Adrian's farm. His name was Cory Wingerter; he was 28 years old and had grown up in Fair Haven, New Jersey.He had graduated from Cornell University with a BS in Hotel and Restaurant Management. Cory was 6'3", a skinny 195 lbs with big bushy blonde hair and a big welcoming smile. They went for a walk to the far pasture and along the way Cory told his story about how he got where he was and his plans for the future. He also lost his father at a young age (Cory was 13 at the time); he had two brothers, one older and one younger and he had a mother who sounded just like Adrian's. He told Adrian about his boss who had hired him in 1975 to work as an assistant manager at his restaurant. His boss told him he should look for a partner because one day Cory should buy him out and he would need a good working partner. Adrian spent the next hour listening to him tell about the restaurant business, what he did, why he wanted to own his own restaurant one day, why he thought it made a lot of money and what he would expect from Adrian. He needed someone who knew how to run a business and help him in the day-to-day operations. Adrian told him he knew nothing about the restaurant business and he didn't cook. Cory said he would teach Adrian.

Adrian then shared his experiences, journey, frustrations in the family tire business and his goals and reasons for looking for something else. They discussed going into business together and were undecided as to whether it should be the tire or restaurant business. The thing that struck Adrian most at their first meeting in the pasture that night was that Cory was brilliant. The other thing that struck him was that Cory was a "Boy Scout." After knowing him for 33 years and being in business with him for 29 years and still counting, Adrian says he is still a Boy

Scout. Adrian calls him, "The Last Boy Scout." He is honest, hardworking, caring of others and innocent to the wicked world around him. At that time, Adrian suspected that if Cory ventured out on his own he would be eaten alive by the wolves outside. Little did Adrian know at that time, and Cory had no idea, that he was already working for one of the most vicious wolves he has ever encountered, Cory's boss. Adrian says that Cory is the greatest business partner he could ever have found. He believes or at least hopes that Cory would say the same about him.

It was decided that Adrian would learn the restaurant business starting at the very bottom. So, Adrian worked his first shift as the "assistant dishwasher" the following Saturday night and just worked and watched the craziness around him. Bartenders and servers were running in and out of the kitchen. Line cooks and prep-cooks were calling out instructions and food orders and always wanting to know why the girls were not picking up the food from the kitchen line faster. Adrian wondered, "How the hell am I going to learn all this?"

The following day, he went over to Cory and Carol's house in Long Branch, New Jersey for dinner and to reconstruct a Profit and Loss Financial Statement based on what information Cory had at his disposal and what Adrian knew would be reasonable parameters for the other business expenses. When Adrian was done forensically reconstructing the financials, he looked at Cory and asked him, "Do you know how much this guy makes?" Cory said, "No, but I know I get paid pretty well." Adrian said he would double-check his figures and get back to Cory. He said that if the figures hold up they should forget about the tire business—"It's the restaurant business!"

The next day, Adrian checked his work and other assumptions and they were correct. He spoke to Cory that week and said, "We need to start my training." Adrian told him he wanted to learn every job in the restaurant and he could work there after 6pm Monday–Saturday and anytime on Sunday. Adrian still had to work in the tire business 60-65 hours per week and he could work about 25-30 hours a week at the restaurant. Cory told Adrian he had to check with his boss to make sure it was okay. His boss said it was okay but he would not pay Adrian. If Adrian wanted to learn the business it would be at no cost to him. That statement did not surprise Adrian who thought that if he learned the business that it would be a cheap college course in restaurant management. They currently train most of senior management the same way, except they are paid. They call it the "Cornell Crash Course in Restaurant Management."

So, for the next year, Adrian worked both the tire business and learned all the jobs in the restaurant, from dishwasher to manager. He worked between 85-90 hours per week for over a year and lost 90 pounds over that time. Also, during this time, Adrian began to buy multi-family rental units in Asbury Park, New Jersey. This was another learning experience he squeezed in during his off-hours. Adrian says that in order to recap that year it would take an entire book. It was one of the most grueling years of his life.

The time had come to approach his boss with a proposal to buy one of the restaurants. He told Cory they should also have a plan to buy both restaurants because Cory was the brains and muscle of the organization. They met with his boss in Adrian's third floor, one bedroom, Spartan-furnished (a TV, mattress and a dresser) apartment in Asbury Park. They proposed a deal whereby Adrian and Cory would buy both restaurants. The meeting lasted about an hour during which Adrian says his boss pontificated on a variety of subjects and avoided a lot of direct questions. The answers he gave often didn't seem quite right to Adrian. He made it clear that Adrian had to get out of the tire business completely or there would be no deal. Though Adrian explained one had nothing to do with the other, his position on the matter was that he wanted Adrian to be a "fully committed partner" to Cory. The boss said he was looking out for Cory's best interests, which in turn would be looking out for Adrian's too. After they both left Adrian sat there thinking and told himself, "I smell a wolf."

After a few follow-up discussions, Cory and Adrian agreed to move forward even though some of their questions were not fully answered.

Adrian decided it was time to sit down and speak with his mother. He was not looking forward to that meeting. She knew he was working at the restaurant but did not understand why. Adrian had told her he needed the extra money and it kept him busy. She said, "You don't even know how to boil water!" He explained that Cory was a friend and he was willing to teach him the restaurant business and she just shook her head. He told her that he had decided to spend the rest of his life in the restaurant business. She went from shock, to thinking he was kidding, to angry. It was rough. Finally, after a few other conversations that were a lot calmer, she conceded to the reality of it all and agreed she would have to sell the business. There would be enough money for her to live on the rest of her life, provided Adrian didn't take any of the proceeds. He agreed, and the only thing he asked was should he need her help in the future that she would help him. She thought about it and said, "I agree to hear you out." It was the best he could get.

From July of 1978 when his father died to July of 1979, they went from losing 30% of their business to regaining the 30% they lost and grew another 60%. Adrian had just turned 20 years old. Over the next five years they grew the business from a mom and pop small business with sales of a few hundred thousand dollars in sales to a million dollar company, grew from one to two locations, developed a nationwide service network that allowed them to service national companies 24/7 whether their fleets operated in New Jersey or California and the premiere 24/7 commercial tire company in Monmouth and Ocean Counties.

In 1984, they sold the business after Adrian put his brother and one sister through college and his mom was able to retire at 50 years of age to her condo on the beach. She bought a brand new 350SL Mercedes which she always wanted to own. She traveled to parts of the world she had only dreamed about and for the first time in her life did not have to work 12-15 hour days as she had since she was 13. For the next 16 years she never had to work another day. She died after her third bout with cancer in October, 2000 at 66 years of age. She was at her beach condo surrounded by her children and grandchildren. She was a woman with an iron will, loving heart and a never-quit attitude that was her hallmark. She trained Adrian to fight with all he had, she gave him street smarts and toughness and taught him how to separate the personal from the business side of things. Adrian says that when you work in most family businesses you are expected to put up with things that no other employer would demand of you; however, you get considerations for your mistakes that no other employer would let you get away with.

When Adrian looks back over his business accomplishments, he is most proud of being able to turn his parents business into the vehicle that allowed her to live her last 16 years in a manner she had always dreamed of when his mom and dad would talk about "the dream." She never remarried and had no significant relationship since his death. He thinks her heart was too broken. He wishes his dad could have been alongside her those last 16 years, watching the sun rise each day on the beach and holding each other at night.

Now that the tire business was sold, it was time to buy the restaurants. Unfortunately the owner backed out and said he couldn't sell that year for "tax reasons" but perhaps he could sell the following year. With the tire business sold and Adrian working in the restaurant for "slave wages," he felt stuck. However, the boss called a week later and informed them that a friend of his was selling a restaurant in Montgomery Township, New Jersey and they could be equal partners with him in that location. They could buy the other two restaurants the following year. Cory and Adrian agreed to become partners in this third restaurant. On January 2, 1985, The Foolish Fox was acquired by the three of them and became known as, The Tiger's Tale.

The boss wouldn't agree to their requests in the partnership agreement except the buyout terms of his stock which he agreed to be on a graduated formula based on time and performance of the operation. The problem with his proposal was that the longer they waited to buy him out the more it would cost them. As they continued to grow and improve the business it became more valuable and more expensive to buy. The boss thought he had them hooked because the deal would require Cory and Adrian to come up with a lot of cash during the year of purchase and even more as time went on. The boss knew they could never come up with enough money to buy him or so he thought. In August 1985, they notified their soon-to-be old boss and partner that they were exercising their buyout option for his stock, which required them to have proof of funds within 30 days. He was quite cordial upon hearing the news and told them that if they had any problems to let him know as he could make some calls for them to some banks. Adrian says that was wolf-speak for, "Good luck you dopes; banks hate financing restaurants. Neither of you have any cash nor will you ever get funding." Little did he know about Adrian's resources, his previous business skills or relationships with lenders.

Adrian made a pitch to his former bankers who quickly told him that if he wanted to go back into the tire business they would gladly help. Adrian says that restaurants are only as good as their last meal served. The banks wanted additional collateral and a co-signer. It was time to ask Adrian's mother for the favor they had previously discussed. He was more nervous about pitching the deal to his mother than he was to the bankers. So, he met his mom at her house, and after about an hour of tough questioning she agreed to pledge assets and co-sign the loan under certain conditions. She wanted the right to examine their books at any time without their consent and without notice. She wanted a second mortgage on both their homes and if they failed to pay any loan back or were late with vendors she could foreclose on her liens. Adrian just sat there with that "What, are you kidding me look on his face?" She just looked back at him with that cold stare he had seen a million times growing up and all the years they were in business together. With her finger pointed she said, "Business is business, and don't you ever forget it. Whether it is doing business with me or your friend Cory or anyone else. Don't be stupid. And don't think I won't do it." Adrian agreed and he knew that Cory would also. There was never a doubt in Adrian's mind that she meant exactly what she said. She never had to exercise her option.

Adrian and Cory notified their soon to be ex-partner that they were funded, with a commitment letter from their lender and wanted to close immediately. Adrian says the attitude of the boss changed quickly and his wolf teeth came out. They had to force the closing on November 2, 1985 and it started a rolling problem for a few years which Adrian says he could write a book about except he is not allowed to discuss it. Now they were free to fulfill their dreams.

In January, 1986 they began to implement their business plan of opening 10 restaurants in 10 years. They never did buy their former partner's restaurants. Their business plan included purchasing the land, building and obtaining liquor licenses which was a tremendous challenge for them. They had little or no money, were in their mid-twenties and in an industry that banks viewed as a very high credit risk. Adrian was able to overcome that challenge because of his gift of negotiating and through his uncommon understanding of commercial banking, lending markets, loan underwriting requirements and tax law. Often competitors could not understand how they were able borrow from lenders when the economy was in recession and banks were not lending.

They next acquired their second location in Howell, Township New Jersey, known as Net Lane's Steak and Seafood House. Net Lane was a successful single restaurant operator before buying his second operation in Howell. He had been in Asbury Park for many years and was quite successful at that location. However, as is the case with many operators who try to repeat the success of their first location, they often run into many problems when growing to more locations. It usually comes down to a lack of certain skill sets and knowledge needed to be a multi-unit operator. They acquired that location on December 19, 1986, after difficult negotiations and trials with Net. Then there was the difficulty of getting a bank to believe in two young men who had been in business less than a year in an industry with the highest failure rate among small businesses.

This location needed substantial renovation which required Cory to become an expert on general contracting so that they could save a great deal of cost. Adrian says that Cory learned the skills that were needed and performed very well. They reopened this location in May, 1987, as The Ivy League. The theme for all their locations was Ivy League school dining hall experiences with casual American cuisine serving chicken, fresh fish and meats, salads and burgers, with many black board specials from which to choose. They offered a complete bar service. They focused on attracting the alumni and their families rather than the current students attending college.

Where the previous six owners had failed, they took off like a rocket. They doubled their sales and assets in less than 15 months and began to build cash reserves. Adrian says there were many elements that were necessary to have in place to put them on their growth path to success ranging from finding the right location, the right deal, the understanding of both micro and macroeconomics and all the various contract, liability and tax laws needed to make their plan work. Now with two locations, 100 plus employees, eight managers with four more in training for another location yet to be identified, they went looking for more locations. The process for locating and making the decision of which deal was best was extensive. It requires not only looking at the project as a restaurateur but as an entrepreneur with a solid business plan and a multi-faceted exit strategy. It was not easy. They looked at scores of deals, frustrated many a business broker and at times Adrian began to question his own judgment as perhaps being too narrow minded and myopic in his thinking. He thought, here are professionals who have had many more years' experience in restaurant buying and operating them who repeatedly told them they would never find exactly everything they wanted because it did not exist.

Adrian knew what he was doing and he and Cory debated each deal like surgeons about to begin a very difficult surgery in which failure would mean the patient would die. Fortunately, none of their patients died as all of the restaurants went on to live fruitful and productive lives. Adrian is quick to point out that he doesn't claim they did everything right. They just made sure they had contingency plans should something go wrong. Business planning was Adrian's responsibility as all the business responsibilities fell to him, he began to learn not only about restaurants but also about real estate investing, tax law, financing and investing. Investing was important because they had excess cash that needed to be invested in stocks, bonds and other financial instruments.

In August of 1989, they opened their next location in the town where Cory grew up, Fair Haven, New Jersey. It was a location that had many years of history to it and was just recently renovated by the Christopher family. Unfortunately, Mr. Christopher had just died and the operation was left to his widow and son which was too much for them to handle. This restaurant required very little renovation to meet their needs and it only took 90 days to reopen. This was their third renovation of a restaurant in three years and Cory had become very proficient at it. They were able to reopen this restaurant in November 1989 under the name, The Varsity Club, which was the name of a dining hall at Harvard University. This restaurant was the largest of their locations with seating for 275 on two floors inside an 11,000 square foot building.

They were now three for three with The Varsity Club taking off just as the two previous restaurants had done. It was now 1989, and Adrian was doing a regular review and amendment to their business plan. He was becoming concerned at this point on two fronts. First, they had grown so large, so fast that they needed to change from two kids buying their first restaurant and dreaming of more, to real experienced operators who now had 150 employees, 15 managers and locations that stretched from five minutes from the Atlantic Ocean to 30 minutes from New Hope, Pennsylvania. The business plan called for adding seven more locations in the next seven years. Second, and the most concerning, was that Congress had just bailed out the savings and loan industry and Paul Volker, Chairman of the Fed, had decided to raise interest rates to cool inflation. US commercial banks were in massive trouble with all their third world and foreign loan debt, which was starting to fail worse than the savings and loan problem, and Congress had no appetite to bail them out.

The storm clouds were gathering and it was not looking good if you were a growing business that was looking for discretionary income dollars to be spent at your business. All the elements were in place for a recession and credit crunch. Adrian says a good business can often survive a downturn in business, even a rough downturn, but a growing small business that is in need of loans from banks to grow must proceed very carefully. Those credit dollars are its life blood and it was about to dry up. Adrian suspected that a recession was on the horizon.

They made the decision to stop growing and focus on reorganization so they could have more controlled and leaner growth. They began to prepare for a downturn in the economy and stopped hiring front-line people. They invested in their business operations side of the business with more effective systems and staff needed to execute the controls necessary to run a much larger organization. They introduced their first point-of-sale computerized systems at the store level. They invested in new software and computers to operate their accounting systems and vendor ordering integration to the store level. They invested in the technology to make them more effective and efficient should they have a downturn in the economy. This process took about 15 months and in 1990-1991 the economy tanked and the first Gulf War began.

Their gross revenue and profits continued to climb as a result of their successful strategies since 1985 and through the 1991 recession. Real estate values declined considerably as a result of the recession and the 1989 changes in the tax laws. They then went looking for a new location while real estate values were quite low. They purchased their fourth location which was located in Howell, New Jersey only two to three miles north of their Ivy League location on the opposite side of the highway. Many people thought they were crazy having two locations so close together; however, it turned out they were right and not only did the market support the additional location but, for the most part, they owned that sector of the market for over 10 years. They got the customer traffic in both directions at key locations and access routes, not unlike the McDonald's strategy.

The fourth location was a local pub that was owned by a local scrap metal recycler who was somewhat of a local character. It was known as JB's Pub and it required extensive renovations which they projected would take six months in order to complete the project and reopen for business. It was the largest renovation they had so far attempted and it included replacing a failed septic system. They renamed the fourth location The Chapter House, and it was very successful. It was now 1992, their seventh year in business. They had just completed their fourth location and they realized they needed to rethink their business needs.

In 1996, they decided to sell The Varsity Club location as market conditions warranted and they went looking for another location. Restaurants are sold every day over and over again. Most restaurant sales are not happy days for the seller other than the nightmare is ending. Adrian described it as when you own a boat. The two happiest days for a boat owner is the day he buys it and the day he sells it. Between those two days the boat owner keeps asking himself, "Why did I do this? Why?"Most restaurant buyers think that it is when you go to sell the restaurant is when you think about when and how to sell it and for how much. The reality is by that time it is way too late. The exit strategy must be configured before you buy, not after. Adrian says there are many elements that must be considered before the deal is made to buy that will allow for maximum options when selling the restaurant. These elements include how to minimize corporate liabilities, maximizing post-tax operating profits during its lifetime, and maximizing post-sale, after-tax profits. He said that alone is a 12 month college program.

They found their fifth location in Waretown, New Jersey in 1999. It was a closed up 9,000 plus square foot location on five acres on a major highway with 185 seats. Cory quickly went to work on renovations and they reopened the location in July, 2000. From its first day it was again clear it was a home run. However, at this location they did not carry on the Ivy League school theme because the demographics did not test positive for that theme. Instead they did it to match the local theme of nature, conservation and love for the outdoor life. They called it The

Thirsty Mallard and inside it was decorated as a high-end hunting lodge with each part of the restaurant dedicated to a wild life conservation focus. Duck's Unlimited, Pheasants Forever, Protect the Shore and so on. It was a great fit for the local client base. Their menu and pricing were universal wherever they opened.

It was now the year 2000, the Y2K hysteria had passed and they looked forward to a promising future. Their staff was now at 258 people with 17 managers and with millions of dollars in reserves. They contemplated what to do next. They were at the top of their game within their industry in their local areas and it was time to think more about their 20 year business plan which was scheduled to terminate in 2004.

Adrian and Cindy married on November 18, 2000.

Adrian had recently married Cindy, an incredible woman, and for the first time in his life he began to think about life outside of business. He had been a workaholic for his entire adult life. Adrian says that society admires workaholics because they often are seen as great achievers, and they usually are successful in their endeavors. However, often the dark side of that behavior is not discussed since it is sometimes viewed as the price one has to pay to be successful. As a workaholic, work and achieving your goals comes before everything. He says that work came ahead of his friendships, relationships, other activities, family, holidays and health. Nothing is allowed to stand in a workaholic's way when he or she is on their path to achieve their goals. Often they will achieve as the result of that behavior or condition what society views as the measure of success, wealth, public recognition of their achievements and the material trappings of success. It is an additive behavior not unlike alcoholism; however, workaholic behavior is admired by society and alcoholic behavior is viewed as destructive. Adrian says that both are equally dysfunctional being a workaholic is accepted by society as a good behavior.

Cindy introduced him to another world. Besides her being perfect or at least perfect for him, she introduced him to the idea of God and His Son Jesus though a series of gentle conversations and a book she gave to him to read called, "Left Behind." It was the first of a series of books to follow over the next several years that conveyed the "Book of Revelations" of the Bible in a modern context. The book read like a Tom Clancy novel and the book it centered on the Rapture event as foretold in the Bible. When he finished the book he asked himself, "What if it is true?" If it was he didn't want to be left behind. This was the beginning of his journey of inquiry of the question, "Is the God presented in the Bible true?" Are the books of the Bible and the information contained in them truthful or the creative writings of men who have come from a time of lack of understanding of the world around them and did their best to explain the nature of man and the world they live in? He had asked those questions with little effort to really get the answers to those questions. The best way he could describe his understanding of God and the universe at that time would be agnostic. He always thought of God as an "Insurance God." He bought into it just enough to cover him in case of an accident (that being He is real; there's a heaven and life after death) but never really cared to understand it fully.

As in everything he does, once he decides something warrants his focus, he puts all his energy with a ferocious drive to learn, understand and master the subject matter to best of his ability. He set off on a yearlong journey of inquiry. He began to study the four major religions, Christianity, Islam, Judaism and Hinduism, which covers 87% of all faiths in the world. Also, during this time his mother began her final battle with cancer which finally took her life. Cindy and Adrian were in the process of moving forward in their relationship toward marriage. To say the least, he had a lot going on that would deal with the question, "Is the God of the Bible real?" The inquiry was wide and deep.Every time he found an answer to his question, it would lead to other questions to which he did not know the answers. He says it felt like he was a gerbil on a treadmill chasing a carrot hung on a string in front of him, just out of his reach. The more he ran, the hungrier he got for the carrot. There were times he felt he would never get that carrot.

Cindy introduced Adrian to the Evangelical Church in 1999. He found the church both uplifting and confusing because he really did not get the whole picture of why they believe with so much conviction. In his heart he wanted to get it, but his mind was constantly wrestling with the concept of faith in a God he did not understand and for most of his life the world around him told him God can be anything you think He should be, as you want Him to be. Adrian and Cindy were married in the church in November, 2000 and he made the decision to accept Christ as his Savior and willingly declared that decision in a public baptism, though a baptism is not a requirement of salvation Cindy joined him in his baptism as a sign of solidarity of his decision. So on that day, they participated in three holy sacraments; their marriage vows, their first communion as husband and wife and his consensual baptism as a person who has been informed of the gift of salvation, willingly accepted Christ as his lord and savior, asked Him forgiveness of his sins and asked Him to be present in his heart and life. When he was fully submerged in the baptismal, then lifted out of the water and opened his eyes, he often tells people he can't explain it other than he felt different.

Initially, he thought it was just the emotions of the moment and the excitement of the day. It wasn't until some months later when he was struggling with the feeling that maybe it's a desire to believe that makes religion seem real to us, and not that God, Jesus and the Holy Spirit are real. He wondered if it was just a mass form of psychological group-think and we convince ourselves it's real because we want it to be real. He thought that maybe the intellectual facts would prove that it's all wishful thinking out of our natural concern about what happens after we die.

In addition to reading his Bible and studying various source information on the various religions (which he felt meant he was being unfaithful to his own newly found faith), he joined a Men's Bible Study that a long-time business associate invited him to attend at his office once a month. After about nine months he sat down with a friend after Bible study and confessed, "I don't get it." Adrian's heart wanted to believe in the worst way, but his intellectual mind was struggling with a list of questions to which he couldn't seem to find the answers. He told the friend he couldn't seem to reconcile all the doubts in his mind. Adrian told him of many unanswered questions he had, and the friend suggested he read a book by Lee Strobel, "The Case for Christ," which he thought might help Adrian find some of the answers.

He read the book and Lee Strobel had many of the same questions Adrian had. Strobel spent two years researching those questions, wrote this book and answered those questions. It was after reading this book that his mind and heart came together as one. It was his second Holy Spirit moment, (his first was when he accepted Christ and was lifted out of his baptismal water). A few months later, on an airplane half-way between New Jersey and Florida, he had an event which is too long to describe here. He had his third Holy Spirit moment when finally his heart and mind seared together as one. God provided him the proof he needed beyond all doubt. Adrian now knows God is real and that He loves Adrian.

Adrian says that having arrived late in life (at 40 years old) in being saved and knowing God, it is both a joyous and sad event. He looks back and sees clearly how often God reached out to him and how he had ignored Him. He recalls how many times God saved him and he thought it was all himself doing the saving. He remembers how many wrongful and hurtful things he did in the name of his own self-interest. He looks back now with his eyes open and wonders how different his life would have been had he accepted God when he was younger. It saddens him at times. Every time he hears "Amazing Grace" it brings tears to his eyes, for Adrian believes he is the wretch he speaks of, and God loves him even with all the sins he has committed. The joy and blessing is that he lived a lot of life during those 40 years that gave him clarity when he did finally accept God. It gave him a very clear line of life before and after salvation. He believes it was needed to get where he is today. Scriptures are very clear that all things work together according to His will, not ours. And all things in His time, not ours.

His religion and faith have so many facets not unlike others; however, there are three things that he knows to be true. First, that Christ is the Son of God, the Messiah foretold in the Old Testament; and that only through acceptance of Him as your Lord and Savior are you saved and will have eternal life in Heaven in existence with God the Father. Second, the Scriptures are the infallible written word of God, written by man in the presence of the Holy Spirit and authored by the Father. Third, the scriptures themselves and their meanings are revealed to those who in the presence of the Holy Spirit seek Him, His love, His will for us here on Earth and His answers to what we struggle and live with each and every day.

In the year 2000, they had opened five restaurants, were operating four, and they were entering their fifteenth year in business and business is good. Their sales and profits were rising, they owned various rental properties and now have millions of dollars in liquid assets that are invested in various stock market portfolios which is accounting for at least a third of the company's revenues. This allowed them to be highly competitive in their marketplace against their competitors who were confounded on how they were able to produce such consistence performance, quality of products and services and such low price points. The strength of their Balance Sheet was rarely seen in the world of independent restaurants and they were both state (NJ Gold

Plate Award) and nationally (NRA Grassroots Leadership Award) industry recognized and award-winning independent restaurant operators.

In spite of all that, they began the process of selling the company. Adrian knew that to do it right and to receive maximum value for the company the timing would have to be right and it would take a couple of years to execute the strategy. He began the process in 2001 and signed their first non-disclosure agreement in November, 2002. They had multiple buyers, which led to extremely complicated deals and it was very difficult to keep it private. They were able to complete the transactions for the sale in March, 2004 with three of the four restaurants being sold. Their original location, The Tiger's Tale, was taken off the market at the last minute as a mutually agreeable arrangement between Cory and Adrian.

As of 2014, they are currently operating that location and in spite of the 2008 stock market crash they have experienced record sales for that location since 2006. They saw the pending downturn in 2006-2007 based on the economic indicators they have used over the last 29 years and began to prepare for it. Although they did not know the exact timing of the event, or what form it would take, they knew it was most likely to occur over the next 24 months. History speaks for itself.

Cindy and Adrian have been in Florida since 2004 and have lived in Florida for the winters and New Jersey in the summers since 2005. They have a wonderfully blended family of four children (Cindy's girls, Jessica 34, with a granddaughter Juliette 4, Ashley 24, with a granddaughter Tabitha 3; Adrian's boys, Aaron 28 and Austin 18). When they first semi-retired in 2004, they were 44 and 43 and they were looking for a part of Florida in which to spend most of their remaining life. Southwest Florida seemed the perfect fit, without the fast pace of New Jersey, yet youthful enough for their stage of life. They had planned to travel the world after retiring and in 2009 they spent a month in Europe and parts of the Middle East with plans of traveling on month-long trips every other year. As is the case with the best laid plans, things change. Their son returned from the Iraq War and started college, their kids got married; then they had grandkids and were turning around asking, "Where did those five years go?"

They got involved in the tennis community at Heritage Palms in 2010 and have met some very wonderful people. Adrian is working on his tennis game and discovered Texas Hold'em Poker with the same love he has for business. He has set some lofty personal goals; by the time he is 60 years of age he plans to be the number one tennis player in his age division in the State of Florida and the 2019 Winner of the WSOP poker championship.

He wakes up every morning living a dream. There are days he just goes outside looks up in the sky and says, "Thank you!" He knows that one day he will go home to his Father's house to a room He has prepared for Adrian. Upon meeting his Savior, he looks forward to what he hopes he will hear, "Welcome my loyal and faithful servant. You are home,your Father is expecting you and all who you have led to me." Adrian has truly achieved The American Dream.

Howard Wright

I met Howard in 1999 while living at The Landings Golf, Tennis and Yacht Club in Fort Myers, Florida. Howard was a very gifted tennis player and I had the privilege of playing on the same team. He and his wife, Ann, are wonderful people and they have a great life story of success. Howard is also one of the nicest people I've ever known. They started with absolutely nothing and through hard work, great sacrifice and determination they have achieved The American Dream.

His paternal grandfather, Millard Wright, grew up in St. Louis, Missouri and became a CPA with Ernst and Ernst in St. Louis. He met his future wife, Beatrice, when he traveled to Bad Axe, Michigan to audit a company. They were married in Bad Axe and lived in St. Louis and later in Bellville, Illinois where Howard's father, Gaines, was born in 1916. Howard's grandfather was very successful and owned several properties in St. Louis. However, he died in 1925 when Howard's father, Gaines, was only nine years old. His grandmother lost all of the properties through foreclosure during the next year. His grandmother never adjusted to big city living so she and Howard's father moved to Caro, Michigan to live with his grandmother's cousin. As a result Howard's father came from very humble beginnings.

His father attended high school in Caro during which he worked at little jobs and he and his high school pal, Jae Kitchen, ran a small gas station together. Gaines met his future wife, Jessie, in 1935 when he was 20 and she was 18 years of age. His mother was born and raised on a farm near Caro. After a one year courtship they were married in 1936 and lived in Caro. Howard was born in 1938 in Caro but when he was only six months old his family moved because Gaines got a new job working in Saginaw for the Gase Baking Co. Approximately 12 years after taking this job, Gase was bought out by Schafer Bakeries and Gaines became general sales manager for all of Michigan.

His maternal grandparents, Howard and Florence Taylor owned and lived on a farm outside of Caro and were wonderful to Howard. In his pre-teen years, he spent about a month each summer helping on the farm during the harvest season. Howard says that was when he learned that farming was really hard work.

After the family moved to Saginaw, they lived in a second floor apartment. They lived there four years and in 1943, they moved into a new home on the west side of Saginaw which cost $5,000. Right after they moved into the new home, his brother Jae was born in 1943. Jim, his second brother, was born in 1947 and his third brother, John, was born in 1950. The house was small and the family included the four boys, Howard's parents and his dad's mother, but somehow they all squeezed in. Howard's dad remodeled the attic where Jae and Howard slept on bunk beds. The boys grew up in that neighborhood and Howard went to Peace Lutheran parochial school which was owned by Peace Lutheran Church, of which Howard's parents were charter members. The school was very small; in fact, there were only four kids in Howard's first grade class. Howard enjoyed school and played tenor sax in the fourth and fifth grades and sang in the church choir.

He played football, basketball and track at Arthur Hill High School. He liked high school sports and particularly enjoyed the fact that he could take showers after practices—he had no shower at home. During his sophomore year of basketball he sprained his ankle so badly that it took nearly 10 years to fully heal. That was the end of his athletic career. He did various small jobs in the summers while growing up. When he got into high school he had to work Saturdays with his dad delivering bread to the grocery stores. He didn't enjoy the fact that he had to get up at 5am each Saturday but he enjoyed spending time with his dad and he learned how to drive a bread truck when he was only 14. Howard says it was really the only time he got to spend with his dad because of his dad's work schedule. During the summer months he would go with his dad on the truck route most days. They discussed a lot of different subjects during those days including Howard's education.

When Howard was a senior in high school he worked in a local pharmacy where his mother worked part-time. The store owner and pharmacist, Joe Faler, convinced Howard that pharmacy school would be good for him. After graduation from high school, Howard attended Ferris State University in Big Rapids, Michigan because it had the largest pharmacy school in Michigan and also because Joe Faler had graduated from there.

Howard and Ann had been high school sweethearts and were both attending FSU in their freshman years, Howard in pharmacy and Ann in accounting. They got married during the school year. Howard said the first year of college was really tough and he sometimes thought he had bitten off a little more than he could chew. Later that year their first child, Bill, was born during his final exam in inorganic chemistry. Howard's mom and dad came and picked up Ann and the new baby and took them back to Saginaw for the summer where they lived with Ann's mother for the summer. After the final exams, Howard joined his wife and baby in Saginaw.

Howard's father helped him to get a job at Schafer Bakeries, where he was employed. Howard worked the entire summer after his freshman year and each summer thereafter until he graduated from pharmacy school in 1960 in a class of 120 students. His job at the bakery was making all of the icing for donuts and rolls. He would mix 100 pounds of powdered sugar with all the other ingredients necessary to make the finished product. It was a great summer job because he was allowed to work about 60 hours per week and made quite a bit of money. The bakery was so hot that Howard lost about 20 pounds each summer. Then it was back to school in the fall. They lived in an apartment near the campus because they could not afford a car. Ann would wheel Bill, their first child, in a wagon to the nearest super market where she would get groceries for the week.

During the school year he had a job at FSU scrubbing floors which he continued every year until graduation. Working during the school year, working at Schafter Bakeries during the summer and some financial help from his parents allowed Howard and Ann to stay afloat and finish college. They lived very frugally. Howard also was able to fit in playing intramural football, basketball and volleyball for three years while at FSU.

Howard graduated from pharmacy school with a degree in pharmacy in 1960 in a class of 120 students. After graduation he interviewed with several pharmacy chains. Howard and his best friend in pharmacy school, Roy Cheever, finally decided on Walgreen Drug Co. because they were the biggest and strongest chain in the country. Walgreen accepted both of them and they became pharmacy interns in Chicago.

Howard's dad showed up with his grandfather's farm truck to move Howard, Ann and their son from Big Rapids, Michigan to Chicago. Luckily, they were able to find an apartment close to the first store where he worked at 59th Street and Pulaski in Chicago. That worked out well because they still didn't own a car. He was in a management training program so he would spend his regular schedule in the pharmacy and extra hours in all other aspects of the store operation. On some of his days off, he worked in other Walgreen locations as a relief pharmacist.

After three years he became a store manager of a Walgreen store located at 41st Street and Archer in Chicago. The store was old and very small, only 4,000 square feet. His office was located in the basement adjacent to the stock room. Howard said that store provided a great learning experience for him. He learned all of the financial working of the company and the handling of employees. Howard says every store is different as to the customers and what they purchase. This store opened at 8am and each morning there would usually be 10-15 Lithuanian ladies waiting for the store to open with shopping baskets in hand. The first week he was there they advertised glycerin suppositories and they went through 25 cases of 24 per case in only four days. He often wondered what those customers did with all those suppositories. Parking at this store was limited and therefore most customers walked to this store. Volume and profit kept growing and after three years he was transferred back to the first store he worked at 59th Street and Pulaski.

Howard worked as manager of this store for three years. One day in May,1969, he got a surprise call from his father telling him that a grocery store back in Caro wanted to have a drug store adjacent to his store. His father got this information from Howard's Uncle Wally, who had a farm outside of Caro. Howard immediately flew to Caro to investigate the possibilities of such a deal. He checked out the competition, the market and the location. The location was great because it would be next to the best grocery store in town and one block from the local hospital. There were four other small pharmacies in town at that time.

After much thought and research Howard decided to go ahead with the deal. Howard's dad knew the president of a large bank in Saginaw which enabled him to consummate the financing quickly with only a handshake agreement. Howard and his dad managed to scrap together enough money for the project to make the bank feel comfortable to finance the remainder. Howard rented this space of 4,000 square feet on a five year lease at a rate of $350 per month for five years with three- five year renewal options. It seemed like a great deal. He discussed the deal with the top brass at Walgreens who warned him of the risks and tried to talk him into staying as manager.

Howard resigned from his job with Walgreens in Chicago and moved back to Caro. His dad once again showed up with a bakery semi-truck to move them to Caro. They rented a small farmhouse outside of town that was hardly livable in the winter. Howard said the average temperature in the winter in the farmhouse was about 60 degrees. The house was cold for two reasons: First, the farmhouse was 100 years old and had spaces between the slats in the wall and the wind whipped right through the wall. Second, they ran out of propane and Howard, now being a city slicker, didn't even realize the house was heated by propane. Once he got the propane tank refilled the temperature in the home zoomed all the way up to 60 degrees again. That first winter was really cold.

Back at the new store, Howard was busy renovating the store and getting it ready for opening day. Until 1985, Walgreen allowed individual owners to enter into franchise agreements and Howard did that until the franchise division was eliminated in 1985. Now, all Walgreen stores are company stores. Howard worked closely with the Walgreen Agency Division on store layout, merchandising and circular advertising. The cost of these services was merely the purchase of merchandise and the circular advertising from Walgreens. It was the best program for independent store owners in the country. It was especially good for Howard because as a Walgreen employee in management for almost 10 years, he had extensive experience with the franchise operation. He ordered fixtures and filed for licenses including his pharmacy licenses. He found a good drug wholesale company which also helped with merchandising. Howard's grandfather came up with a great carpenter to build the pharmacy department and a local electrician for the store.

Because of their extended family living in Caro, he was able to hire new employees from these contacts. The store finally opened in November, 1969. The store opened with three part-time clerks, a part-time relief pharmacist and his oldest son, Bill, was the stock boy and janitor. He also had one helper and Ann was the bookkeeper. Howard worked in the pharmacy and ran the store from 9am to 8pm Monday through Friday and limited times on Saturdays and Sundays. Howard says that after that first year the store was really doing well.

In the summer of 1972 an opportunity presented itself to open a second store. Again his dad came to him with this deal. It seemed that the owner of a strip shopping center wanted to rent his vacant building next to a supermarket in Sebewaing, Michigan, located 20 miles north of Caro along the Saginaw Bay. He thought a drug store next to his grocery store would be a good fit. Again Howard was off to check out the deal in Sebewaing which was a small town with a population of about 3,000. Howard immediately liked the possibilities as his pharmacy would be adjacent to Luke's Supermarket which was the only grocery store in town. There was one other pharmacy in town. The vacant building was 5,000 square feet and Howard and the lessor agreed to terms. The lessor's attorney drew up the lease and Howard noticed that the lease had a critical error in that the lessor and lessee were reversed. As a result, the lessor agreed to let Howard have his own attorney draw up a lease. This new lease called for a triple net lease with no increases in rent or other pharmacies in the shopping center for the duration of the lease. A triple net lease means that the lessor is responsible for payment of real estate taxes, insurance and maintenance of the mechanicals. He hired Ralph Elsner who was working in Kalamazoo, Michigan for Walgreens as a pharmacist. Ralph worked out well because of his previous experience with Walgreens. Howard worked part-time as a pharmacist on Ralph's days off. The other staff was similar to the other store. All of the same procedures in opening a drug store were in motion again. This store opened for business in late 1972.

In 1975, about three years after the Sebewaing store opened, Howard met with Jerry Rich, of Jerry's Foodland, who was in the process of building a new supermarket in a shopping center just outside of downtown Sandusky, Michigan. Sandusky is a town of about 4,500 people. Howard says that Jerry and he hit it off right away. Howard had meetings with Al Loding, the developer of the shopping center, and there were conditions that the store be located next to Jerry's Foodland and that Howard must own the building. At first Howard didn't like the idea of tying up so much cash in real estate but he was finally persuaded. He would own the 6,500 square foot building at a cost of about $150,000.

The deal came together at 8pm in the office of the developer with the local bank president, Al and Howard in attendance. Again the financing was agreed on by a handshake. Howard was able to negotiate, with Al's help, a 20-year term mortgage with a low interest rate with no payments during the first year of operation. They did a construction and end loan requiring a 20% down payment. The third store was finally opened late in 1975. There was one other pharmacy in town and he was able to hire the pharmacist from the competition and also hired a great staff that were all from Sandusky and knew everybody in town. As a result the store took off and gained momentum quickly. Howard says this store turned out to be a blessing in disguise as it was the strongest location he had. The building was paid off in 10 years and when Howard later sold his business to Rite Aid they signed a lease paying him an annual gross rent of $8.87 per square foot.

During those years, Ann and Howard had dinner with his mom and dad about twice a month and mostly they discussed their businesses. In 1980, Howard and his dad attended a buying show in Chicago and his mother told Howard that his dad was having difficulty swallowing. Howard was concerned and sent him directly to the Mayo Clinic in Rochester, Minnesota for a checkup. He was diagnosed with esophageal cancer. Ann literally spent the next 18 months taking care of his dad.After a lot of cancer treatments and a real fight, his dad passed away in 1981. That was a terrible blow to Howard because his dad had been instrumental in Howard's success and they had so much in common. Howard says he really misses him. His father had a lot of influence on him and was the perfect sounding board for Howard.

The fourth store was formed with a partner in Hemlock, Michigan, a town with a population of 2,000 in 1985.Several interesting developments occurred with this deal. This was an existing store of 2,500 square feet, which was owned by Perry Drug, a 100 store chain in Michigan. This deal was brought to Howard by Gilbert Caten who represented Perry Drug. Three years prior, Mr. Caten had negotiated with Howard for Perry Drug to buy his stores. The deal eventually fell apart because Howard really wasn't ready to sell and Perry ended up buying an auto parts chain in Arizona. This was a bad move for Perry because they ended up losing a lot of money on that deal. So now Perry was a seller rather than a buyer. Perry wanted to sell this store because of its size and location—they wanted to rid their company of small stores in small markets. Howard liked the deal because it was the only store in town and there was no big chain competition in the area. The hooker in the negotiation was that Howard had to make a decision to buy the Hemlock store within 10 business days. He agreed and assumed the lease that Perry Drug had with the landlord.

Ironically, his first and only choice as a pharmacist to run the store was a man named Bob Bell. In the mid-1970s, Bob worked in Howard's first store in Caro but later left to move to South Carolina. After several years in South Carolina, Bob moved back to Michigan and worked as a pharmacist for K-Mart in Saginaw. Howard knew Bob well and also knew that he had grown up and knew everyone in Hemlock. He was the perfect fit. He met with Bob and his wife at Bob's home in Hemlock and discussed a deal over the kitchen table. He offered Bob a 1/3rd interest and they became partners. They were able to retain all the Perry Drug employees who had worked for many years at that location and also knew everyone in town. Howard says that these deals just prove that you can't burn your bridges with anyone.

The fifth store happened back in Caro in 1990 when the supermarket next to his first store built a new supermarket on the main drag just outside of Caro. Howard opened the new pharmacy next to the new supermarket which was the largest supermarket in town. The new pharmacy was 7,500 square feet. The store was operated by one full time pharmacist, one part-time pharmacist and two pharmacy techs. The store hours were 9am to 8pm Monday through Friday, 9am to 6pm on Saturday and 10am to 4pm on Sundays. He continued to own and operate the other Caro store.

Howard had a very busy schedule. He tried to work in each store one day per week when he could. He usually worked Sundays in Caro because that was the only one of his stores that was open on Sunday. He says he had terrific employees who were dedicated to their work and dependent on their jobs. He had experienced almost no turnover of employees. Howard believes that the key to his business success was giving good service to customers, hiring the best people available and taking good care of his employees. He also believes that timing is another important key, plus you should never burn your bridges.

Early in 1994, Hook Drugs came to Howard and wanted to buy his stores. Hook owned approximately 1,000 stores and was headquartered in Indianapolis. He had several meetings with the vice president of store operations both in Caro and in Indianapolis. Howard says that selling to Hook Drugs was the most difficult and important decision of his life except for his marriage to Ann. At that time, he was not that old and really liked running his stores. He was also very concerned about his employees. He ended up striking a deal with Hook and sold his stores in June 1994 for cash with the stipulation that all of his employees would be retained. Looking back, he believes that selling his business when he did was a good move. There was a lot of consolidation in the industry and within two years of the sale of his business Perry Drugs and Arbor Drugs were bought by Rite Aid, both Michigan chains.

The Hemlock store was not part of the deal with Hook Drugs because his partner was still young and wanted to continue the operation. Howard and Bob struck a deal in 1995 which allowed Bob to purchase Howard's 2/3rd interest in the store. Howard financed the sale over a 10 year period.

During the almost 10 years Howard lived in Chicago he played no tennis as he was just too busy. When he bought his first store back in Caro in 1969 he started playing again. One of his best friends in Caro, Steve Williams, played with him for the next 35 years. They played at night on lighted public courts from about 9pm to 11pm because they were too busy during daylight hours. During the last 15 years they played on Steve's tennis courts which he had built in his back yard. In 1994, Howard attended the Professional Tennis Registry at Hilton Head Island and became a certified tennis instructor and began teaching tennis at Bay Valley Tennis Club in Bay City, Michigan.

Howard and Ann now spend most of their time in Ft. Myers, Florida at The Landings Yacht, Golf and Tennis Club which is the premier tennis club in the area with a total of 15 HarTru courts. Howard says he also plays some golf, which he describes as the most unforgiving game on the planet and sings in the Cape Chorale, a barbershop chorus. He also sings in two barbershop quartets and in The Landings chorus. Howard and Ann spend the summer months in Caro where he still teaches tennis and until recently did some summer relief work as a pharmacist.

Last year they sold their home in Caro requiring Howard to get rid of all his tennis trophies. Howard's most memorable victories were winning The Century Cup at Bay Valley Tennis Club in Bay City, Michigan five times with his tennis partner, Roy Walker. He took the plates off the trophies and gave them to the coach of the Caro Tiger's tennis team. Howard worked with this team getting them ready for their tennis seasons. They plan to go back to Michigan for about three months this summer. They will live part of the time in their son Bill's log house on Torch Lake, which is near Traverse City in northwest Michigan. They will also spend some time in Caro visiting family and friends.

Howard and Ann have three sons: Bill, age 56, who works for Walgreens, David, age 50 and Steven, age 49. David and Steven live in Grand Rapids, Michigan and Bill is in the process of moving to Raleigh-Durham, North Carolina from Lavonia, Michigan to convert a chain of drug stores which Walgreen purchased in that area to the Walgreen's logo. All three of Howard's sons worked in the Caro store during their high school years. Howard is grateful to his entire family for those years.

Howard and Ann spend considerable time visiting their sons and their families. They especially enjoy spending time with their grandson, Mike, and their great granddaughter, Haley, who is now five years old. Life has been good to Howard and Ann and they certainly deserve their retirement after achieving The American Dream.

Brian and Bev Nelson

I've known Brian and Bev since 1972 when I was Brian's banker and he was my accountant in Rockford, Illinois. At that time, Bev owned a bridge center and I took bridge lessons from her. They went on to become owners of a chain of retail stores in Indianapolis, Indiana and achieved The American Dream. Later, they started a bridge center in Fort Myers which became the fifth largest bridge center in the United States. They've done it all.

Brian's father, Stege Nilsson, was born in 1909 in Sweden and immigrated to the United States in 1923. He was 14 years old and came along with his sisters who were ten and seven and a brother who was only three. His mother, Alice Goranson, was born in Rockford in 1913. His father changed his last name to Nelson and met his wife, Alice Goranson, in 1930 and they were married in 1933.

Brian was born Nov 25, 1946 at Rockford's Saint Anthony Hospital. His sister was born in July, 1934 in Rockford where the family lived until moving to Naperville in 1939. They lived in Naperville from 1939 to 1941 when they moved back to Rockford. His dad was employed at National Lock for a long time and worked his way up to the title of "head engineer" with 100 men under him. Brian says his dad made a lot of money.

Brian began his formal education at Rolling Green School in Rockford, Illinois in the fall of 1951. He believes it was the first year Rolling Green was open and was built for all the new baby boomers. Brian was only four years of age when he started school and was the last kid in his class to learn to skip. He went to kindergarten in the mornings and was taught by Miss Brown. Many of his fellow classmates attended class with him all the way through his senior year at East High School. He lived at the western boundary of Rolling Green School which was 23rd Street.

Most of his neighborhood playmates lived on the west side of 23rd Street and went to Hallstrom School. It was too far for a four year old to walk and nobody had two cars at that time. So, a group of parents got together and six or eight kids who lived in the outlying areas were transported every day by a taxi. Brian said, "Hey, I thought everyone went to school by taxi." Many years later, he was going through some old papers and found his parents bank statements with cancelled checks. There was one check for $2.17 to Yellow Cab for taxi services for one month. Imagine being picked up and taken home 20-22 days a month for $2.17.

Brian and his mother went everywhere on the city bus. They could catch the Broadway bus going away from town on 17th Avenue and 23rd Street and it went all the way to the edge of Rockford at Broadway and East Gate Parkway. It was years later that Rockford Transit started the Broadway buses going all the way out to Five Points. When they rode the bus it was usually to go downtown. To catch the bus they had to walk two blocks up to Broadway and 23rd where they would have to wait 5-10 minutes for the next bus.

Gate's Grocery was located half a block from the corner of Broadway and 23rd Street which is where they got all their groceries, etc. Brian said it was a little mom and pop store that you can't find any more. Don and Audrey Gates and all their children, there were six or seven of them, lived in back of the store and knew everyone by name. Brian's family had a charge account there and when his dad would pay the bill at the end of the month, Audrey would give them a half a gallon of ice cream for being "good customers." Brian told his dad to be sure to pay Audrey because the other clerks wouldn't offer any free ice cream. Brian said there wasn't a sweeter person than Audrey Gates. He knew that a lot of people paid cash, but he loved the fact that he could go in there and charge almost anything to S. B. Nelson.

And they also lived only a few blocks from Broadway and 20th Street, a hotbed of retailing. Mrs. Gus owned the Rockview Confectionery where she sold penny candy, sodas, shakes, ice cream cones, newspapers, milk and bread. Brian says she was a bit of a crab, but she still got all of his birthday and gift monies. He remembers Lik-m-aid and little dots of candy which were dropped on adding machine tape paper. She had the best ice cream for cones—Oak Brand Ice Cream which was made in Freeport, Illinois by the Credicott family.

Also at Broadway and 20th was Madden's Drug Store, Freeburg's Swedish Bakery, Gus the Barber who supposedly was married to Mrs. Gus at one time. Madden's also had a lot of candy as well as comic books which were 10¢. Brian wishes he still had those old comics. He saved them for years and years, but they got lost in the shuffle when he moved out of the homestead years later.

On Saturday morning, they would go to Freeburg's Bakery and take a number—there must have been a dozen ladies clerking. The place would be packed, but eventually your number would come up. Brian said you could buy Cardamon rolls, Cardamon Coffee Cake, Swedish Smolandskaka, almond tarts, Swedish Rye Bread, and a whole host of yummy things that smelled marvelous. They would run the bread through the electric slicer right in front of you and the bread would still be warm when you got it home. They world wrap it in white paper and wind a bunch of string all around it. They would use a paper bag to write down all the prices of what you were buying and add it up by hand. Then that bag would be one of the bags they'd use to send you on your way. And the total, even though you had a sack full of goodies, was but a dollar and some cents.

Madden's Drug Store had a pay phone which had an earpiece you would put up to your ear. You would talk into the fixed mouthpiece sticking out of the wall-mounted phone. Brian would always check to see if someone had left money in the coin return. Every once in a while, they had, and his day was made. He remembers that long distance calls were considered very expensive.

Brian went to school for kindergarten and first grade at Rolling Green School but second grade was at a little two room school on 26th Street and Broadway and then back to Rolling Green for third and fourth grades. He attended Hallstrom School for fifth and sixth grade. Then he went to seventh, eighth and ninth grades at Jefferson Jr. High School and then went to East High School for his sophomore, junior and senior years. Brian thought it was a little strange that he attended so many different schools even though he lived at the same home the entire time.

It was after his junior year of high school that he learned to play duplicate bridge. When he started, he scored at the bottom time after time but perhaps a few times came in next to the bottom. He began playing in July of 1963, and continued playing into August and September. He finally came in fourth in a five table Howell and won .06 master points and he was so happy. He began running games on Saturday and Sunday afternoons. Then he remembers playing on November 22, 1963, the day President Kennedy was killed, and there was a game that night of seven tables in which he played with his mom. They were first with a 63% average game and won with a 79.5 game. Then he started playing Tuesday evenings in DeKalb, Wednesday nights in Rockford, Thursday nights in Janesville, Wisconsin or in Sycamore, Illinois. He played Friday nights in either Beloit, Wisconsin or Freeport, Illinois. Brian said he was so busy playing bridge that he barely made it through school but he graduated in the top half of his class, 305 out of 625.

After graduation from high school in 1964, he went away to Champaign, Illinois to the University of Illinois for his freshman year of college. Brian realized after one year that college was not for him so he came back to Rockford and attended Rockford School of Business for three years. Brian did well there.

After graduation from Rockford School of Business in 1968, he played bridge all the time. That is when he met Bev Brodd. She started playing bridge a little bit in1965 when she and her husband came to the bridge club and played on a Friday night in November. They had a nation-wide game with 17 tables in play at a place where they only had room for 12 tables. They played one table on the stairs half way between the first and second floors, another two tables in the ladies room (outside the toilets) and two more on the second floor outside the men's room. In 1966 Bev started playing a lot of bridge and was becoming a very good player. Bev and Brian started playing together in late 1966 and they won everywhere they played. They continued to play together until Brian graduated from Rockford School of Business and he decided to go to Europe with a couple of friends. Brian had been working at National Lock while attending business school and for a while after he graduated. One night he left a note for his boss saying that if he had to work one more night at National Lock it would blow his mind. That is when he left for Europe.

Bev says she had an unhappy childhood with parents who both drank constantly. She was an only child, alone a lot and frightened of being alone. As she grew up, she knew she had to escape this environment, so she married her high school sweetheart, Loren Brodd.After having one child, a son, and separating for about eight months, she went back to her husband and had another son. Bev said that by this time, her father had left her mother and had married twice to nice women. His third wife had six children and Bev ended up raising one of the children, Janie, a girl, in her own home. This girl grew up to be a fine young woman and she introduced this girl to Brian. They dated for over a year but they eventually broke up, leaving Janie with a broken heart.

While Brian was on his trip to Europe he sent post cards talking about the gals they had met and Bev felt some jealousy which she didn't quite understand. While he was in Europe, Bev and her husband separated for the second time and were in the process of a divorce. When Brian returned from his European trip, Bev said she was overly happy when she saw him. They continued to play bridge together again and started to get close. They started a relationship but they had to keep it quiet because Bev's divorce was not yet final. Eventually Brian went to her former husband's office to discuss their relationship and to assure the former husband that his relationship with Bev did not start until after divorce proceedings were initiated. He said he believed that and Bev and Brian were married September 12, 1969.

Bev was close to Brian's mom for years as they had played foursomes bridge in Bev's home so she could be with her children while her husband was out drinking until all hours of the night. Bev felt that she needed to be home with her children in the evenings so she only played bridge outside her home one or two nights per week. Bev says that Brian's mom and his sister gave stellar support of their relationship. Without the support of Brian's mom and sister their marriage could never have happened. She says their love set Bev and Brian free to tell the world.

Upon his return from Europe he started his own accounting firm on East State Street in Rockford. It was slow at first but within three years the business became profitable. During this time, Bev was running bridge games at his office during evenings and weekends and they were doing well. In 1976 Brian was asked by Gary Maitland to be his accountant for a new business he was starting. Gary said he had just returned from California and found that waterbeds were a big thing and he wanted to open a waterbed retail store. Brian thought Gary had lost his mind and tried to discourage him. He told Gary he was afraid he would lose all his money but since he was so determined, Brian agreed to become his accountant. Gary opened a retail store at the corner of Harrison Avenue and Alpine Road called The Bedroom. Bev says she recalls Brian telling her "he wouldn't put a red nickel into that business." She said he later had to eat those words.

At this point I must say that Gary Maitland had been a friend of mine since we were freshmen in high school. Gary made his living as a truck driver, but when he received a sizeable inheritance he decided it was time to become an entrepreneur. Since I was his friend and banker, he came to me with many different ideas and I was able to talk him out of them. After a trip to California, he came to me with an idea to start a waterbed store. Initially I thought it was not a good idea, but he asked me to do research with him. We went to the Rockford Public Library and tried to find out everything we could to see if such a business was viable. Eventually he won me over and we got together at my house on several occasions to write a business plan. During that time my former wife came up with the name for the business, The Bedroom. Gary asked me to be his partner, but I declined at that time thinking that the business wouldn'tbe that successful. I suggested that he work with my accountant, Brian Nelson.

Brian saw Gary making money hand over fist, month after month, and in June,1978, Gary asked Brian to be his partner. Brian had to come up with $100,000 to purchase a half interest in the Rockford store. This was no easy task. They now had three children. Bev had two sons from her other marriage who were now ages 19 and 14 and another son born to Brian who was then seven. They didn't have anywhere near that kind of money. Luckily the previous year they had purchased $5.000 of Wendy's stock which, after one year, had grown to $25,000. They sold it. Right after the sale, the stock started to decline and went back to $5,000. Bev says it was quite a break as they just happened to be in the right place at the right time. Then, Bev's mom, Irene, died leaving her with her mom's home which Bev sold for $38,000. Bev and Brian were able to borrow another $35,000 from a friend of Bev's. This totaled $98,000.

It was about that same time that Gary asked Brian to fly to Indianapolis with him because Gary thought that was a wide open market for waterbeds. He felt there was little competition and they could make a lot of money there. This is when they allowed three additional partners to come in so they could raise another $100,000 and to have management in place to open two stores in Indianapolis. Gary, Brian and a third partner each put in $26,333 and two other partners put in $10,000 each. One of the new partners was a couple from central Illinois, one was a longtime friend of Gary's and the third was a guy who worked in the Rockford store.

Next they had to find a location and waterbed retailers were not the most desired tenants by many landlords. They were turned down by several landlords but finally they found someone who would take a chance on them in Speedway, Indiana, a suburb of Indianapolis. This was not the greatest neighborhood but they were grateful that someone would take a chance on them. Eventually, as the business grew, this waterbed store became this rich landlord's largest tenant.

So, the three new partners went to Indianapolis and they opened their first store in Speedway, Indiana in August, 1979, called The Bedroom. In a short time they were fighting like cats and dogs and didn't get along at all. They ended up firing one of the partners and buying out his interest in the business. After another couple months they kicked out another partner and bought his interest. Gary and Brian knew this wasn't going to work and one of them needed to move to Indianapolis to get things on the right track. Gary, although not married, said he wouldn't move from Rockford and Brian said he couldn't move because he had three children and a wife to consider. In the end it was Brian and Bev who had to move. They had borrowed to the hilt to become a partner and everything they had was tied up in this business. They had to move to save the partnership and their investment.

Brian and Bev sold their home and packed up everything they owned, and with their two youngest children, Chris and Jay, headed for Indianapolis in May,1979. The oldest son, Mark, then 20, stayed in Rockford to be with his girlfriend, Joy, who eventually became his wife. They stayed in a motel room for a few days which was very small for the four of them. They purchased a home under construction and while it was being built they rented a home. This home was sold so the builder moved them to another home just down the street from their new home. This home was also sold, so they moved into their new home before it was completed. It was a great home with the nicest view in town and surrounded by trees and open air all around them. Unfortunately it didn't have carpeting and a lot of other things you take for granted in a new home.

After getting settled in their new home they opened up another store in Indianapolis. After a couple months they got into a disagreement with the partners who were a couple and bought them out. Now it was just Brian and Bev running Indy and Gary running Rockford. Bev started working part-time, 12 hours per week, and she became the leading sales person in the two stores. That is when they asked her to become the manager of one of the stores. After school their son would come to the store and play in Bev's office until it was time to leave for the day. One day Bev attended a bridge tournament and someone gave her a chocolate chip cookie which they told her contained marijuana. She put the cookie in her purse intending to give it to Brian. She left it in her purse and one day her eight year old boy ate it and they found him stoned on her office floor. Bev was shocked that she had actually drugged her precious child.

In March, 1990, their oldest son, Mark, was killed in an auto accident. Bev says he was a great person in the business and was really missed. It was very difficult for Bev and she decided to give up and move to Florida in December, 1990. They had owned homes in Fort Myers, Florida since 1984. They owned one property from 1984-1987 and another from 1987-1995. Bev lived in Florida full time starting in 1990 and Brian went back and forth from Indy to Florida until 1997. They ran a bridge club in Fort Myers from 1990 until December, 2000; it was called McGregor Point Bridge Club. They started with two games per week and it grew and grew. It was the fifth largest bridge club in the entire country. In the winter, they ran over 50 games on Monday through Sunday including Monday, Wednesday and Friday nights. It was one of the nicest clubs in the United States. It started out real slow but after five or six years business was booming. The business got so big and successful that it was affecting their marriage. They sold the business in December, 2000 to another couple who was employed there and it continues to operate under the same name.

Eventually Gary and Brian and Bev split up the operation so that Gary owned all of Illinois and Brian and Bev owned all of Indiana. In 1982, the waterbed business in Rockford was struggling. Gary asked me to join him in the business to help straighten it out and we brought in my friend Dennis Roop to be CEO. We became equal owners in the corporation. Dennis was a very successful banker who I had worked with for many years and he did a great job. He improved operations and efficiencies and instituted sound business practices. We started opening other branch stores in Illinois and by 1988 we had seven stores in Illinois and Wisconsin. At this time, I decided the waterbed business had its run and was no longer a good investment. Also, I was uncomfortable that we had a "line of credit" with my bank for $500,000 for which I was personally responsible. I sold my interest back to the corporation and the bank released me from any personal responsibility on the line of credit. The waterbed business limped along until 2003 when it was closed. Dennis and Gary also opened and operated several waterbed stores in the Virginia Beach, Virginia area. They did well for several years, but eventually they met the same fate as the other waterbed stores.

The waterbed business in Indianapolis grew to a total

of 13 stores and was also known as The Bedroom. Bev and Brian were a good team with her expertise in sales and his in accounting. During their time in Indiana, there was a great change in the competition in the sale of waterbeds. Soon the mom and pop retailers were driven out of business and replaced by regional and national chains. The competition became very keen and retailers had to adjust and become more efficient or they failed.

Bev says, "It was a whiz of a thing." When profits were good they didn't want to sell and when profits were bad they couldn't sell. The business lost money every month for the last 10 months of 1990 and it lost money every month in 1991. The bank became concerned with their losses and in January, 1992 their bank asked them to sell nine of their 13 locations. Brian agreed to sell one store but he told them the other 12 stores would be okay. Brian says, they had learned how to get smart in the business. They spent 1990 and 1991 trying to get lean and mean and were in a good position starting in 1992. In January, 1992 the bank demanded that Brian pay their line of credit down from $1,250,000 to $1,000,000 within three months. So, Brian agreed to give up their 13th store in Evansville. They had a January-February sell out during which Bev and several employees from their other stores helped out. In Evansville they usually sold about $50,000 per month but during this sale they sold $250,000 of furniture at only 10% off and closed the store. At the end of March, they paid the bank down to $1,000,000 as it had demanded.

Then the bank came around and said they wanted the line of credit reduced by another $100,000 within the next three months. Brian told them he couldn't do it but sales improved and he was able to pay the loan down by $100,000 to $900,000 during July of 1992 just as the bank had requested. Next the bank told Brian they wanted the line reduced by another $100,000 and Brian was furious. However, three months later they paid the bank down by another $100,000 to $800,000 in October 1992.

It was at that time that they changed banks. The year 1992 turned out to be a very good year but 1993 was even better. However, their best year ever was 1994. Brian considered selling at that time to his two vice presidents, Jeff and Paul, but they weren't interested. Brian said that at one point he would have given it away for $1,000 but finally at the end of 1997 his employees bought it for $2,000,000. They agreed to pay $950,000 down and $25,000 per month for seven years. That totaled $2,000,000 principal and $1,050,000 in interest for a total of $3,050,000. Brian told Bev they might never get the money they agreed to pay. After five years, they asked Brian to reduce the interest rate to 9% since interest rates had declined a lot. Brian refused to reduce the interest rate so they got a bank loan and paid Brian and Bev the balance still owed. Five years later the business closed and Brian and Bev felt real bad for them.

Brian and Bev sold their home in Indy in 1997 and both lived full time in Florida and worked in the Bridge Center until it was sold. In September, 2004, Brian was diagnosed with a brain tumor and was given one year to live. Brian says he started drinking carrot juice like there was no tomorrow. He was told by Hallelujah Juice to drink a ton of juice, so he did. He drank 25 pounds of carrot juice every five days. Brian says it worked because he got better and better. He went to his doctor every eight weeks for five years until the doctor said he didn't need to come anymore. It has been over nine years since his first diagnosis and Brian says he's still kicking. He says he can no longer read anything because his brain is pretty much gone. However, he can still play a decent game of bridge as long he can play a pretty simple game.

He plays bridge every day. About half the time he plays at the Elks Club and the rest of the time he plays at his old club, McGregor Point Bridge Center. Bev also plays bridge every day and achieved one of her goal of accumulating 2,500 bridge master points by her 75th birthday in February, 2014. Their son, Chris, and his wife, Beth, moved to Fort Myers in June, 1999. They have two children born in 1995 and 1998. Their son, Jay, moved to Fort Myers when Brian was scheduled to die after the first year. Joy's son, Keith, moved to Fort Myers and is getting married in March of 2014 at age 26. Brian is now 67 years of age and Bev is 75. They will be married 45 years in September of this year. Life is good.

John Failes

John Failes

This is the life story of a man who has always done the right and proper thing his entire life and rose to the position of owner and CEO of one of the 10 largest CPA firms in the State of Virginia. He always worked hard and played by the rules and volunteered his time and talents for the benefit of the community. In the year 2000, John sold his firm to one of the largest CPA firms in the country and at age 55 he had achieved The American Dream and retired. Since then he has spent his winters at Heritage Palms Golf and Country Club in Ft. Myers, Florida where he enjoys golf and tennis and still maintains his home in Virginia where he spends about six months each year.

John's paternal grandfather was a blacksmith and his paternal grandmother was a housewife. They were a hardworking lower middle class family that stressed religion and a strong work ethic. John's father, N. Warren Failes, was born in the mountains of western Virginia in 1914, the youngest of four children. John's mother was born in Portsmouth, Virginia in 1917 and was raised by her elderly grandmother. She never knew her parents as they passed away when she was very young. Her family was very poor but she graduated from high school at the age of 16. She worked her way through college by small scholarships and working as a waitress and graduated from college at age 19.After graduation, she taught school for over 40 years. During that time, she went to night school and earned a Master's Degree from William & Mary College. John's parents were married in 1941 after a two year courtship. John was born March 5, 1945 in Portsmouth, Virginia

John's father worked in electronics at the Naval Air Station in Norfolk, Virginia and retired in 1970 at age 56. John says his father was a very good man and a hard worker but he was limited by his formal education and never made more than about $6,000 or $7,000 per year. John says his father was a very easy-going man who was never really given a chance to display his skills in his job.John said his mother was just the opposite. John and his mother were often at odds with each other because she was rather demanding in that she was always pushing John to do better as she had pushed herself in life. John believes that his mother achieved great success in life because she drove herself so hard and also expected a lot from those she loved. John remembers her coming home from teaching school all day and helping his dad fix dinner and then she would go off to class when she was working on her Master's Degree. She was always busy and intense because she was always working hard and trying to improve herself and her family.

John has reflected on his relationship with his mother since her passing several years ago. He believes she had a great influence on his success by the way she pushed him all through school. This made John very determined to make good and he was consumed with worry that if he didn't push himself that he might not be successful. His parents chose to have only one child so as to be able to help John get a good education.They lived in a nice lower middle class neighborhood and, back in the 1950s, everyone on his street was shipyard-oriented and hard working.

John graduated from the public school system in 1963 and subsequently attended Virginia Tech.He graduated with a Bachelor's Degree in Finance in 1967 and spent 1968 and 1969 in the U.S. Army in the infantry and finance corps.He went back to Virginia Tech in 1970 on the GI Bill and received a second degree in accounting.At the end of his military service, he married Mary Benn Underwood to whom he has been married for over 44 years.Mary taught school for 20 years and was instrumental in his success in the business world. John says, if she had not been working his first few years in business that he would not have made it. They had close to zero net worth in the early 1980s and as his business grew his expenses had to be paid as they were incurred because his accounts receivable was collected later. This put a real squeeze on their personal finances. Consequently, he worked long hours with no cash compensation.

John and his wife first met when he was 10 and she was six at a Methodist Church where their mothers taught Sunday school.Because of the friendship of their parents, John and Mary remained close friends until John graduated from college. It was at that time that they started dating and later married in July, 1969. Her father was a test pilot in the U.S. Navy whose plane crashed when she was five years old and her mother was a school teacher.

John's initial employment in the early 1970s was with a CPA firm that evolved into KPMG and subsequently a large local firm in Hampton Roads that was formed in 1926. John became a junior partner with them in the late 1970s and in the early 1980s started his own firm with several young people that grew to over 80 individuals by the time he sold the business in August 2000 at age 55 to one of the largest CPA firms in the country.During his tenure, he ranked consistently as one of the 10 Largest CPA firms in the State of Virginia. Virginia Business Magazine recognized him as one of the "Who's Who of Virginia CPA's".

John says that much of his success was attributed to good fortune in addition to some of the following reasons:

- A strong work ethic
- All clients, no matter how small in terms of fees, were equally important.Some of his best referrals were from individual 1040 tax clients
- He joined many non-profit and civic organizations in order to meet people and to give back to the community
- He opened offices in four different cities with Virginia Beach being his core office. He wanted to be convenient to his clients and none of his offices were ostentatious, but very comfortable.
- He noticed early on that most business partnerships do not work out long-term.So, he decided that any partners he had would be 10-15 years younger and could become 1% owners for $100 and if they left they got their $100 back.At the time of the sale of his business, he had six partners who he rewarded on the sale at his discretion.All the partners over the years enjoyed the ego of being a partner and having their names on the letterhead so, consequently, they were a smooth-running organization without the conflicts that many partnerships suffered.

- Most CPAs that he knew were not very good business people.They were quick to brag about how fast they could add one and one but were unaware of what many clients really wanted—they wanted sound business advice. Most of his clients knew their trade very well but were neophytes in how to run a business efficiently and how to bank and invest their money productively. He tried to do that as well as the traditional tax, accounting and audit work of a CPA firm.

The years of fear of not being successful and losing what he had achieved was a very strong motivator for John. To this day, he still thanks so many of his clients for their support over the years.They knew he would go to great lengths not to let them down. His fees were always middle of the road, as he did not want to get rich off any one or two clients.John says that if you treat people fairly then they will treat you fairly. As a result, he rarely had a client go elsewhere.John says, the moral of that story is, if you do not lose clients and continue to pick up new business you will continue to grow. He was able to grow because he realized early on that 90% of the work was pretty simple stuff and the other 10% was not, but extremely important. The 90% of the work that was routine was done by his staff but clients did not know or really care who did the work as long as they felt like they had his attention and his signature on their tax returns.Most of his competitors did not operate this way and tried to do 100% of the work, but were limited as to how many clients they could deal with because of the number of hours in a day.

To summarize, his parents and his wife had a strong work ethic that inspired him at times to overachieve. Beginning with his teen years, he always had a job working in the summers and during Christmas holidays, such as mowing lawns and delivering newspapers and mail.His roots were instrumental in helping him to treat everyone with respect and equally, and he expected all people to give their best efforts to society.

In 2007, John was asked by his alma mater, Virginia Tech University, to be chairman of the Hampton Roads $50 Million Campaign.Their goal was to raise $50 million from various individuals and businesses. The campaign was very successful and it was an opportunity for John to give back to the university which John feels has done so much for him. He has been very generous with Virginia Tech with his own money having given the school over $250,000 since 1992. This was his way of thanking Virginia Tech for the great education he obtained, which he believes was one of the big reasons for his success in the business world. He says that Virginia Tech was a pedestrian type school, not a preppy school, but rather sort of a melting pot of the students in that area. It was sort of a mixture of all kinds of people just like in the business world, so it enabled John to mix, interact and feel comfortable with everyone.

Early in John's career he joined a lot of organizations so as to meet people and get his name out into the business world and to try to build a book of business.He feels these many organizations were very helpful in bringing him a lot of business from his peers at the time. As his reputation grew, his firm grew and he was asked to get into more organizations because of his perceived business acumen. He was a volunteer with Commonwealth College where he was Chairman of the Board for a period of time where they helped young people to get jobs in various trades. John felt that not everyone could benefit from education and that these various jobs and trades offered a chance to earn good money and become successful.

John was one of six trustees of the Beazley Foundation which has been around for over 50 years. It has given well over $100 million for education to organizations such as the Sugar Plum Bakery, which teaches individuals how to become productive members of society. Many of these individuals have Down's Syndrome or similar type disabilities and helps make them feel good about themselves. His business success gave him the ability to help distribute the money appropriately. A personality trait that helped him in business is that, although shy by normal standards, he is actually gregarious compared to most of his CPA competitors and peers. It was a useful trait in the business world where he was able to interact with other business people whereas some of his competitors chose to stay home rather than volunteer and get known by people in the community.

He believes his jobs as a youth such as having a newspaper route, cutting lawns and later his military experience were all helpful in his career and made him want to be in charge and live or die by his own sword. He said he had enough confidence in his ability in the accounting arena to believe he could be a success. If he wasn't successful, he would only have himself to blame.

During the last 10 years or so of being in business he turned away quite a few clients who were going into business for themselves and came to him for assistance. After years of working with entrepreneurs, John knew quite well what it took to be successful and could tell on the front end whether someone had what it takes to be successful in business or was pursuing the right type of business. He didn't feel right encouraging those who were putting up their life savings to go into business so he would tell them how he felt about their chances of success. He said in his final 10 years in business he probably turned away about 90% of those who wanted to start a new business. I wonder if it is only a coincidence that according to the SBA about 90% of businesses do fail in the first 10 years.

John said that early on in his career he took on all clients and didn't try to make decisions about whether they were likely to become successful entrepreneurs. This was because at that time he didn't have the knowledge and experience which he developed over his career.After seeing businesses succeed and others fail he got a sense of what it took to succeed and wanted to prevent giving encouragement to those who he expected would lose everything. John felt it would be dishonorable to give these people false hope. He suspects that most of them went to another CPA and got the help they wanted. He believes that most of them probably failed in their business but he certainly hopes they made good.

In one case, he turned town a client to go into business, but John did his Form 1040 tax return for a fee of $250 annually, and he ended up referring a new huge client to John. So, John says that sometimes good deeds do pay you dividends.

In 1999, John was one of 16 founding corporate directors of TowneBank, which now has nearly $5 billion in assets.He currently serves as vice-chairman of the bank.John has served as chairman of many different committees. He says it has been delightful to watch the bank grow so rapidly and feels good that he has contributed to its success. In the beginning he got lots of his clients to invest in the bank at around $3 per share and the price 15 years later is over $15 per share, with a dividend of about 3%. It has been a great investment for all of them.

Here is a resume of his background:

EDUCATION

1963 Graduate of Woodrow Wilson High School, Portsmouth, Virginia

1967 Graduate of Virginia Tech in Finance

1970 Graduate of Virginia Tech in Accounting

WORK BACKGROUND

1968-1970 U.S. Army Infantry/Finance Corps

1970-1972 Staff accountant for Berry, Dale & Drinkard (KPMG)

1972-1983 Staff accountant and junior partner with Edmondson, Ledbetter & Ballard

1983-1985 Partner of Roberts & Failes

1985-2000 Partner, Sole Director and CEO of Failes & Associates, P.C.

AWARDS & HONORS

Distinguished Super CPA by Virginia Business Magazine

Director of Year by Princess Anne Bank

Founder & CEO of one of ten largest CPA firms in the State of Virginia

Chairperson for the Virginia Tech Hamptons Roads $50 Million Campaign, "Invent The Future"

PAST OR CURRENT BOARD OF DIRECTORS
TOWNEBANK (Vice Chairman)

Princess Anne Bank

Hampton Roads Chamber of Commerce

London House

Portsmouth-Chesapeake American Cancer Society

Virginia Tech School of Accounting

ODU School of Accounting

St. Christopher's School
Commonwealth College (Chairman)
Girl's Club of Portsmouth (Chairman)
Virginia Tech Student Aid Foundation
Cedar Point Country Club
Eton Group
Envest
Towne Insurance (Chairman)
Monumental United Methodist Church
Portsmouth City Retirement Board
Virginia Beach TowneBank Executive Committee (Chairman)
Towne Financial Services Board
TowneBank Financial Services Board Executive Committee
Beazley Foundation

PAST OR CURRENT MEMBERSHIPS
Portsmouth Elks Lodge
Portsmouth Assembly
Portsmouth Sports Club
Virginia Beach Rotary
Virginia Venture Group
Virginia Beach Vision
Princess Anne Country Club
Greenbrier Country Club
Cedar Point Country Club
Harbor Club
Town Point Club

Churchland Rotary
Virginia Tech Ut Prosim Society
Hokie Club (Endowed and Lifetime Member)
American Institute of Certified Public Accountants
Tidewater Chapter of Certified Public Accountants
Virginia Society of Certified Public Accountants

Klaus Tiessen

I've known Klaus and his wife, Ulla, for about 15 years through playing tennis at The Landings. It is amazing that in their late 70's they are so very active. Ulla has the same beauty that made her mother a beauty queen. This is the story of a German nurseryman who immigrated to Canada when he was 20 years of age. He didn't speak a word of English and with $25 in his pocket he continued his quest of owning a "garden center" in North America.Through hard physical work, seven days were week, from dawn until dark, he finally made his goal in 1989 and achieved The American Dream.

His garden center, Glen Echo Nurseries, Inc., is a family owned and operated business that was established in 1961 and has grown to be one of the premier garden centers in Ontario. It is situated on a 38 acre corner property located on a major road in a continually growing area in Caledon. The garden center has knowledgeable and loyal staff ready and willing to help with any of the many facets of the business. Glen Echo is a retail garden center as well as a tree farm with 20 acres of growing nursery stock. They also provide award winning landscape design and build services. They sell annuals, perennials, large and small trees and shrubs as well as large and small landscape materials and natural stone.

The premises include over 19,000 square feet of retail store and offices, a 3,600 square foot maintenance workshop, a natural pond, extensive irrigations systems, six detached hoop houses and a three bedroom quality home with a pool. Glen Echo has invested nearly a million dollars in machinery and equipment.

Klaus was born in 1936 in Windbergen, Germany where his ancestors were all farmers. His maternal grandfather, Opa Groth, was the mayor of Windbergen, population 2,000, which was located approximately 100 miles north of Hamburg, Germany.Opa's main occupation was farming—he owned and operated a 100 acre dairy and potato farm. He had French and Polish prisoners of war working on his farm during the War who were unguarded. According to Klaus, the prisoners were treated well and had no reason to escape and anyway there was really no place for them to go. Klaus' mother, Marianne Groth, was born and raised in Windbergen. She had three siblings which included one brother and two sisters.

Klaus' paternal grandfather, Opa Tiessen owned and operated a 200 acre farm but his main occupation was that of the owner of a brick manufacturing plant in Nord Hasted, Germany which had a population of 3,000 people. His factory was the largest employer in the town.

Klaus' father, Heinrich Tiessen was born in 1919 in Nord Hasted, Germany and his mother Marianna Groth was born in 1925 in Windbergen. Heinrich was the postman for the Windbergen area where he met and married Marianna who was a beauty queen. Klaus had three brothers and two sisters. During World War II his father was a medic serving mostly on the Russian Front. Klaus remembers only a little about the War which started in 1939. There was an oil refinery about 20 miles from his home and there were many bombers from the Allied Forces in England which came to bomb this refinery. He remembers the formation of planes flying over their home and thinking the planes were headed to Hamburg but they circled back and bombed this refinery. There was a lot of smoke which came from the fires as a result of the bombing of the oil refinery. Klaus said that except for the bombing of the oil refinery they were untouched by the War.

After the War the German citizens in that area were protected by British soldiers. Klaus was about 11 years of age when he started jackrabbit hunting with some of the British officers on his uncle's farm. Many of the British soldiers came to that area to hunt with the German citizens after the War. The German citizens had a very friendly relationship with those soldiers.

Klaus was born and raised in Windbergen and attended public school there until he was 12. When Klaus was 12 years of age, the family moved to Meldorf, Germany because his father received a promotion to postman in that town. Klaus attended public school in Meldorf until he graduated in 1952. In Germany, after public school, all the children learn a trade. Klaus decided he wanted to become a nurseryman. He entered a three year nursery apprenticeship program in which he attended school one day per week and worked at a nursery the rest of the week. The nursery was located in Elmshorn, Germany, which was about 30 miles north of Hamburg. That area gets plentiful rains and the soil is very good for growing plants. His employer had a mail order business where customers would order trees, plants, shrubs, grasses and seeds from salesmen all over Germany and other European countries. The trees were transported by train and packaged in straw bales. Today that nursery would be called a "garden center."

His teacher was very proud of his former students and he showed the class pictures of nurseries throughout Europe and the United States where his former students were working. He took the students on trips to Holland and Belgium to visit other successful nurseries. Plants have Latin names so that the names are universal throughout the world with nurserymen. One of his former students sent pictures from a magazine of a nursery in Toronto and it impressed Klaus that perhaps that was something he might also do. It was at that point that Klaus decided on his goal of owning a garden center in North America. Klaus was a very eager student because he was obsessed with success. He worked very hard and learned all that he could. He and a friend would visit other nurseries on weekends to learn about different plants and to get new ideas.

Klaus had an uncle in Nebraska who had a large farm and he hoped to immigrate to the United States with his uncle as his sponsor. However, he found that with all the paperwork it would take about two years to get to the United States. He realized it would take only two months to go to Canada so he decided to go to Canada first and then later to the United States. He applied for legal status in Canada and since they needed nurserymen they even loaned him $200 for the fare for the trip to Canada.

In 1956 Klaus arrived in Quebec City with $25 in his pocket and went from there by train to Toronto.He was amazed at the various church groups which met the train that helped the immigrants. They took the immigrants to their churches, fed them and helped Klaus and a friend get a room they shared for $8 per week. The next day they arranged for the immigrants to interview with the Canadian Immigration. They got jobs right away with a landscaper doing different jobs—Klaus was paid $1 per hour and his friend, a bricklayer, was paid $1.30 per hour. They were laid off each December and after being laid off in the second year they went north hoping to get jobs during the winter months in the copper mines. It was a bad time because nobody was hiring. Klaus went back to Toronto and answered a newspaper ad from a telegraph office looking for someone with a Volkswagen to deliver telegrams. Since

Klaus owned a Volkswagen he got the job and delivered telegrams in the northern part of Toronto.

Klaus worked from 7am to 5pm five days per week at the telegraph office and he also had a part-time job as a driver for a chicken restaurant called the Swiss Chalet as a deliveryman. He worked his part-time job four nights per week for three hours each night. In his spare time he rented one acre of ground and grew evergreen cuttings. Klaus got the cuttings by visiting cemeteries and clipping off a twig of the plants of many different species and planting them on his rented land. The man who rented Klaus the land allowed Klaus free use of the equipment he needed to plow, plant and weed the plants. After two years he was able to harvest 1,000 plants and sold them to large nurseries for two dollars each.

Shortly after taking the job with the telegraph office, Klaus was promoted to dispatcher and was required to wear a tie. This was uncomfortable for Klaus as he was used to hard physical work and wearing a tie was uncomfortable for him. After about two years, spring came and Klaus couldn't take it anymore and told his boss, Joe Brennan, that he was leaving. This turned out to be a big break for Klaus as he and Joe had a detailed conversation about Klaus' future plans and goals. Joe had a lot of respect for Klaus because of his work ethic. Klaus told him he was a nurseryman by trade and had a goal of owning his own garden center. Joe wanted to help and offered to help him financially and with business advice.

At this point in 1960, Klaus had saved a total of $5,000 by living frugally, working two jobs and by selling the evergreens. During this time, he was also able to pay off the debt on his Volkswagen and the $200 that Canada had loaned him as the fare to travel from Germany to Canada. Klaus and Joe started looking for land to start the garden center. He was advised by a friend of a new town being built in the suburbs of Toronto called Bramalea. Klaus and Joe investigated this area and Joe bought 10 acres for $20,000 from a farmer. Klaus was able to borrow $5,000 from a bank, with Joe's co-signature, to erect a building on this property. The son of this farmer soon started working for Klaus and, now at 70 years of age, is still employed there as a truck driver.

It was at about this time that Klaus met his life partner and love of his life, Ulla Harth. They met in 1961 when she was visiting her sister in Toronto and they were married in 1962. Ulla was born in Essen, Germany in 1934. Essen was a major industrial center of Germany and during the War was the target of over 270 air raids by the Allied Forces. This bombing destroyed 90% of the city and 60% of the suburbs.As a result, her family fled Essen and relocated to the southern part of Germany near the Swiss border.

When they started the first garden center, the plan was for Klaus to pay back half of the money for the land as soon as he could so that they would own the land jointly. The garden center opened for business in 1961. Klaus worked from 8am until dark every day including Sundays. After seven years, 1968, Joe told Klaus he had an offer for the land of $100,000 from Esso Oil Company. Klaus tried to negotiate a deal with Joe for him to buy the land but was unsuccessful. In their separation agreement, Joe paid Klaus for all of the money Klaus had invested in leasehold improvements including the buildings, well and parking lot. So, they parted on very friendly terms and he continued to give advice to Klaus for many years. That was the end of his first nursery.

It was at about this time in 1970 that Klaus finally made it to the United States on a nursery tour from Toronto to Detroit. The purpose of the tour was to see other nurseries and learn what the competition is doing in various places. This was the first time he visited Detroit and was told to be careful because it is a very rough area. The leader of the group said, "If you must go out please stay close to the hotel and don't go downtown." However, Klaus and two others decided to go downtown and see for themselves. They were sitting at a bar, having a beer, and all of a sudden at the rear of the bar in walks a bunch of black guys with baseball bats in their hands. Klaus thought they were about to meet their maker. He told his friends, "See, the teacher told us to be careful and not to get into a situation like this."They came closer and closer and all of a sudden they realized it was just a baseball team and they were really ashamed.

After the split with Joe, Klaus had $50,000 in cash plus his equipment. He found a 10 acre parcel of land just 1,000 feet from the old nursery for $100,000 which he wanted to buy. By this time, the highway had expanded to four lanes with lots of traffic. The new town of Bramalea was growing rapidly which was very good for business. He talked with his brother-in-law about helping him finance a new garden center. His brother-in-law said he would rather become a partner in the new business. Klaus' wife, Ulla, was in favor of this because she envisioned Klaus having to work fewer hours and would then be able to spend more time with their family. Klaus agreed, so in 1970 the two men formed a partnership as equal partners. They each put in $50,000 and purchased the land. They obtained a loan from a bank for working capital and to erect a building. They built 15,000 square feet of retail space and an additional 20,000 square feet of outside sales area. They would plant whatever plants were purchased from the garden center but they didn't do landscaping. They had landscape crews available on a contract basis.

In 1974 Klaus' brother-in-law wanted out of the business. The long hours that were required were more than he was willing to maintain. Klaus found an investment group that wanted to buy the land and business but only on the condition that Klaus would stay and continue to run the business. One of the investors, Harry Smith and his wife wanted to work in the business and Klaus thought his background would be helpful in the business. Klaus really wanted out of the business too but he agreed that if the investors would own 70% and the Smith's would help with the management that Klaus would agree to stay in for 30%. Both he and Ulla thought that with the smaller percentage of ownership and the Smith's helping with the management that he would be able to spend more time with his family. Finally, they agreed to a sale price of $750,000, so the brother-in-law walked away with $375,000 and Klaus took his $375,000 and reinvested $225,000 in the new corporation.

Layout of Glen Echo Nurseries

So, in 1975, the Smiths and later two of their children started working in the business. This arrangement didn't work out the way Klaus had hoped. Eventually he became dissatisfied with this arrangement and in 1985 he met with a lawyer to discuss his future. During the discussion with the lawyer, Klaus disclosed that his dream was for his family to own a garden center completely with no outside partners.As a result of this conversation Klaus decided to work towards getting out of the second garden center and starting a new one on his own. In 1986, he purchased 38 acres about 10 miles north of the location of the first and second garden center. The new center had 1,000 feet of frontage on Toronto Airport Road and 700 feet of frontage on a side road. This property was located near the Tiessen family home and was operated as a branch of the second garden center.

In 1989 the investors and Klaus sold the land and business of the second garden center for a price of $4 million to a group from Iraq. Since Klaus owned 30%, he walked away with $1.2 million. After 30 years of hard work Klaus had achieved financial independence. He finally owned his own garden center which had been his lifelong dream.

The third garden center, Glen Echo Nurseries, Inc., is owned by Klaus with his son Derrick and Ulla as equal partners. Klaus chose the name Glen Echo because he saw that name on a Norwegian lodge north of Toronto. He liked the name and had it registered. He is glad that he did because now he has the exclusive rights to the name. It is the largest garden center in the area. Sales now exceed $5 million per year and they have a crew of 18 employees. In the garden center they sell annuals, perennials, shrubs, evergreens, stone, concrete products and plant installation. His other son Andrew works out of this nursery with his own business known as Northern Echo Landscaping, Inc. Derrick is now 50 years of age and his brother Andrew is 46 years of age.

One of the unusual things about this garden center which distinguishes it from the competition is that of the 38 total acres he has 20 acres devoted to various trees. When he started this garden center in 1990 he planted 4,000 small trees of various sizes and species that were mostly 8-10 feet tall. At that time they cost about $20 each. Since that time, whenever he sells a tree he replaces it with another tree. Some of these trees have grown to as high as 30 feet and are worth $2,500-$3,000 retail. Klaus says the average tree of his 4,000 tree inventory is worth about $500 retail and they increase in value $50-$100 annually. Presently his 4,000 tree inventory is worth approximately $2,000,000 at retail prices. Klaus has all the equipment including a tree spade to dig out the trees and plant them on the customer's property. The garden center has a John Deere Gator which seats six people that he uses to drive prospective purchasers of trees around in his forest.

Life has been good to Klaus and Ulla who are now 77 and 79 years of age, respectively. They have now been married for 52 years. Klaus says that 50% of his sales occur between April and June so by the end of summer he and Ulla can spend considerable time traveling and Klaus and his sons spend some time hunting. Klaus and Ulla enjoy meeting people in their travels and have many friends both in the United States and Canada. Klaus and Ulla owned a condo in Key West, Florida but since 1997 they have been spending their winters in Ft. Myers, Florida at The Landing Golf Tennis &Yacht Club. They are both good tennis players and each play on two different tennis teams which travel to other clubs in the area on a weekly basis for tennis matches. In 2004 they bought a 400 acre hunting farm in Bruce Peninsula which is a three hour drive north of Toronto. Klaus, his sons, and their friends spend much of their free time hunting bear, deer, coyote, ducks, geese and other game hunting on this farm.

Klaus said his dream was always to own a garden center, travel and hunt. He still works hard and plays hard. He is quite an amazing man. I don't know anyone who has worked harder. He says that for him hard work and good service is what has made his business such a success. He also gives credit to a book he read by Dale Carnegie entitled "How to Win Friends and Influence People."

Congratulations to Klaus and Ulla for achieving financial independence and The American Dream.

Glen Echo Nurseries

1965 Klaus Tiessen with son Derek in truck

1996 Derek Tiessen with son Tyler in truck

Mike Fisher

I've known Mike Fisher since about 1980 when I became his banker. He is a very nice and caring person and was a benevolent selfless entrepreneur. He was a man of his word and I thoroughly enjoyed working with him. In high school, Mike became interested in communal living and his ideal was to have a commune own and operate the business and for everyone to share equally in the profits. Although Mike is an idealist he is also a pragmatist and pragmatism usually won out. Mike worked hard and was very skilled in the wood products industry which allowed him to start and grow Heartwood Creations to $5 million in sales when he sold the company at age 49 to an employee/friend in 2007. Mike had achieved The American Dream.

Mike's father, Bill Fisher, was born in Oshkosh, Wisconsin in 1925. He helped in his father's custom tailor business as a child and loves talking about those times. He was drafted into the Army in World War II and served in the infantry, earning both the Bronze Star and Silver Star. After the War, he finished his college education and earned a Bachelor's Degree in mechanical engineering from the University of Wisconsin at Madison in 1950.

Mike's mother, Rachel, was born in 1926 in Mills City, Montana. The family moved to Osh Kosh, Wisconsin when she was nine years old. She met Bill while both were attending the University of Wisconsin and they married in 1950. After their marriage they moved to Rockford where Bill began his great career at Sundstrand Machine Tool in

Belvidere, Illinois. Rachel died eight years ago but Bill is still going strong.

Mike was born in June, 1958 and has two older sisters. When he was five years old his dad painted the outside of their house. He gave a small brush to Mike and asked him to paint the batons between each of the boards on their garage. His dad rolled the wide surfaces and Mike sat there with the brush and painted the batons up as far as he could reach for the entire day.It was such a new thing for Mike and he remembers getting $2. It was a Saturday and the next morning they went to church and Mike put $1 in the offering plate. Mike remembers that it was satisfying in learning to work for a living and also being able to share what you have.

Mike's first experience with the business world was when he was six years old. He grew gourds up the side of his house and onto the roof one summer.His dad strung up the strings to make the gourds grow high and even built a little wooden shelf at about Mike's eye level for a really giant gourd that was too heavy for the string to hold.At the end of the summer, he put those gourds in a little red wagon and headed down to Highcrest Shopping Center selling door to door.He sold them for from 10-25 cents each and sold his entire gourd inventory in the first 15 homes.Mike says it was a pretty easy sales job when you're a little kid, missing a tooth so that he had a slight lisp when he spoke, when he offered to sell the gourds on the cheap.

Mike had a childhood experience when he was about 12 years old that he has reflected on many times as a business person.One day he was riding his bike in his driveway in circles and had this revelation that the only way he could find out what the smallest radius of the circle he could ride was to keep riding in smaller and smaller circles until he fell over, which he did.He says now that he thinks the sense of understanding what the limits are of something has struck him many times. He has tried to find ways to make things that were unusual or beyond the normal scope for which a particular machine was designed or to make different products.It has taught him to push the boundaries of what can happen.

Mike's dad was a mechanical engineer and designed metal working machines.He was one of the early inventors of numerically controlled machines and talked joyfully of his business accomplishments.He made their simple bedroom furniture when Mike was 12 or 13 years old. His dad had a $30 table saw that was metal and wood construction. He made simple plywood dressers and beds for Mike and his sisters. His dad never had the patience to teach Mike anything about woodworking but he keenly watched his father as he worked and enjoyed the finished products. Mike says his designs were clean and Utilitarian. Mike finally got to start using the old table saw in the garage along with some old wrenches and bent screw drivers.He was never allowed to use any quality tools and that always bothered Mike.

When Mike was about 13 years old, he and a friend, Steve Anderson, had a summertime worm business. They lived close to Sinnissippi Golf Course and would walk there at dusk every night and with a flashlight and search for night crawlers on the greens of the golf course.He remembers one night they caught at least 200 night crawlers. It was about a one mile walk from his house through the woods to the golf course and Steve's mom let them use their extra refrigerator to store the worms.They got little Chinese carry-out containers somewhere and put 12 worms in each container which they priced at 45 cents each. He bought some buss bedding which is a product designed to mix with water to keep worms in so they live longer. He did not want to use dirt which would have been a cheaper option. They made plywood signs to direct people to Steve's house.Mike isn't sure they sold many worms but the refrigerator was full at one time and had many customers come knocking on their door.

When Mike was 14 years old there was a neighborhood guy named Joe Gleesh who showed special interest in neighborhood boys.He worked at a scrap and metal company and one day as he was having dinner on his screened porch he offered to set Mike and Jim Doege up in the scrap metal business. The next Saturday, they drove his station wagon down to Joe Behr's metal business on Seminary Street. They weighed his car as he pulled into the giant scale and then they drove over to a humongous pile of electric meters. They loaded the back of his station wagon up with these broken metes and weighed the car again as they drove out of the scrap yard. Joe paid two cents per pound for the meters and Mike and his friend were to re-pay him. They took this giant pile of meters to his friend's garage and set up tables. For most of that summer they hired other neighborhood kids to help them disassemble the meters into various metals. They had yellow brass, red brass, copper, steel, aluminum and the highly coveted sliver content. As Mike now recalls, the brass sold for about 25 cents a pound and the small amount of silver sold for about $2 per pound.Mike says it was a highly entertaining summer job.

He got his first real job when he was 14 years old at an unusual factory in Rockford, Woodward Governor Company. They had a "recruit program" in which they hired 40 fourteen year-old boys each year from schools throughout the city. They announced in January of the year that they would be accepting applications for the summer program. Hundreds of students from across the city applied every year—it was a prestigious job to get at the time. Mike went through a series of tests on five Saturdays in a row as they eliminated possible candidates. It ended with a personal interview around a big table with four or five adults in suits. Mike got the job and started working the first week after school. It was a very unusual place in which you had to get your hair cut every 13 days and wear a bow tie when you walked into the building—you had to take the bow tie off when you left the building. They taught you the "Woodward way" to push a broom and the Woodward way to mow the lawn and the Woodward way to do just about everything. Mike was part of a lawn crew which worked on the executives' lawns and he also worked on the lawns of their church. They were trying to groom them to work there for the rest of their lives.

The program included four years of high school work and then four years of college work with a promise of a job after college. Mike got paid $1.60 per hour and Woodward took half of his gross pay and put it in a college savings account that he was not allowed to touch until he went to college. Mike had to go to classes on Tuesday and Thursdays afternoons for two hours. Mike remembers them teaching them about the free enterprise system and Mike said, "If it's free enterprise, why do I have to get my hair cut all the time." The teacher told him he was free to quit if he wanted. Mike only lasted seven weeks.

Mike says he's not bragging but he thought that he had already learned as much as he was ever going to learn there and had no intention of spending the rest of his life with Woodward. So, he quit and got a job as a bus boy at a country club for the rest of the summer. Mike says he really respects what Woodward did and believes it was the most important job he ever had in terms of sense of what they were trying to create. They really wanted to take care

of their employees so for that he respected what Woodward was all about. They had their own dentist, their own
barbershop and their own doctor. They had a great bonus
system in which they shared the profits with their employees. Mike believes a lot of things they did were right and
they built a good sense of culture and trust. They were just
a little too controlling for Mike.

After watching his dad make things out of wood and
having access to a table saw, he started making Christmas
presents when he was 14 years of age. Each Christmas and
birthday, his parents would give him a new Sears Crafts-
man power tool. He was given an electric drill one year,
then a router and then a belt sander. He made simple tables
for the router and belt sander. He also had his grandpa's
little grinding machine in his basement.He continually
got sawdust all over the clothes washer and dryer and he is
amazed that his mom put up with him all those years. His
parents were very supportive of his interest in woodworking from an early age.

When Mike was 15 years old, his youth minister at
the Congregational Church gave him the idea of painting houses for a summer job.Mike enlisted another church
friend, Gary Sleighball, to be his partner.They painted
the youth minister's house and three other houses.He remembers painting a neighbor's house, Nick Parrinello, for
$175.They ended up making $1.40 per hour which was not
great pay.The neighbor saw how cheaply they were willing
to work and that they did such a good job that he gave
them a job painting the inside of his garage. They had to
paint every 2x4 stud white and then the wall in between
the studs a dark green color. The neighbor didn't care that
they were working for peanuts.

Something happened to Mike when he was 15 years
old. He started to form a sense of my core beliefs. It might

have been a combination of his girlfriend Mary and his youth minister, Dan, at the UCC church in Rockford. They had a hippie youth minister who never mentioned Jesus or the Bible but had meaningful discussion groups every Wednesday about life and values. Mike remembers he took them on a meditation and mysticism retreat when he was 15. He led them on a guided meditation that he will always remember.

Mike grew up in the 1970s but early on something inside connected with the culture that felt business was inherently evil. He grew up feeling that people should share what they had and started to take an interest in communes and living self sufficiently. He took on the hippie ideals in many ways. When he was 16 he discovered a place in Rockford called Sunshine Life Works. It was an old house on Whitman Street, set up as a social service agency to give young people positive and meaningful activities to do. He spent a lot of time there. He took meditation from two different instructors and was actively involved in encounter groups. He also took woodworking and stain glass classes. When he was 18, Mike wanted to buy land in Wisconsin. It was in 1976 that he got this large catalogue of rural land for sale from Stout Realty. He asked his dad if he could sell all of his dad's Army memorabilia and use the money to buy land. He had a goal of spending $10,000. He found someone that would buy his dad's Army stuff for $4,000. Somehow he never followed up with that dream to buy the land. But it marked a lifelong yearning to be in nature.

Mike graduated from Guilford High School in 1976 and had planned to attend Blackburn College in Carlinville, Illinois.He chose this school because it had a work program where every student worded 15 hours per week to help run the college. This offset the cost of an otherwise expensive liberal arts school. Mike was registered for his freshman year but decided to travel instead. He had spent two years sitting in Latin class looking out the window wanting to have an adventure so when he finally graduated he chose instead to travel for three and a half months.A friend had an old 1968 Pontiac Lemans that served them well as they drove 13,000 miles throughout the western United States camping for free every night.Mike says he really got a sense of the beauty of the west and how many people were on this Earth. He returned to Rockford at Thanksgiving unsure of what to do next. He moved back in with his parents and was quickly offered a job repairing furniture at the local Ethan Allen furniture store. The old guy who was repairing furniture was 80 years old and his eyes were going bad.Although they wanted Mike to work full time he only wanted to work part-time and spent the rest of his time making wood products in his parent's basement. He did this until the fall of 1977.

After taking off the one year for travel and to get his thoughts together, Mike attended Northern Illinois University in DeKalb, Illinois.He lived in a dormitory and had a great time.He got on the Dean's List, took art classes and classes in the industry and technology department.In the second semester, he took 19 hours of classes and was loving woodworking design class, craft classes and the general education classes that were required.He loved college and life in the dorm.He tried to get into a co-ed floor that was geared around a sociology class that everyone had to take to study human relationships.He didn't get into that dorm but he did get into a co-ed dorm.After one year, his friends were all either going to walk to Peru or move to Eugene, Oregon so he decided he was done with college too.He saw no reason to get a degree in furniture design, his chosen possible major.So, he quit after one year.

He was very anxious to get out in the world and start

doing stuff and kind of saw college as a waste of time. He went home on May 12, 1978 and told his parents he was quitting college and was going to make wooden boxes in their basement.He knew they were broken hearted but they hardly showed it.They said, "You can do whatever you want and we will support it." Mike started making wood products in his parent's basement.He did his very first craft fair at Edgebrook Shopping Center that summer with his next door neighbor. He worked for 25 hours making a lamp that he tried to sell for $100. He still has the lamp. Mike made little boxes with sliding dovetails and carved his initials in the bottom of the slat. He sold one box for $12.50, of course, it was his mother's friend who bought the box and that was all he sold that day.

Towards the end of the summer he realized he didn't want to live with his parents any longer so he talked a friend he had traveled with into moving to DeKalb to continue college at NIU and work.They found two other guys and rented a house that had a basement where he could set up a woodshop.He took classes part-time and continued to make mostly boxes. He kept pushing and pushing to find places to sell them.After the first semester he started getting busier with his woodworking.He registered for a few more classes but eventually had to drop out because his woodworking was taking so much of his time.In that year of living in an old house in DeKalb with three roommates he officially created the name Heartwood Creations by filing an assumed name with the State of Illinois in October of 1978.

Mike decided to move back to Rockford and where he rented 1,000 square feet of shop space on Cedar Street. He found a roommate to rent an apartment and settled back into his home town. He started getting pretty busy with orders from gift stores and ended up hiring 10 friends within two months. He was only 20 years old and had these high school friends who never went to college who were just hanging around town working for him.This was the birth of his idea of a social and economic world where people worked together and shared their lives together. Mike says, he promised them the stars but could barely provide them with the treetops.

He chose an early hero, the guy that started Celestial Seasonings Tea Company. His name was Mo Siegel. Mike wrote him a couple letters trying to see if he would talk to him about his business ideals. He never replied. Mike says, "Good heroes are hard to come by." Mike wanted everyone at work to have a flexible and free schedule. He truly believed that work was not the most important thing in people's lives but their freedom and enjoyment was paramount. He would let people come and go as they chose. One guy, Doug Fourze, would come in at work at 4am and leave at 8am. He worked whenever he wanted to. Everyone had a key to the place. People gave them a few cats that lived in the shop. He looked long and hard at a large house that had 10 bedrooms on South Main Street. It was supposedly a former gangster hangout from the 1920s. He thought of buying it and making a place for everyone to live in. That never happened.

Mike says that reality is just what it is. He always chose the practical route and says his ideals never seem to win out in total. They all worked together and hung out together after work. They had many dinner parties, camp outs and vacations together. He wanted it to be a family of people that worked and lived together. One of the toughest realities of those years was after about 1980 when the work slowed down and he had to lay off two employees/friends. They could not believe that Mike would lay them off after all the good times and closeness they shared. It was the first time in his life that he made an enemy. Someone that he was close to and cared about actually just did not like him anymore and it hurt Mike deeply. One guy came to his house at 8pm begging for his job back. Mike gave him part-time work but after a few months he still had to lay him off. Again, being practical he laid off the people that were the least productive.

It was the hardest time in his early business life and a very formative time at that. It was a time where he chose, out of necessity, to become a bit hardened to the world. The first year at Cedar Street they grew from 1,000 to 2,000 square feet. They were busy most of the time and his 10 friends enjoyed their jobs. Some left and some just worked a few months. It was a fun time. Mike says that sadly all those people are now gone except Scott. Scott and Mike have worked together since 1978. Mike says now that he guesses that to get one dear friend and co-worker from those early years is all that can be expected in practicality.

After one year on Cedar Street they needed a larger space. Jim Stormont, owned the most incredible building in Rockford. It was the old Rockford Brewing Company on Prairie Street. In May of 1980, Mike leased and moved into 7,000 square feet on the third floor of this old building. Mike says, "This building was way cool." The day they got the keys, about 10 of them spent all night in the building. They built an employee lounge that night as well as had a general good time in that incredible old building. The building is right down the river, had a six story tower and a very cool basement where the landlord used to shoot rats when he was a kid. The old timer, Jim Stormont, the landlord was a great Scotsmen that you couldn't help but love. Short on words but big of heart, he became a hero of sorts to Mike. He loved what Mike and his company were doing. Mike paid the rent on time and gave him a bottle of scotch every Christmas. The only thing they ever did wrong in their eight years in that building was to paint his naughty pine off his walls white when they remodeled to create a retail store called Heartwood's Emporium in the front of the building. This was a rambling 88,000 square foot building with nooks and crannies galore. They ran the store in this freshly painted nutty pine front room for one year. Sales only reached $26,000. It was fun but just not practical. The woodshop was on the third floor so they had to run down to the first floor to serve the store. In the off season it was a pain. They were also trying to do custom woodworking and sell lumber.

After one year they made a large corporate decision to dump the store, the custom work, the lumber sales and just focus on their core product lines. The fun was over for that part of the business. The Brewery Building was absolutely incredible. Mike had countless dreams about that building for years after they moved out in 1988. Heartwood's eight years in that building was some of the most fun, engaging and spirited times of Mike's life. Mike says, "That building had spirit." That building goes back to 1848 and had been added on a few times. Mike says, it was like an old cathedral that had thousands of life experiences, you could feel the spirit and energy in that building and it carried with him for so many years afterwards. In their eight years in the building, three other wood workers moved in and it became a place for them to celebrate life.

During the spirited years at the Brewery Building, Mike did a five day visit to a commune in Tennessee called The Farm. He was 22 years old and he had given hard thought to donating the woodshop to the farm and moving there. Mike took a Greyhound bus to Summertown, Tennessee falling asleep that night in the bosom of a fellow passenger, a large African American woman. He spent just four days at the farm which was enough to get to know the place. At that time they had many visitors. They all camped out just behind the gate house. His fondest memory of the farm was a concert they had on Saturday night. There must have been 500 people out to enjoy eight different entertainers with a real stage and real sound equipment. The difference was everything was free, there was no money exchanged. It was just a celebration of life. That's the part that impressed Mike and that stuck with him. The next morning was Sunday and he got to hear Steven Gaskin give his Sunday morning sermon which was well attended by well intentioned people. The woodshop was pretty rough. Mike remembers the floor was made out of little scraps of plywood all cut and fit together like a mosaic. He talked to a wood worker there for a while who told him that in life the most important decisions need to be made from a spiritual level. Mike took the bus home and kind of fell in love with a girl on the bus named Cathy Glover and never chose to move to the farm.Mike says, that again, practicality took over.

Mike found himself in charge of this group of people making wood products and he kept searching for a basis on which to operate from—he was looking for a moral compass. In high school he thought business was evil yet he found himself running this small business. He remembered something that his wonderful sixth grade teacher, Mr. Nelson told the class. He told them never to slouch in their seats, to be very thankful they were born in this country, how lucky they were to have so much opportunity and to always trust someone until they give you a reason not to trust them. Mike really believed it at the time and he still does. He believes in basic goodness and from that hopeful vantage point he chose to trust people in every capacity of running that business. Mike says that part of it was selfish because he wanted to delegate so as to get out from under the responsibilities.

After a few years in business, he wanted to escape and live out west and do something different. But a fear of failure and a sense of responsibility kept him from leaving Heartwood Creations. None the less, he chose to empower those around him mostly by inherently trusting that their basic goodness and skills would allow them to do what they would do best. He feels he has always had a good ability in finding what people are good at and then allowing them to do it. He tried to teach them as little as possible and gave them the freedom to do what they did best and gave them the space and the freedom to make mistakes. He remembers one guy who felt so bad because he made a mistake that he returned his keys and said he was quitting. Mike said, "Hey, forget about it, you know we all make mistakes." There have been employees who have cheated and stole from Heartwood Creations and those people still work there and have become great lifetime employees. Some people make too big a mistake but in general it's worked out to forgive and to accept and to allow people to be themselves. In many capacities that have given them a sense of security and belonging that has made their culture healthy as a company.

Mike kept looking for ideas that would stick and would make sense out of his responsibility for running a small business. In the early1980s, he watched a TV show about Mazda and the Wankel engine—the Wankel engine was a rotary engine that failed and cost the company greatly. The top management took the largest hit out of their paycheck. In the documentary, a guy said a great line. He said, "Management gets the labor it deserves." And that became a guidepost or an anthem to Mike for the rest of his career. Another movie at about that time was Michael Moore's first movie "Roger and Me" about Roger Smith, the CEO of General Motors, and how he closed factories in Flint, Michigan. Finally, at one point in the documentary a General Motors executive looks at Michael Moore and says, "What do you expect? Do you expect the corporation to guarantee lifetime employment?" Mike thought the executive's statement was correct and there was a moment when Michael Moore was at once an idealist but not a pragmatic. To offer someone lifetime employment is on the face of it somewhat ridiculous. To find yourself employing someone for 2, 5, 10 and 20, 30 years is very sobering. At what point do you say it is your obligation as employer to do whatever it takes to offer lifetime employment? Mike says, to that end there was a great company called Lincoln Electric which made red electric arc welders. James Lincoln wrote a book in the 1950s about the philosophy of business which became a case study in college business classes. In that book, he stated that it's the business director's obligation to continue to find work for their employees throughout the lifespan of the company and to give the employee six months notice if for any reason they feel like they cannot find employment for their employees. James Lincoln operated in the wonder years of the 1950s and 1960s when business was booming. Mike agrees with that philosophy. In about 1989, Mike took a keen interest in Ben and Jerry's the ice cream makers. He called their offices in Vermont about 15 times in a 10-month period requesting their company handbook. He got to know an HR person there and a lawyer was rewriting their company handbook during that time. At the end of those months of phone calls she finally mailed him a copy of their company policy. It was his intention to try to be like them. His largest curiosity about Ben and Jerry's was their "compressed compensation ratio." It was their somewhat Japanese ideal of only paying the top person 5-10 times what the lowest paid person was paid. Mike always thought that was a sensible concept. Over the years Ben and Jerry's kept raising that from 5 to 7 to 10 times the lowest paid person and finally they abandoned that as they outgrew that business model.

Mike still thinks that the concept is very sensible and has tried to use that in thinking about how people are compensated. Mike believes that equity or compensation is one of the most important measures of job satisfaction. People need to feel like they're treated fairly. In about 1990, his former wife and business partner, Judy, and he traveled to the Omega Institute in Rochester, New York to attend a weekend retreat with Ben Cohen of Ben and Jerry's and two other inspired people. The weekend retreat was called "Zen And The Art Of Business As A Force For Social Change." Mike said it was his honor to hear Ben Cohen talk and to sit next to him and share lunch with him. Ben Cohen talked of the two part bottom line that is the combination of profits and people.A co-facilitator at the retreat was Bernie Glassman, a former NASA scientist and a Zen Buddhist Monk who explained that there are two ways to solve a mathematical problem. One is to maximize and the other is to optimize. It supported Ben's idea of a two part bottom line—that if you optimize a mathematical equation in the long run you come out ahead. If you maximize and you only try to solve for one piece of the equation you generally end up with a solution that is not sustainable in the long term nor is it healthy for all parties concerned. Interestingly, 25 years later in talking to a young woman involved in the Indie Craft movement also known as a DIY movement or the Etsy movement, explained that it's really a three part bottom line—people, profits and planet. Mike thinks that thought was well said.

Mike kept trying to think of what is the best form of a business. He still came from the vantage point that people are more important than profit and that jobs should be a part of one's life in a rich and meaningful way. His college friends were living in Eugene, Oregon so on a business trip to hire gift sales reps, he spent five weeks driving out west, stopping in merchandise marts and hiring gift reps that charge 15% to sell your products. When he got to Eugene, he spent a week with his dear college friends. Eugene had many co-ops at that time, mother truckers, restaurants, other food co-ops, etc. He was involved in food co-ops in college and was very drawn to that. He had conversations with people that worked with co-ops while in Eugene and remembers them talking about having to be in a lot of meetings to make decisions. He came home from Eugene inspired about co-ops and in researching industrial co-ops he bought a bunch of work books about industrial co-ops and started meeting with his 10 employees every Tuesday night at his secretary's house, Kate Kush. They tried to talk about what it meant to start an industrial co-op. They had these workbooks to try and work through some of the decision making process. He is not sure if anyone really grasped the concept, including himself. At that time, he learned of a guy named Christopher Hill who wrote a book entitled "The Golden Egg." Mike said he was this amazing guy that started cooperative businesses; one was called The University of The Trees Press in Walnut Creek, California. He called this company and started talking to whomever answered the phone and asked what it took to be part of a co-op? The woman on the other end of the line said, "Well a co-op really needs to have a spiritual level to it. It needs to have a spiritual leader." And that is the exact point in which he bailed on the whole concept.

He never felt he had the strength to be such a leader to connect people on a spiritual level. So he left that idea and that was the end of their Tuesday night groups.

Mike always wanted to stay clear of banks if he could. He had two perspectives on banks. One is that if some guy is going to let him borrow the bank's money, he better do his best at using it wisely and paying it back timely. It gets back to trust, Mike says. He knows it's just business but this guy is trusting him to handle that money and he felt a supreme obligation to do his best to use it wisely and to pay it back as soon as he could. The other side of banking was that Mike didn't want to be owned by a bank. He really felt that it is better to grow slowly than to be in debt. So it was his intention to self finance throughout the years. Every time he made a profit was a time to reinvest in machines and in experiments in the market place. Mike felt that every step of the way was an experiment, was taking a chance on the unknown and trying to ride your bicycle in a smaller circle until you fall down. Mike can't imagine what percent of money he misspent over the years in making mistakes and taking the wrong turn and falling down. It gets back to his friend that says, "You just have to outlive your mistakes." The point is you have to be tireless in taking a chance.

Another high point of being in business was at year-end. Heartwood Creations was profitable every year except 1982. Each year they made 6% or 7% on sales before 401k and bonuses. Mike believes it's the owner's responsibility to divide bonuses fairly. He had a worksheet each year that he used to balance the bonus distributions with part for management and part for the non-management.He really tried to be fair and equitable in the division of profit. Each year they had a Christmas party and luckily in the wonder years from about 1985 to 2000 they had profits to share. For many years they played Bonus Bonanza. For their small company the bonus pool would average $100,000. They would carefully divide that among the people who worked in the shop and office based on their level of importance to the company. Bonus Bonanza was this game they played where they would put everybody's bonus check upside down on the table at the Christmas Party. People would walk up one by one and if they drew their own bonus check from all these envelopes lying on the table they would get an extra $100. If not they had to give that $100 to the person whose name was on the check. Bonus Bonanza was the highlight of the year.

The year 2001 was a difficult time in business, things started to fall off. That year they chose to buy another little woodworking product line out of Madison, Wisconsin called Wilderness Woods. It was a slow payback but it kept people working and added to their offering. It did not fit the look and feel that they were part of but it was in keeping with their responsibility to find work for their shop. As their hippie dippy mailman said one day, "Hey now you have something to sell to the Hillbillies." In other words it was a real different look than what they had before.

In early 2000, it became apparent that they needed to continue to reach out beyond their quickly shrinking contemporary American craft marketplace. In 10 years, their trade shows went from two trade shows to one trade show and from 1,600 exhibitors at the winter show to 750 exhibitors. The trend was obvious. People weren't going to these boutique style and expensive American hand craft stores any longer. They were finding their loving gifts elsewhere. That is when Heartwood entered the souvenir industry. It started with one product, a simple lighter sleeve made of wood and laser engraved. They added more products and found out that the souvenir industry was not only new to them but also slightly recession proof. People still went on vacation to Yellowstone Park and still spent $7 for some little item that said Yellowstone on it.

The problem was the price point was very low and the markup was high. Yellowstone wanted to buy it for $1 and sell it for $3. In about 2003 the writing was on the wall—Heartwood Creations had to import the wood components from China and add value by laser engraving Yellowstone and destinations on the product. It caused much internal strife and debate but finally they started importing wood products from China to laser engrave. Heartwood now buys items from China and imprints on them. Importantly Mike found a formula that works. At this point the woodshop is still able to function at full capacity. People come to work every day and make wood products from raw boards to finished product in their shop. They get a living wage, good health insurance and a 401k plan. Some of that is subsidized or bolstered by the fact that part of their business model is now imported items from China that are sold in the souvenir market. Mike says that at some point you do what it takes to stay in business and to keep people employed.

Mike started doing retail craft shows and learned how to wholesale to gift stores. Not content with that, he kept trying other markets. Someone from a local corporation, Sundstrand, called one day wanting to buy corporate gifts. Mike ended up really liking the guy he dealt with for many years whose name was Dave. So, for sometime Heartwood made corporate gifts for the executives at Sundstrand and learned about the advertising specialty market from his friend, Dave. Eventually Mike got annoyed with Sundstrand because Dave would call and expect Mike to make some silly gift for the CEO's wife in a 24 hour turn-around

Mike Fisher In His Office

Six Head Wide Belt Sander

period.At some point Mike felt like he was really working for the man.He ended up walking away from that business. However, Heartwood did spend 14 years in the advertising specialty industry laser engraving on corporate gifts. Sure enough they made a desk set for Roger Smith, the NRA, Pat Robertson and others with whom Mike did not really like. Mike had to wear a suit coat when he went to a trade show for the advertising specialty marketplace. At their

Clamp Carrier

CNC Router #1

CNC Router #2

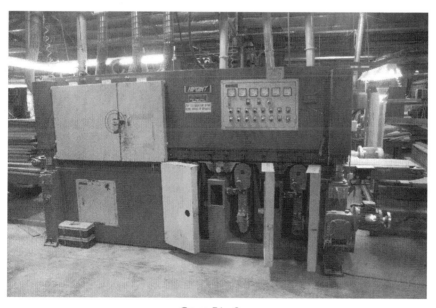

Gang Rip Saw

Moulding Machine

peak, Heartwood was only doing $1,000,000 in sales in this industry but Mike felt an obligation to keep this business because he had people employed doing that work. It literally took five years to unravel from that industry and figure out how to dump it by slowly letting the sales go. He found very little pleasure in being a part of this market.

Mike started out in the gift industry and tried so many different things to find sales over the years. He always enjoyed what a knife maker friend in central Illinois once said. He said, "I'm just busy trying to outlive my mistakes." And Mike thought that was so realistic. You just keep trying and trying, maybe essentially out of the fear of failure, but you just keep trying endlessly to find out what works. It's like what his dad taught him, "Never fall in love with your product." He meant never think that you have such a great item that the next guy's not going to beat you tomorrow. It's that constant running like someone's just two steps behind you. Mike really believes that the fear of failure is what kept him in business for many years. It's not an exciting way to look at it but it sure is a motivating force.

There are two aspects of his working career that are the most inspiring. Number one is those times when there were five or six people sitting around a table talking about a possible new idea when no one owned the idea. It was those rare times when there was an absolute synergy in the room. Ideas flowed freely without ownership and one idea built on the next idea. That was a moment of living in a commune for Mike—a moment of being with others in their spirit. Mike says that may sound cosmic but he knows there were times when a group of peoples' ideas and thoughts were able to connect without ego and in those times the best of thoughts flourished.

Heartwood Creations has enjoyed a home in a very sweet little piece of the gift industry—contemporary hand-crafted marketplace, for 35 years. During that time they also ventured into the advertising specialty industry for 14 years, the office products industry for four years, the Christian bookstore market for one year and the souvenir industry for the last 10 years. They have also spent time with a retail store doing custom woodworking and furniture making for people, selling lumber, etc. They have put thousands of products into the market and Mike has always said the market never lies. It is brutally honest. It either accepts your product mildly, embraces your product or ignores your product. The feedback mechanism is powerful and immediate. It is very easy to listen to the market. The market wants creativity and it also needs the basics—a decent product at a decent price with good service. Mike always believed that if you are an honest and hardworking plumber you should get business even in the hard times and so be it with any aspect of the business world.

In his early 20s, Mike observed three old business men in Rockford that were attached to their businesses for what he thought was way too long. He bought a building from Ed Laue who at 85 still sat in the vacant building everyday pretending he was at work. He had closed his industrial baking business eight years previously but still showed up. Mike met his daughter years later who called him an obsessive workaholic. He also met Anton Geoleto from Geoleto Sheet Metal Works down the street who at 80 something years old still wanted to look at every order and try to tell the 25 year old foreman how to cut a piece of sheet metal. Mike saw the exact same thing at Quality Paper on Sixth Street. The old man was breathing down the secretary's neck making sure she typed every invoice just right. He saw that as being ridiculous that he didn't want to be a part of it. He's so glad that he was able to trust people and to want his freedom enough to empower others around him to do what they knew how to do better than he could.

Mike worked for a good part of his career to make himself obsolete. He feels very lucky that he inherently trusts people and was able to empower others to take over daily business operations from an early point. He really wanted to get out of the business from early on. Fear of failure kept him going. He feels very blessed that there was one individual among the hundreds of people that worked there for any length of time that had the drive and the gumption to run the business. Warren had worked for Heartwood Creations since he was 14 years old. He went on to get a Bachelor's Degree in mechanical engineering and a Master's Degree in economics. He came back after college and two years in the corporate world to work at Heartwood. He helped make the business what it is today. When it was obvious that Mike was burned out he was the only one with the ability to step up and say, "Hey why don't I buy this business?" So, in 2007 Heartwood Creations had $5 million in sales and 50 full time employees and Mike decided it was time to retire at age 49. He had achieved financial independence and The American Dream.

When Mike started his business in his basement and stayed there for about nine months. In 1979 he rented 1,000 square feet on Cedar Street in Rockford. In 1980 he rented 7,000 square feet which he increased to 13,000 square feet in the Old Brewery Building from Jim Stornmont. In 1988 Mike bought the old Rockford Bakery from Ed Laue consisting of 40,000 square feet which has been the location of Heartwood Creations ever since. It was a great purchase because it is located behind Lincoln Junior High School and close to Swedish American Hospital. He believes that if the new owner ever wanted to sell that Swedish American Hospital would be a likely buyer.

When Mike sold the business and the building to Warren in 2007 they considered asking a bank to finance the building. He was skeptical of dealing with a bank because he was fearful that if the bank was bought out by a larger bank they might try to change the terms of the loan. Mike felt comfortable in financing the building himself which made it easier and better terms for Warren to buy it. Mike says that he and Warren are like family so trust was not an issue. Mike was happy to wait to get paid in full and he has such a keen interest in Warren and seeing to it that Heartwood Creations prospers because he spent all of his adult life, 35 years, in making it succeed.

Mike says it was the luckiest day of his life to sell Heartwood Creations. He believes that it added 10 years to his life the day he sold the business. Mike's wife took him to the burrito place where they bought a hippie burrito with tater tots and went to the Botanical Gardens to celebrate. Running a small business is tireless. Once you get hooked into it and have employees you have this painful obligation to keep it going. There's almost no easy out. It is as much a matter of stewardship as it is a matter of ownership to be in charge. You must be a good steward of the organization. Mike feels blessed that he had someone who wanted to take over the reins. This gets back also to the notion of equity and fair pay.As much as he worked to make sure that everyone got their fair pay each year and the management did not get overpaid, in the end he still owned the stock and the company and the building from which the company operated. And for that he was able to sell and get paid beyond a normal paycheck so he feels lucky and almost too lucky to be in that ownership role.

It has been 35 years. There are many people that have worked there for 25, 30 and 34 years. It's getting to be the end of the game for some. Heartwood had a simple employee retirement plan known as a Sep IRA and then a 401k Plan for the last 20 years. Mike wonders if that will be enough? Will the people that are 58 continue to work until they are rightfully tired and ready to stop working? He surely hopes so for that is the end game of a small or large business. The Japanese used to believe in lifetime employment and Mike wanted to provide that as he believes that is the only gracious solution to one's work in life. He hopes that Heartwood's future decisions will allow for their core people to work into their comfortable retirement and that they have the choice to ease out when they see fit. As always, it will be management's decisions to make that possible.As mentioned before, Mike believes that management always gets the labor it deserves.

Kenneth White, Jr.

Ken and Norma live in Heritage Palms where they are very active playing golf and tennis. I've known Ken for over 10 years as a teammate on my tennis team. This is the story of a man who started with absolutely nothing and who quit high school when he was 16 years old. Through hard work and determination, Ken was able to become successful in the construction business and ended up achieving financial independence through free market capitalism. Ken achieved The American Dream and retired at age 59.

Ken was born December 21, 1937, the oldest of five boys, to Ken and Helen White, Sr. He grew up on a small farm in South Windsor, Connecticut. Ken and his brothers did all the chores that were typical on a farm such as milking cows, driving tractors, bringing in the cows from the pasture, etc. When he was about four years of age, his aunt came to visit and brought a little sailor suit for him as a present. He was quite proud of that outfit and strutted around in it quite often. His family started calling him "Skipper" and the nickname "Skip" stuck with him all through school, including high school.

His parents always struggled financially so his paternal grandparents moved in with them to help out. Neither of Ken's parents had any formal education, but they were hard workers. Ken's father and paternal grandfather both worked on the railroad and his grandmother helped Ken's mother with the cooking, cleaning, washing, canning and other chores required for this large household. They really had their hands full with all the chores and raising five rambunctious boys. Ken said they never had a bathroom in the house until he was about 17 years of age.

Ken says he will never forget the time when he and his brother, Ed, who were age four and five at the time, went into the barn and found some old oil-based paint. They took off their clothes, and painted their entire bodies different colors, pretending to be Indians. They were having so much fun playing cowboys and Indians until their mother found them. They got the worst spanking that Ken can remember. However, the most painful thing was trying to get the paint off. Their mother took rags soaked in turpentine and scrubbed their bodies, which was quite painful. Ken thought she was going to burn off his skin.

Ken and his brothers had guns and were hunters by age seven. One day Ken and Ed were hunting with some neighbor kids when one of their guns went off accidentally and his brother went down. He had a bullet wound under his eye and was not responsive. Ken thought he was dead and started screaming; a neighbor heard the ruckus and called his mother and an ambulance. The kid who shot his brother started running and Ken went running and shooting at him. Ken says that he was hysterical and he thanks God that he was such a bad shot. His mother got their before the ambulance so they put his brother in the back seat of their car and raced to the community hospital. They worked on him for quite some time and then he was transported to a larger hospital in Hartford. Ed remained in the hospital for months with possible brain damage, a shattered cheekbone and loss of vision. He finally returned home but with severe memory loss.

Back then, special rehabilitation was unavailable for poor families and he had to learn again to talk, count and read, etc. all over again. Ed missed two years of school and was never able to catch up. He ended up quitting school when he was 16 years old. He eventually got a driver's license, although he could barely read, and got a job with Pioneer Parachutes in South Windsor, packing parachutes. He was good at packing and folding parachutes and was chosen to pack the chute for a famous Lunar landing. He was interviewed on television and he just smiled a lot. They were all quite proud of him.

Ken remembers at a young age, his father and grandfather would sometimes kill a few of their chickens. They laid the chickens out in the back yard on a chopping block and chopped off their heads with an axe. Ken was watching the headless chickens jumping all over the place and as they got close to him he thought they were chasing him. He ran away screaming and was terrified. They had a special chicken which was deformed and they called him "Henry." He stood and walked upright like a hawk. Ken entered him in a contest at the county fair and won first prize.

At age seven he started working on a tobacco farm. Connecticut Valley was famous for growing some of the best tobacco leaves for cigar wrappers. At age nine, he was driving the tractors and trucks on the tobacco farm and by age 13 he was "spearing" broad-leaf tobacco for $20 per day. At that time, he was actually making more money than his father. He was allowed to keep $10 per week to buy school supplies and clothes and the rest was given to his parents.

Every Friday night, Ken's grandmother held an all-night poker game at the farmhouse. It included his grandfather, father and a few friends. His grandmother was the only female while Ken's mother stayed in the living room crocheting beautiful doilies and tablecloths. She had no interest in their night of gambling. They never had alcohol in the house except on card night. Ken said this was his first chance to make some money. The guys would send him downstairs to fetch them a beer and they tipped him five cents for every trip. The game would continue until 9am on Saturday morning and then his grandmother would make breakfast for everyone. Ken and his grandmother really looked forward to Friday nights. It was her only form of entertainment after working hard all week and Ken could make as much as $2 per night.

When Ken was a teenager, he suddenly realized he was too cool to ride his bicycle all over town. He traded his bike to a kid at school for his pet monkey. Ken thought it would be neat to have a pet monkey instead of a dog. When his mother found out he thought she was going to kill him. This mean-spirited animal made a mess of everything. "Little Bastard," that was Ken's pet name for the monkey, ended up by biting everyone in the family at one time or another. Ken says he can't remember whatever happened to that monkey but he hopes it died a slow and painful death.

Ken started playing little league baseball for the only team in South Windsor called Sheppard's Short Seconds. They traveled to neighboring towns to play ball and he loved it. Ken decided he would become a professional baseball player until he met his high school sweetheart and fell in love. In high school Ken got a part-time job in a bowling alley as a pin setter. He became a very good bowler and started winning money bowling against some "big time bowlers."

In his junior year of high school his mother died suddenly and he had to quit school and go to work to help support the family. He started work in a potato warehouse loading freight cars and packing potatoes into 10 pound bags. Ken hated every minute of it. He heard about a company which was hiring carpenter apprentices but you had to be18 years old and belong to the union. Ken lied and told them he was18 and paid $25 to join the union. He started installing acoustical ceilings for $1.20 per hour. He traveled throughout the states of Connecticut, Massachusetts and New York doing this work. He was paid for travel, so much per mile, and they carpooled. Ken said his travel money was tax free and sometimes equaled his salary. While working full time, he attended night school to finish high school and got a diploma.

Ken married his high school sweetheart, Norma, in 1957. So many people tried to discourage them because they were so young but they had big plans. They were both working and making decent money and planned to buy a house. Neither of their parents ever owned a house and even the farmhouse where Ken grew up was rented. Norma worked at the Probate Court and later became a legal secretary. They had $880 in their bank account when Ken had what he thought was a brilliant idea. He had a chance to buy an old Army Jeep for $700 that he intended to equip with a snow plow and start a part-time business plowing snow. Norma thought he was crazy and didn't want to use their savings so Ken decided to borrow the money from a bank. It turned out that the banker thought he was crazy too and denied the loan.

Ken finally talked Norma into using their savings to buy the old Jeep.Norma was very nervous about this because they now had a daughter and another child was on the way. Ken had a lot of confidence in himself and was never afraid of hard work. He secretly prayed for a lot of snow that winter and his prayers were answered. The Jeep did not have a top so when they had a heavy snow Ken first had to shovel out the inside of the Jeep before he could even drive it. This was a part-time job as he was still working over 40 hours per week as a carpenter apprentice.

He got so many plowing contracts that his brother-in-law bought a snow plow and joined him in the business. They did so well in this business that they bought new Jeeps with heaters and decent plows. They eventually hired two more people and continued plowing for 15 years. By then they had three children and their first new house.

Ken was asked to take an inside job as the new warehouse foreman.It involved a raise in pay and he immediately accepted.He stayed at this job for approximately two years working 70-80 hours per week.Ken was then promoted to construction manager, overseeing approximately 125 men and about 50 jobs. In 1968, Ken was promoted to vice president of construction. This sounded great but it involved traveling to oversee jobs in Connecticut, Boston, New York City and Long Island. He also went to Puerto Rico to start up a company branch. They had jobs at the Caribe Hilton, a hospital at Santurce Naval Base in Ponce, etc.He also went to Trinidad to teach natives how to install specialty ceilings for the Central Bank Project.

The pressure of the long hours, the traveling and a very demanding and arrogant boss prompted him to walk out and quit during an argument with him. Ken offered to work until they found his replacement but he was so furious with Ken that he told him to clean out his desk and not return. In retrospect, Ken says that argument turned out to be the turning point in his career. Norma was really nervous this time. Ken didn't know just what he was going to do but was confident things would work out. He thought about starting different businesses including a restaurant but decided he should stick with what he knew.

He decided that instead of the actual construction business, since he didn't have a crew, that he would just sell building materials. He put an advertisement in the telephone book with the name of his company, "Interior

Construction Supplies" and had a business phone installed in their dining room. They waited three weeks for the phone to ring and got really excited when they received their first call. When he started receiving orders, he would have the supplies delivered to his garage and then he would transport them in his car to the construction site. Soon he started getting more and more orders and he had to rent a small office and warehouse. He also had to hire a driver and buy a truck to deliver supplies.He checked the local newspaper for truck sales and found a Ford owner who said his truck had been stored in a barn for two years and he had no further use for it. Ken went to look at it and found it in great condition. The price was fair and he bought it on the spot.

They started talking and Ken told him he was starting a construction business, installing acoustical ceilings, drywall, taping, hanging doors, etc. The truck owner sounded interested and said he owned a few businesses and wanted to build an upscale used car showroom and maybe he would give Ken a call. About two weeks later, he called Ken and asked Ken to give him a price on installing the ceilings in the new showroom. Ken won the bid and then he panicked. He did not have a crew and was a one-man operation. He called one of the former carpenters that he had trained and he agreed to do the job. That was Ken's first actual job. After this first job, he became friends with this prominent car dealer and did numerous jobs for him. By then, six months had passed and Ken was getting very busy, mostly by word of mouth but also from past friends and former associates in the trade. He was getting calls from various hospitals, schools and corporations such as United Technologies, Aetna Insurance Company, GTE, etc. They not only bought a lot of building materials but also wanted them installed.

Ken persuaded his brother-in-law to become his partner and together they hired some of the former carpenters they had known over the years. The main business was selling construction supplies but eventually they had to do some of the construction jobs—mostly commercial projects like schools, hospitals and some small home improvements. At times they had as many as 14 employees. Ken ran the company for 20 years until he retired at age 59. Ken says that Norma panicked and was wondering how they were going to cohabitate peaceably after his retirement. She kept reminding him that "she married him for better or for worse but not for lunch."

Ken's father remarried a woman with four adult children. They were together for about 15 years until he died in 1979.Ken has lost contact with two of the four step-sisters and step-brothers as they have moved all around the country.

It is quite amazing to Ken that being the oldest of five boys that they have all predeceased him. His youngest brother, Bob, was killed in Vietnam when he was only 19 years of age. The next youngest, Larry, was a Marine, earning two Purple Hearts. After he got out of the Marines he worked as a security guard. He was a bachelor and lived with their brother, Ed, the brother who was shot as a kid. Larry died unexpectedly from a brain aneurism. Another brother, Jerry, was also a Marine who served in Vietnam where he was also wounded and received a Purple Heart along with several other medals. Jerry died of complications from C.O.P.D. and diabetes in 2013. There was talk of his health issues being the result of Agent Orange but it was never investigated.

Ken says the strangest and most mystical story is that of his brother, Ed.After Larry died, Ed lived alone and kept his job at Pioneer Parachutes. Ken and Norma looked after him—having him over for dinner once a week. He brought all his bills with him and Ken would pay his bills and make his various appointments. After dinner they would play a game called "set back" which Ed loved.Norma would make extra food to send back home with him.

When Ken and Norma started going to Florida for the winter, Ed would send his mail down and Ken would take care of it. They invited Ed every year to visit them in Florida but he was terrified of flying. Before they left for Florida in 2004, Ed came for dinner with his mail. They tried to talk him into coming with them as he had just retired but he still declined. Ken and Norma drove for two days and after arriving there were hurricane warnings. Since they lived on Sanibel Island, just where it was headed, their children were insisting they fly back to Connecticut as the warnings were getting more and more serious. Finally their daughter called and said she had bought them airline tickets for the next day. Many people were evacuating so they packed a bag and flew back home.

Ken tried calling his brother but there was no answer. They stopped at his home and although his car was there he did not answer the door. With that they called the police, who found him dead on his couch the result of a heart attack. If not for their daughter insisting on their coming home, they don't know who would have found him or when. They made all the final arrangements, cleaned and sold his house and then returned to Florida. The hurricane never did hit Sanibel Island.

Ken believes in honest and fair work ethics and says that is why his business was successful and he had the same repeat customers over the years. He has been successful and he and Norma have accumulated some very valuable real estate over the years. He said, to him, success is not measured in how much money you have accumulated or how many properties you own but rather the love and success of your family. He has three children and six grandchildren and they are all very close and loving. He says he has to be reminded not to brag about them all the time. They have a beach house in Rhode Island that everyone enjoys. During the summer, most of the family shows up at the beach house on weekends and they have loads of fun playing games, making puzzles and trying new gourmet recipes besides enjoying beaching it during the day.

Their oldest daughter, Lori, was a nurse and left that profession to become a special education teacher. She worked as a teacher for 10 years until retiring last year. She now tries to travel with her husband who is a national sales representative. They have three children. The oldest is married and works as an elementary school teacher. Her brother graduated from Boston University and is now working in advertising. Their younger daughter is attending Boston University and is majoring in business.

Their second daughter, Kellie, was also a special education teacher but has recently started her own business. She is co-owner of "Graffi-tee Studios and has a web site describing their art work. They started an art design company, licensing designs for destination apparel. They have two adult children living in New York City. Their son graduated from Boston College and also studied in Barcelona. Now he works for Major League Baseball. Their daughter is an aspiring actress/singer. She has performed since she was very young and attended the Academy of Arts in Hartford, Connecticut where she starred in many of their productions. She has graduated college and has recently performed at the Bitter End, Joe's Pub and soon to sing at 54 Below. In between auditions and productions, she works at a prominent restaurant in New York City.

After graduating from college, their son, Michael, has

taken over the construction business. He has several hobbies including golf and tennis—he was a scratch golfer at one time. He has another hobby which is playing poker; Ken thinks he inherited this from his great grandmother. Five years ago, he was on television playing in The World Series of Poker and out of 600 players, over a period of three days, he made it to the final table. This consists of the last six players and he won $250,000. They have one daughter still in high school who hopes to become a doctor.

For Norma and Ken's 50th wedding anniversary, the entire family went on a cruise, 14 of them, and made many happy memories. They are so proud of each and every one of their children and grandchildren and would do anything for them. Next spring Norma and Ken will celebrate their 57th wedding anniversary. Ken says he believes in God, honesty, hard work and love of family. They feel so blessed!

Robert Decore

I met Bob in their beautiful home located on the 6th hole of the Royal Golf Course here at Heritage Palms Golf and Tennis Club to discuss writing his life story. I've known Bob from playing golf with him on many occasions. Bob and his wife, Donna, split their time between Fort Myers, Florida and Huntley, Illinois where they reside in a Del Webb retirement community during their summers. Bob has a great personal story of coming from a very modest background, went to college, learned a trade, worked hard and was promoted to various management positions with different companies. These experiences helped him when he eventually started his own successful Tool and Die business. His company builds dies (tools that are mounted in punch presses to produce metal components) for many different industries, such as automotive, computers, medical, etc. This business has grown to be one of the premier shops in the Chicago area and Bob and Donna have been fortunate to have their children work with them in achieving The American Dream.

His paternal grandparents, Frederico and Anna DeCore, were born and raised in Naples, Italy. They had two children: his Aunt Nancy and his father, Harry, who was born in 1908. When Harry was only one year old his mother passed away. His father remarried a few years later and he and his new wife relocated to the United States leaving Harry and Nancy to be raised by relatives in Italy. In 1923, when Harry was fifteen, he and Nancy left Italy and immigrated to the United States to be with their father, his new wife, three stepbrothers and two stepsisters. Frederico, Bob's grandfather, was a barber and had his own barber shop located in Chicago. Frederico passed away in 1932 and Harry's stepmother died a few years later.

Bob's maternal grandparents, Carmen and Carmella Ciancio, were born and raised in Calabria, Italy. They had one son who was born in Italy before they immigrated to the United States and settled in Denver, Colorado in 1907. Carmen was a construction worker during his early years in this country. The family moved to Pennsylvania and finally settled in Chicago in 1910. He later started a business selling fresh fruits and vegetables from a horse-drawn wagon. His grandmother was busy raising their children which included three daughters and five sons. Bob's mother, Eva, also born in 1908, she was the second of eight children, five boys and three girls. Bob's grandmother passed away in 1934 at the age of 47. His grandfather remarried and died in 1971 at the age of 84. Bob only knew one of his grandparents, his mother's father Carmen. He was a typical Italian grandfather—a disciplinarian, strong-willed, very independent and stubborn. He even made his own wine. Bob got along well with his grandfather and remembers some good times with him. His grandfather spoke very little English but somehow they were able to communicate.

Bob's dad, Harry, had a rough childhood being raised mainly by relatives. The family he lived with was very poor and he never had a lot while growing up. When Harry and Nancy immigrated to the United States by boat, they landed at Ellis Island. The boat trip took about four weeks. They cleared customs and then traveled to Chicago and to meet their father, stepmother and new siblings. Bob says he finds it hard to visualize how his father and his father's sister could come to a new country at their age, not knowing the language and be able to find their way to Chicago and reunite with his father and new family.

His father, Frederico, taught Harry the barber trade. The two of them worked together in Frederico's shop until shortly after Bob's parents (Harry and Eva) were married. Harry and Eva met at a dance and dated for more than a year before they married. While dating they each said they had other names. Harry told Eva his name was Jim, and until his death, he was known as Jim or Harry depending on the person. Eva said her name was Andrea but that name only lasted a short time. Bob was not sure why they used different names but it was a joke when the families got together. After their marriage, Harry got a job in a large barber shop in downtown Chicago, There he was earning more money and they were able to get their own apartment. This was during the Great Depression and jobs and money were scarce. He eventually started his own business and had his own shop until he retired. Bob says that for the limited education that his father had, he was successful in his business and provided well for this family. He was a good father but typical of those times was working a lot and did not get very involved in raising the kids. His mother had that responsibility but when they misbehaved or got in trouble Harry was very stern.

Bob's mother also had a hard childhood. She had to drop out of high school during her sophomore year due to her mother's health. With her being the oldest daughter, she had to assume the household chores of making dinners, cleaning the house and helping raise her younger brothers and sisters. Because of this, she was very insistent on her own children going to school and getting a good education. She encouraged Bob and his brothers to do their best and set high standards and goals. She was the disciplinarian of their family and, although small in stature, she carried a big stick. Besides raising the family and running the house she handled the finances of the house and Harry's business.

After her mother died she became the matriarch of the family. Her brothers and sisters and their families would be at Bob's parents' house often. Their home was where Bob's aunts and uncles would stop to visit on the spur of the moment. She would always put on a pot of coffee and had some type of cake or cookies to go with it. Many of the holidays would be at their house with her brothers and sisters. She loved to cook and have people over. When Bob and his brothers had families, this tradition continued, as they would also stop over at any time. They would go to his parent's home for dinner on many Sundays and holidays.

In 1976, Bob's mother had a massive stroke and died a month later. This really changed their family structure and the family tended to drift apart. She was a great lady and mother and is missed by all. Bob's father then retired and moved to Elk Grove Village, Illinois where Bob was living, and bought a condo. He lived there until he passed away in 1985. Bob was glad he lived long enough to see the start of Bob's business.

Bob was born on June 14, 1938, the middle child in their household. His brother Fred was four years older and his brother, Don, was eight years younger. Since his dad owned his own business as a barber, most years growing up were spent living in the back or above his barber shop. His dad changed locations a number of times but it was always to a better neighborhood and apartment. They lived on Fullerton Avenue by Avers Avenue until Bob was six years old and then moved one block east, also on Fullerton. They lived there until Bob was 10 years old and then moved to Albany Park on Pulaski Road. They stayed there until Bob's junior year at Roosevelt High school when they moved to Elmwood Park. Bob lived there until he got married in1958. Because of the frequent moves, Bob went to three different grammar schools: Darwin, Mozart and Haugan.

In 1948, Harry had to sell the building and barber shop because of business conditions. He went to work at a friend's barber shop and the family had to move in with his dad's sister and her family. They had four children and Bob's family had three, so all together there were eleven people living together. The home was not very big and they had to share a bedroom. Bob and his older brother slept together in a single bed with their heads at opposite ends. His younger brother slept in a crib and his parents had their own bed. They moved there in March when Bob was ten. For Bob to continue at the same school until the end of the semester, he had to take a city bus to school and back. Bob says it was quite an experience living with that many people in the same house. Luckily, in July of that year, his parents bought a two story building with a store on in Albany Park on Pulaski Road. His dad and a couple of uncles built an apartment behind the storefront into which the family moved. Between his dad's business and the rent collected from the upstairs apartment, life got easier financially for the family.

After the move, Bob developed some great friendships and to this day still keeps in touch with many of them. He developed a great interest in sports, especially baseball, football and basketball. He played all three sports in high school and also on many neighborhood teams. Bob had some miscellaneous jobs and saved to buy a used bike. He was then able to get a job as a paperboy. He did this for a couple of years. In his freshman year of high school, he and a few of his friends worked for a small company that sold packing goods. Their job was to unfold newspapers. They would unfold them and stack them. They were paid by the height of the stack. The stacks looked high and they thought they were going to make a lot of money until the boss came and compressed the stack to measure it. Another job he had was working for his dad cleaning the barber shop on weekends. This included washing the floors, the mirrors, windows and counter tops. For that job he was paid about a $1 per week.

He started high school in 1952 and during his first year he did not apply himself very well and his grades showed it. Two things happened to him just before finishing his freshman year in high school. He met the love of his life, Donna, and dated her until she became his wife. The other was that he broke his ankle while playing baseball and was in a cast for six weeks. Being in the cast meant he couldn't do much, so between boredom and his mother pushing him to put more effort into schooling if he wanted to succeed, he began to read a lot. He developed an interest in mechanical things, trying to figure out how they worked, working with his hands and building things. This was an eye-opener for him because in grammar school he did not have to put in a lot of effort to get good grades. It worked and the rest of his high school years his grades improved.

After his sophomore year, his parents moved to Elmwood Park, a suburb of Chicago. Since there was no high school in Elmwood Park, he was able to finish high school at Roosevelt. This worked out well, since he kept the same friends and was at the same high school as Donna. To get to high school from Elmwood Park, he had to walk a mile to the bus stop and take two buses. This was about an hour trip each way. He would leave for school at 6am and get home about 5pm or later depending on team practices and other after-school activities.

His parents did not drive, so the family never owned a car until his older brother was discharged from the service and bought a car. He taught Bob to drive and let him use his car a few times after he got his license. This made commuting so much easier for Bob that he knew he wanted to earn enough money to buy his own car. During his junior and senior years, he worked at a gas station on weekends and saved enough money to buy a car in his senior year. This made it so much easier to get to school, play sports, spend time with Donna and go to work. He worked Friday night, as well as Saturday and Sundays at the gas station. During the school week, he often had team practices after school so he had a pretty full schedule.

After graduating from high school in June 1956, Bob and a few of his friends went to work at Avon Products for the summer. They had a great time working there loading and unloading boxcars. One day near the end of summer, while driving to work, they decided to go to the beach instead. Each of them called in sick, had a doctor appointment or came up with some other lame excuse. When they returned to work the next day, they were all fired. It worked out well since college was starting in a couple of weeks.

Bob attended the University of Illinois at Navy Pier in Chicago after high school but was not sure what he wanted as a major. He considered majoring in education or mechanical engineering. After discussions with relatives and a counselor, he decided on mechanical engineering. During the summer, after his freshman year, 1957, Donna and Bob got engaged and decided to marry the following summer. She had just graduated from high school and was starting her career as a comptometer operator. Bob went back to school for one more semester in his sophomore year and then quit and found a job as a junior engineer at Automatic Electric Co. in January, 1958. They had a great in-house training program. Automatic Electric also assisted with tuition for night school classes. He stayed in their program for a couple of years but did not enjoy the work he was doing. He did not see a bright future working at that position and was looking for a career change. He completed their in-house training program and went to night school at Wright Jr. College. He then applied for an apprenticeship at Automatic Electric in tool and die. He had a brother and two uncles who were in the trade, knew a little bit about the trade and thought it would be something he would enjoy. There were about 30 applicants for this program but he was the only one selected. This turned out to be a great career move, because he enjoyed the work and felt he could have a great future in it. He took advantage of this opportunity and was fortunate to advance successfully.

Bob and Donna were married in the summer of 1958 and lived in Chicago's Jefferson Park area for the first two years of their marriage. Donna worked at Ditto Manufacturing Company for the first year of their marriage and then became pregnant. They had a beautiful girl, Terry Lee, in August of 1959. Donna stayed at home to raise their daughter and Bob worked part-time two evenings per week and on weekends to make ends meet. He also attended night school two nights per week for a year or two. Two years later, Donna was pregnant again, so they moved to a larger apartment in the Albany Park area of Chicago. In 1962 she gave birth to their first son, Scott.

In 1963, after he finished his apprenticeship, he changed jobs and they bought their first house in Elk Grove Village, Illinois. They went from an apartment paying $90 per month to a house with payments of $145 per month. At Bob's new job with Andrick Tool and Die, he was able to work 55 to 60 hours per week. The overtime pay really helped them financially in their new house. In 1966, Donna gave birth to their second son, Rob, and in 1968 they had their last child, Jeff.

Bob's tooling career started with four years in the Tool and Die Apprenticeship Program with Automatic Electric, He became a journeyman and left Automatic Electric and worked for four years as a journeyman at Andrick Tool. He enjoyed the work but knew that to really advance in the field he would have to become a tool designer. He decided to take classes in that field instead of pursuing his engineering degree. This was the start of many career and job changes that led to career promotions for him. He went from a toolmaker to a tool designer with Andrick and in1968 became manager of that department. Andrick closed in 1971 and Bob went to work for DuPage Manufacturing Company as head of their tool and manufacturing engineering department. DuPage's main product line was producing adjustable steel-hose clamps for the automotive industry. While with DuPage he headed a project to reduce the cost of the product. He and his team redesigned the product, revised the manufacturing process, modified and/or built new tools to produce the revised product and automated the manufacturing process. This project came in under budget and increased the production rate by 125%. They also reduced the material usage, and the internal cost of the product was reduced by 33% without adding any people.

He left DuPage Mfg. in January of 1972 and went to work for Electri-Flex as plant manager. This company was much closer to where Bob and Donna lived and reduced his travel time about an hour each way. This job gave Bob experience in scheduling, inventory control, union negotiations and personnel. Electri-Flex employed about 100 people and manufactured electrical flexible conduit. This is metal conduit with a PVC outer skin which is used as an insulator when wiring high-voltage equipment. He stayed there a little over a year and left because of some differing management philosophies especially relating to how employees were treated. He did not feel comfortable in this environment and was unable to change the owner's view.

In late1972, he went to work for Fel-Pro, which manufactured gaskets for the automotive industry. He was hired as a designer and after a year he was promoted to manager of the tool room and the tool engineering department. Within a couple of years he was given the project of starting and managing a new Process Engineering Department. Of all the places he worked, Bob believes this company was the best. They were family owned and rated one of the top 100 companies in the nation for which to work. Their products had a great reputation in the field for quality, delivery and price. Their employee benefits were among the best in the nation and when Bob started his own business he tried to follow their example. They influenced his thinking in terms of how to run a business and how to treat employees, vendors and customers. People working there felt appreciated and respected.

Bob says that he and Donna like to have changes in their lives. They have moved often, bought and sold five houses, bought and sold two summer cottages, and many cars and boats. In most cases there were financial gains by these moves. Their friends joke with them about the number of homes they have bought and sold, the number of jobs Bob had, the activities they are involved with and always running somewhere. They can't believe Bob retired from such a great job and company and started his own business.

The starting of the business came about inadvertently.

Bob had a good friend, Al Butkus, who had a small tool shop. Bob worked with Al earlier in his career and they kept in touch. He often helped Al when he needed advice, design help or assistance on some complicated tools. Bob's oldest son, Scott, had graduated high school and had no desire to go to college. He was not sure what he wanted to do for a living and Bob talked him in to trying tool and die. Al was ready to retire and wanted to sell the business. Al wanted Bob to buy it, but Bob was happy and successful working at Fel-Pro. He was not ready to leave Fel-Pro until he was fully vested and able to receive their retirement benefits.

Another friend of Bob's, Don, knew of this and wanted Bob to go into business with him. They decided to form a partnership and have Scott work with Don to learn the trade. Bob worked with Al to buy his business and equipment by paying him a monthly sum which he used for his retirement. This helped Bob and Don get started and gave Al a nice monthly income to supplement his retirement. The idea was for Don to work there full time and Scott work there as an apprentice. Bob would handle the sales and engineering and Donna would do the office work. Bob and Donna did this without pay to help grow the business and buy new equipment. They did this for three years and then, as many partnerships go, both partners decided it wasn't working out as planned and decided to end the partnership and remain friends. They split the equipment, customers, supplies and money and each went on their own.

Bob and his son took their half and started a new business called Dec Tool Corporation. Scott only had a few years of his apprenticeship completed but was excited and confident they could make it work. Bob went into the shop in the evenings and on weekends to help out and guide Scott. They would plan out what he should do the next couple of days. As business improved, they decided to hire another toolmaker. Bob hired a friend who was an experienced toolmaker, who at one time was Bob's foreman. He took Scott under his wing and helped teach him the trade. These were some trying times especially with cash flow. Luckily Bob was employed at Fel-Pro and used their savings and household money to cover expenses and fund the business.

Somehow it came together and they grew from a one-man shop to 12 people in eight years. When Dec Tool first started they rented about 1,000 square feet of Al's 5,000 square foot building. As time went by they rented more of the building and then eventually rented the whole building. About six years later, 1991, Bob bought the building and the remainder of his equipment from Al. As they grew, they needed more equipment and decided to buy the latest technology equipment they could afford. As with most small companies, the cash was not available so they financed their first CNC Machine which cost about $85,000. This was a big step and hard to do, but Bob knew the only way to grow was to keep updating the equipment. They put 25% down and financed the rest. Bob was somewhat cautious and wanted to finance only one piece of equipment at a time in case a downturn in business occurred. The early 1980's was such a time but they were able to stay in business because of minimum debt.

Bob is really proud at how Scott matured and took on the responsibilities of the business. That experience helped him a lot when Scott started his own business later. That is also true of his two younger sons as to how they got into the business and now have bought and are running Dec Tool.

As the business grew, his other two sons grew up and went to college. Rob, his second oldest son, graduated from

Illinois State University with a finance degree. His youngest son, Jeff, received an Associate Degree in mechanical engineering from Harper College. They both eventually went to work at Dec Tool. Jeff started in 1990 and programmed and ran their first computer numerical control (CNC) machine. This machine would drill, bore and machine openings in steel to programmed specifications. It had an automatic tool changer and once programmed and set up would run by itself. Bob next bought a computerized wire electrical discharge machine. Jeff was trained to run and program this machine, and they hired an operator for the CNC machine. Jeff did the programming for both machines. The wire EDM machine uses a brass wire to electrically cut through hardened steel by eroding a preprogrammed path to a tolerance of + or - .0002. This machine once set up would run by itself.

Rob started with Dec Tool in 1991 and worked with Jeff and ran the CNC Machining Center. It worked well having the three boys working together for a couple of years, but it was difficult to have Scott, the oldest brother, being the boss and telling the younger brothers what to do. This was especially true of Scott, and the youngest son Jeff. Besides Bob's three sons working in the business, Bob's two brothers also worked for Dec Tool part-time along with his wife, Donna. It was hard for her to be an owner, run the office and also be a mother. Bob would get many calls from family members and try to reason with each one with limited success. Donna would get involved and try to solve their differences as a mother and not as an owner. This only made it harder to have a set chain of command.

Bob always felt it would be nice to have a family business but didn't realize all the problems that come with it. In 1994, Bob retired from Fel- Pro and began working full time at Dec Tool.

Home office of Dec Tool

Shop floor of Dec Tool

He hoped he could help the boys work it out but after a couple of years realized a change had to be made. Scott felt the same way and was getting frustrated with trying to run the shop and the family disagreements over work.

He decided to start his own tool and die business so as to be able to grow and make his own decisions. He left in 1996 and with the help of his wife has built a wonderful business that now employs about 20 people. Scott's son, Bobby, now works for him and is taking an active part in their business. This was hard for Bob to accept because Scott was such an integral part of the start and growth of Dec Tool. Deep down Bob knew that Scott made the right decision and his company is doing great. Scott's son, Bobby, will probably eventually take over their business as Bob's sons did his.

Dec Tool has continued to grow and update their equipment and manufacturing procedures, along with the office. They have computerized most office records, payroll and job time recording. At first Donna was against this but slowly she fell in line. They have hired a full time secretary for the office. She has brought in more computer programs and updated their records for job reporting, inventory, purchasing and job analysis. Bob and his sons developed a computerized program to aid them in their quoting process, which has reduced time to quote a new die by about 50% plus eliminates some errors in the process.

They also have done some long-range planning and have put together a five-year business plan and wish list. Bob reviews this plan with his sons on a regular basis to keep everyone focused in the same direction. It has worked well because they accomplished most of what they projected. The company has become completely computerized. They do all their designing on the computer using Auto Cad and other design software. They also have added more computers for the shop toolmakers to help them in their job. The cad/cam designs along with the numerically controlled machining centers (CNC) and wire EDM machines require the toolmakers to become more computer literate.

They started some in-house training on the use of the computer in design, programming and building of dies.

In 1997, Dec Tool got to a point where it outgrew its facility in Bensenville. Bob sold the building in Bensenville and built a new 15,000 square foot building in a new industrial area in St. Charles, Illinois. When they first moved into the new building, it seemed so big that Bob thought they would never fill it. Today it is full to the brim and they are considering moving to a new building of about 25,000 square feet.

Besides building dies and tooling, Dec Tool has purchased some punch presses and has started to run stampings for some of their customers. Computers, Cad Cam design, CNC machining and CNC wire electrical discharge machines have revolutionized the tool and die trade. Bob's plan was to keep up with this new technology and grow with it. Luckily they did and today Dec Tool is one of the most modern tool shops in the country. They have their own cad/cam design department, five CNC machining centers, a CNC lathe and eight wire EDM machines. They employ about 30 people and their customer-base includes many large companies. Bob believes in diversification and never wanted to have the company too dependent on one main customer or industry. Dec Tool presently services over 60 companies and many different industries, such as automotive, medical, construction, computer, furniture and building. They have customers in many states and also have some international customers. DEC Tool works with them to update their manufacturing processes by automating many functions. They have produced manufacturing lines where assemblies take place in the dies or parts are transferred from the die with robots and assembled in an automation line.

Bob and his sons have also developed some products to be used in the tool industry which they are starting to sell. Their hope is to get a product line of their own that they could sell to retailers and other manufacturing companies. They have invented and developed a fixture to prevent slug pulling in dies to eliminate scrapping many parts with slug damage. This is a patented design and the fixtures sell for about $6,000 each.

When Bob looks back as to how the company has grown while some of their competitors had to close during the recent downturn in the economy, he feels fortunate and proud of what they have accomplished. He knows the growth and continued growth in both companies is partially due to the work ethic he and his sons acquired while growing up. Bob was taught that with hard work, honesty and treating people as you want to be treated you could accomplish a lot. Somehow, between Bob and Donna they were able to instill these values in their children.

Bob believes that another important factor in building a successful business is to treat your employees and customers fairly and with respect just as you would like to be treated. Companies are successful because of their employees and the relationships established with their customers. Bob says it takes years to develop a good workforce and good customers and only a moment to lose them.

Bob started with a goal to be one of the biggest and best tool and die businesses in the Chicago area. Dec Tool still has that as its goal. Bob worked with his son who has the finance degree and prepared a five-year growth and financial plan in order to achieve this goal. Their goal was to have a 10% growth in sales every year and still maintain their profit margins. They prepared annual and monthly budgets and sales forecasts which supported the plan and reviewed it monthly. If they found their forecast or budget was not going to be reached they adjusted accordingly and tried to figure out why. They wanted to be proactive and not reactive to potential problems. They also review their employee benefits every year and try to adjust and add perks when they can. An example is they give each employee one day's pay on their birthday.

They do things to help the employees achieve their goals and give those who put forth extra effort advancements when possible. They encouraged them to take computer classes or other industry-related courses or seminars. They have an apprenticeship program through the Tool and Manufacturing Association. Apprentices are required to complete three years of night school, two nights a week, at the Association. They try to give employees as many benefits as the company can afford, knowing it's easy to lose a good employee but hard to replace or train a new one. They review their customer base yearly and evaluate them on profitability, receivables, and ease with which to work. They try to weed out customers that score low on this evaluation.

Bob considers himself to be very fortunate to have met and married such a wonderful friend and wife in Donna. They started dating when Bob was a freshman in high school and she was one year behind him in school. They dated all through high school and spent many evenings talking about their dreams for the future. Her goal was to have four children, which they did, own their own home in the suburbs of Chicago, which they did, have two large dogs, and they had two golden retrievers (the mother and one of her puppies) and live on a ranch and own horses. Bob's dream was to be successful, have a great marriage and own his own business. They accomplished many of their dreams but never had a ranch or owned horses.

Bob's goal when they first married was to earn $10,000

per year. He told Donna that if they could reach that level they would have it made. When Bob earned that amount he realized it wasn't enough. He knew to have some financial stability he would have to be successful in his job, be promoted into a management position and eventually start his own business.

Bob believes he and Donna were very fortunate with the way things worked out. They have four wonderful children, a daughter who is married to a great guy who graduated from Notre Dame and is very successful in his career as CFO of a publicly held company. They have three sons who all followed Bob in his field of work and now own their own tool and die businesses. They have 10 grandchildren ranging in age from three to 26. Two have college degrees and their oldest grandson has an Associate's Degree and is working with his father in his business with the goal of taking over the business when his father retires. The other grandchildren are still in school and all achieving very good grades.

In 1982, their daughter, Terry, married Dave Baker. They had their first grandchild in 1988, Shannon, and she graduated from North Central College and is now pursuing her Master's Degree. In 1983, Scott married Carol Potts and they have two children, Amanda and Bobby. Amanda graduated from DePaul University and has a degree in accounting. She recently married (November of 2013) Dave Aremka. Bobby went to Elgin College for a couple of years and is now working with his father, Scott, in their tool and die business.

Their second son, Rob, married Tina Kirstein in 1990. They have three daughters who are still in school. Ashley is a senior and Carley is a sophomore at Batavia High school. Their youngest daughter Hailey is in sixth grade. All of their girls are doing well in school; they are very active in sports at school and on traveling teams.

Their youngest son, Jeff, married Darla French in 1996. Darla is from Kansas City, Missouri, is a CPA and worked for the McGladrey LLP accounting firm until they had children. They have four children; Brooklynn who is in seventh grade, Austin who is in fifth grade, Madison who is in second grade and Jackson who is three years old. Their children also are doing very well in school and in sports. Bob and Donna feel blessed to have four wonderful children and their sons and daughters-in-law. Of course the joy of their lives is their 10 beautiful grandchildren.

A few things that really helped Bob develop personally was becoming a member of the local Jaycees and teaching night school. He joined the Jaycees because of friends and to play on their baseball team. He did not realize the personal growth he would also get from the Jaycees by running and working on non-profit projects for the community. This gave him more confidence when speaking to a group and the confidence to do new things. A benefit of the Jaycees that he never anticipated was that Bob and Donna met many people who became great friends who were very influential in their lives. Bob had always been shy and did not like to speak in front of a crowd. The projects he ran as a Jaycee forced him to do that and helped him overcome some of his nervousness at speaking. Donna was very active in the Women's Jayceettes and loved to get involved with their projects and social events. She also loved to do crafts, sew and make clothing, cook, decorate for parties and make fancy cakes and hor-duerves for affairs. Bob taught night school for the Tool and Die Manufacturing Association for two years: 1976 to 1978, and this also helped him overcome some of his shyness and taught him a lot about people, their different backgrounds and abilities.

Bob's plan when he first considered starting his own

business was to develop the business to a point where his children could take it over and live a good life with few financial worries. This has happened, and his younger two sons have bought Dec Tool from Bob and Donna. They purchased the business in 2003 and paid it off in 2013. Bob and Donna financed the sale and used this money to help them enjoy their new retired lifestyle living in Heritage Palms. Rob and Jeff's next objective is to buy the building where Dec Tool is located. Bob is in the process of setting something up for them to accomplish this. Bob and Donna will probably finance this sale and work with them when they decide to sell the building and use their equity to buy a larger building. Scott also has his own building in Carol Stream and has much of the same equipment as Dec Tool.

Many of Bob and Donna's personal goals have been met and the remaining ones are very dependent on their health. Donna had breast cancer in 1990, and it was in remission for many years but she recently had a reoccurrence and is taking chemo treatments for it. It has negated much of the feeling and movement of her right arm, but she is handling it well and they are hopeful the chemo will continue to work. Because of this, they have changed their lifestyle and future goals but are enjoying what they have. Bob says it makes one realize how important our health is to us and our families. They try to enjoy every day and do the things they want while their health allows them to do it. They want to travel more and have some wonderful trips planned.

They also realize the importance of religion and belief in God. Bob remembers the saying and believes "I'd rather die believing in God and finding out I was wrong than not believing in Him and finding out I was wrong." Bob is really enjoying retirement and life in Heritage Palms with many friends from Illinois. They have a dog, Angel, which has changed their life and enjoy her very much. He still likes to visit the boys at each of their businesses and takes great pride in seeing what they accomplished. He also likes to fix things, come up with new ideas and products. Both he and Donna enjoy traveling and had a motor home in which Angel loved to travel. They recently sold it and now hope to do more traveling on cruises and travel tours. They have taken some of their grandchildren on trips and hope to do more with the younger ones. Bob also would like to work on his golf and tennis games. He also would like to learn more about computers, smart phone and other new technical items.

Fred Cox, Sr.

Fred Sr. & Fred Jr.—Fred Jr. is the second generation of this company

Fred invited me to his beautiful home located on the 5th hole of the Sable Golf Course at Heritage Palms Golf and Country Club to discuss writing his life story. I play tennis with Fred and was delighted when he consented to allow me to write his life story for my book. Fred is a real go-getter and an idea man. He is also a leader and when Fred decides to do something everyone wants to participate with him. Through free market capitalism, Fred was able to achieve financial independence and The American Dream. He has also been very successful in his personal life which Fred believes is much more important. Later in life, he became a politician and accomplished many things for his community in the Toronto area of Canada.

I find it very interesting that Fred got into his business, National Event Management, almost by accident. He was running a retail carpet business and was just looking for better and more economical ways to market his business. Initially he did weekly music shows in the park and that success resulted in a home show and that success developed into all kinds of different trade shows. This is the miracle of free market capitalism.

Fred was born November 4, 1942 in Toronto, Ontario where his family lived in a modest three-bedroom home in Leaside, a suburb of Toronto. Fred says his mom and dad were your normal middle-class family members. Fred has a sister, Gaille, who is one year older. Apparently when he was born his head was shaped like a peanut, so, as he was told by his mother and father, they called him Peanut for the first three or four years of his life. His father served in World War II and when he came back from the war Fred asked him who won. His father replied, "We did," and then Fred asked for the score. When he looks back on that exchange it sort of shows Fred that he had a competitive side at a very young age.

His mother was a housewife who stayed home and made sure they had enough groceries on the table and did the cleaning of the house, etc., like all good mothers used to do in those days. His father went to work six days per week in the insurance business—he was a claims manager for a company called Shaw and Begg and rose to be vice president of that company. He doesn't remember much about his early childhood other than he can recall playing a lot of ball hockey on the streets of Leaside. He also recalls his mom and dad buying him what they called "Bob Skates," which were skates that had two blades on each foot and that is how he learned to skate.

In the summer, his parents would rent a cottage up at

Georgian Bay, where they would live for two weeks each year. Fred recalls the good times playing with all of the other kids up there in the big sand dunes and running around on the beach and in the warm waters of Georgian Bay. When he was two years old, a good friend, John Simpson, lived up the street, and they became best buddies. They are both 71 years old, and they still live within two miles of each other, golf with each other and share a lot of happy times.

Fred's four grandparents came from different parts of the world. His maternal grandparents came from England while his paternal grandmother came from Scotland. His paternal grandfather always told Fred he did not know where he came from but believed his origins were in India. However, he could never be sure. He did have darker skin as did Fred's father so it is very possible that he did come from India.

Some of Fred's early memories of living in Leaside were that both sets of his grandparents were alive and they would come over every Sunday for dinner. Fred's paternal grandfather was a sergeant major in World War I with regiment number 007. He was the seventh man in all of Canada to sign up to serve his country. He did tell Fred later in life that he lied about his age, as he was only 15 and you had to be 17 to sign up without parental consent. Fred is very proud of his grandfather for doing a remarkable job for Canada and the rest of world. Some of the war stories that his grandfather used to tell him on Sunday afternoons sitting around the fireplace, long before television, were horrendous. Fred once asked him what it was like to kill somebody and his grandfather told him that most of the time when he was in the cavalry, before they went out on a mission, they would offer him many shots of scotch or some other type of drink. The Major, at the time, would always ask, "Do you want to drink before you go on the mission or after you come back?" His grandfather would always take it before the mission because only about half of the soldiers would come back from the fight, so there was plenty to drink when they got back. His grandfather said they knew from their advance men where the German foxholes were. He would describe in great detail how they would creep up on the Germans in the mud and the rain, and when they got within about 20 yards they would pull the pin on their hand grenade with their teeth, count to three, and then throw it into the foxhole. His grandfather would yell, "Share that amongst you, you bastards." One of the gifts from his grandfather at Christmas was a hand grenade.

Fred went to kindergarten and grades one through eight at Rolph Road Public School in Leaside. He says he was only an average student but had lots of friends and played lots of sports. One of the things that Fred recalled immediately was being ejected from the school choir in grade seven because the choir director told him he had the worst voice that he had ever heard. On a positive note, he won the public speaking contest for his school in grades five and six. He remembers in kindergarten that they would have a rest period during the day and the children had to lie flat on their back during this time. Fred says, that in those days, they all wore breeks with braces on them and to this day he remembers the terrible pain in his back from those braces. He can still remember the teacher, Mrs. Robinson, saying, "Lie still Freddy."

In first grade, he had a teacher, Miss Palk, who is responsible for his poor penmanship today. Fred says he has the world's worst handwriting skills. In grade five, he had a teacher, Mr. Franklin, who made him write 500 times, "A word to the wise was not sufficient."Fred can't recall what he did to deserve this punishment. Many times Fred has thought of that in raising his own four children but couldn't bring himself to make them do something like that. In grades seven and eight he had a fantastic teacher, Mr. Barrett, who started to teach the class what life was all about. Fred respected him because he was very firm and strict but also fair. He was one of the best teachers Fred ever had. He remembers many good times at recess and at noon hour playing in the schoolyard. Whether it was soccer, hockey, baseball or lacrosse he had such a good time with his fellow classmates.

After school, they had a great group of guys who never stopped playing hockey, baseball or football, depending on the season. Fred had very supportive parents all through public school even though most report cards came with notes like, "Could do better" or "Not working up to his ability" or "Much room for improvement." Fred's father served as chairman of the Parks and Recreation Committee for the town of Leaside. This committee established a series of playgrounds at the various schools in Leaside. In the summer, Fred would play at these playgrounds with his friends playing ping-pong, soccer and baseball and they also played against the other playgrounds in a very competitive manner.

In grade seven, Fred had a paper route consisting of 125 customers and he had to get up every day at 5am to deliver these papers which he did for five years. His best friend, John Simpson, helped him for two and a half years before he retired in grade nine. Fred's dog, Skippy, used to help him with the papers every morning until one morning he collapsed and died after eating some food poison on the route. It was a very sad day for Fred and something he will never forget. One of the downsides of delivering

125 papers every day is collecting for the subscriptions. He had to collect every week from each customer so he could pay his bill to the newspaper company.He says he met a lot of good people and it taught him at an early age how to run a business and how to deal with people. Fred knew those 125 customers were counting on him every day to provide a service and he was determined to not let them down.

One of Fred's best memories was one summer day driving down to Cleveland to see a baseball game between the New York Yankees and the Cleveland Indians. What a thrill that was. It was the only trip they made as a family while Fred was in public school. Fred attended St. Cuthberts Anglican Church on Bayview Avenue and he remembers one year the priest put together a baseball team and they went down to the intercity to play a couple of teams which he remembers fondly. Fred says that, all in all, he had a very happy childhood when he was in public school while living in a very stable and supportive home. He says he had the best of all worlds—family, friends and a great school.

Fred graduated from college in the Spring of 1966 and in June he married Anna. After the wedding they went on a six-week honeymoon in which they toured all of Europe and camped most of the way. Fred says it was quite an experience visiting all the foreign countries, as neither Anna nor Fred spoke any language other than English. They met several very interesting people at all the campsites they visited but unfortunately the weather was not very good and their camping gear got completely soaked. When they got home, Fred started working for British International Finance, which had just started a new mutual fund called York Fund. Fred became a sales representative for this fund. This was a real learning experience for him as he had to find all of his own leads and every night he would go into peoples' homes and try to convince them that they should invest with this company $10, $20, $30 or more each month in order to build up their retirement savings plans. He found this quite a challenge and learned very quickly how to sell. Although Anna, his wife, was a school teacher, Fred felt some pressure to do well to pay the rent and put food on the table.

He remembers one day his sales manager called Fred into his office and told him how well he was doing, but he couldn't figure out what motivated him. The sales manager said he should be motivated by money and Fred said, without hesitation that, money did not motivate him. Instead the motivation was making the sale every night to different individuals. To Fred the important thing was putting people into the right product as opposed to considering what commissions he would make. He remembers, to this day, that the sales manager was flabbergasted that Fred was a commission salesman and was not motivated by money. It is one of the principles, that Fred strongly believes today, that money should not drive an individual. He believes that everyone has to have a passion for what they do and with a bit of luck, success will follow.

Fred really enjoyed this job, as every evening he was sitting with different families encouraging them to invest dollars every month and he would project how much money they would have when they retired. In other words, he was painting a very positive picture for them when retirement was upon them. Unfortunately, the parent company of the mutual fund ran into some financial difficulties and the company started to close down.

Fred had a few contacts in the insurance industry at the time and he was hired by JW Randall & Associates, an insurance adjustment company, and he became an adjuster for the next four years. Every day he would talk to many people who had been involved in car accidents and as adjusters they would try to finalize the financial implications. They also did a lot of liability claims with some of the major hospitals in the Toronto area including the doctors. As an example, in some cases a doctor who was supposed to perform a left hip operation might instead do the right hip. When something like this happened, both the hospital and the doctor would be sued and Fred's employer would represent them. Obviously, in these particular cases, they did not have much of a defense. He really got to know the human nature of people and what they will do and how they will react in a time of crisis in their lives. They caught many people lying about how accidents did occur. They caught them trying to cheat the system by saying they had whiplash or other injuries and trying to take advantage of the Workmen's Compensation Act in Canada. Fred says that some people will do almost anything for a dollar—human nature has no boundaries.

After being an insurance adjuster for four years, an opportunity surfaced for him to start his own business which he called Canadian Tel-A-Views. He, along with his brother-in-law, developed a product that looked like a television but inside it had a rear-screen projection system whereby they put slides in the back of this so-called TV box and through a system of mirrors and prisms an image would show on the screen. They got a contract with a major financial institution in Canada and placed 30 of these machines behind the bank tellers so when people came to do their banking, while they stood in line, they would see a different image appear on the screen every 10 seconds.Fred and his brother-in-law were partners for approximately two weeks when his brother-in-law decided to quit and Fred took full control of the company.It was very difficult to move the company forward at the time because their product was a static slide presentation. At the same time, videotape was coming into play and the banks were now going to an upgraded machine with videotape. Fred tried to keep this company going for more than one year, but financially, it did not make any sense. By this time, Anna and Fred had two children and she had quit teaching school, so money was tight.

He happened to see an ad in the newspaper from a carpet company looking for sales people to go into homes every night and sell carpet.He applied and got the job, and for the next four weeks he was given leads by the owner and Fred would go into two or three homes each night and try to sell carpet to the homeowner. It was very challenging and also very rewarding. People got very excited about covering all their floors with carpet and Fred found it to be an easy sale with very big commissions. After four weeks of working with this owner, he decided to open up his own carpet company.

Fred started his own carpet sales company called Direct Broadloom.Every Monday he placed a full-page ad in the Toronto newspaper from which he got 50 to 60 leads. He made appointments and every night he would go into peoples' homes to sell them carpet. He made arrangements with all the carpet companies to supply him with carpet and he found some installers to install the carpets. He also lined up a finance company to finance the purchases for those who could not pay cash. This proved to be very lucrative and Fred enjoyed running this small business out of his home which gave him freedom and flexibility to do what he wanted. He operated this business out of his home for four years and then he moved the business into a retail store in Unionville, the neighborhood where he lived. He then changed the name of his company to Unionville

Broadloom and Interiors and catered to the people in the Markham and Unionville areas.He rented space on the second floor of a building and their slogan was "We are on the second floor to save you more." They successfully ran Unionville Broadloom and Interiors for a number of years with a staff of nine people.

Fred was always looking for new ways to present and market his business to the community other than by traditional advertising methods. One nontraditional advertising method used was musical concerts. Murray Edmonds, a local roofer, and Fred put on musical concerts in the local park every Sunday night in the summer. Over 1,000 people would attend for free with their families and Fred made sure every Sunday night that all of those people knew who presented these concerts. Fred believes this was the best form of advertising that they could do.

Once, in the middle of the night, a thought came to Fred that literally made him sit up straight. The idea was that his company, Canadian Tel-A-Views, should start a home show in the Unionville area whereby Fred would set up a booth along with other merchants in the area to display their products to the local people.At that time, there was only one other home show in Toronto, the National Home Show. The next morning, when he awoke, he started giving it serious thought and rather than just do the little community of Unionville he decided to call it the Markham Home Show and target all of Markham which had a population of 80,000 people.

The next day, he visited the Markham Fairgrounds and inquired about renting some space as it had five different buildings. The general manager said that no one had ever rented the buildings before and the only thing that the Markham Fair Board approved was the Annual Agricultural Fair. Fred requested and got an appearance before the board of directors and somehow convinced them to rent Canadian Tel-A-Views their buildings in the third week of October for the Markham Home Show. Fred signed a contract with the Board and hired Jane Simard to assist him in selling to all the merchants, advertising and promotion and the operational aspects of producing a consumer show. She was very instrumental in making this all happen.He knew very little about producing a show and he learned by the seat of his pants and by talking to a lot of people. The first annual Markham Home Show was a tremendous success and all the merchants did extremely well getting new leads for their products. The people of Markham really enjoyed seeing all the different products and services available within their local area. This was the start of something really big.

To back up in time, shortly after they started Canadian Tel-A-Views, he realized that his family needed more money to survive. Fred started another company called Fredrick Studios. He had a couple of cameras and knew a little bit about photography so he went into different condominiums and apartments at night, knocking on doors. He would ask to speak to the homeowner, saying that he was a photographer and he would take pictures of their children and bring the pictures back in a couple days. This was very profitable for about six months, and it allowed Fred to get over his financial hurdle. This was a very valuable experience for him in negotiating with people and trying to sell parents pictures of their children.

After the first Markham Home Show, his staff of three people wondered what Fred would do next?After a couple of weeks Fred came up with the idea of producing a rodeo and an outdoor living show which really was nothing more than a home show with a rodeo.He didn't know anything about rodeos, so he went to Edmonton to watch the world championships and made a lot of contacts in the rodeo business, learned a bit about horses, bucking broncos, calf roping and bull riding. He convinced the Markham Fairgrounds to rent Canadian Tel-A-Views, Fred's company, its facilities for this event. He contracted with another company in northern Ontario that had produced rodeos. They put the rodeo on under contract about ten months later. At the same time, Fred put on an outdoor living show with about 300 exhibitors which was another great learning experience that he had at a young age.

It is very difficult to market and advertise two products to the same people at the same time. People came in droves to see the rodeo, but they never did bother walking through the buildings to see all of the merchants that paid good money to exhibit their products and showcase their services. Because this was billed as an Outdoor Living Show and Stampede, many of the animal rights people boycotted this event, because they believed rodeos were cruel to animals. They even spray-bombed Fred's office with paint and picketed the front gate so people had difficulty buying tickers. It was a tremendous learning experience, but Fred lost over $200,000 producing this event. He realized that what you name something is of utmost importance and you will always learn more from your mistakes than from your successes. The lights went on in Fred's head, and he suddenly realized this business wasn't as easy as it appeared on the surface.

Canadian Tel-A-Views produced the next Markham Home Show again the following year and it was a tremendous success. After the second successful home show he made a decision to go into producing shows full time, and as a result, he sold Unionville Broadloom to one of his employees. He then started to develop other shows including the Metro-North Business Show which they did in Markham. He brought several companies in the region of York together to showcase their products and services to all the business people in the area. This was a medium success story and after two years, Fred realized it wasn't going to grow or be very profitable in the future, so he sold this particular show to a chartered accountant and the show folded one year later. His oldest son, Fred, Jr., was attending the University of Western Ontario at the time and was taking courses leading to a business degree. He joined them for three summers assisting them with the Metro-North Business Show.

When Fred, Jr. graduated from college, Fred had a discussion with him about joining Canadian Tel-A-Views or pursuing other career opportunities. Fred, Jr. decided to work for his father and they started another show called the Financial Solution Show which they produced in Halifax, Ottawa and Calgary.Fred, Jr. was in charge of the show and sold the exhibit space to all the financial institutions, such as banks, trust companies, mutual funds, etc. Then they marketed the shows to all the people in the various cities. This was a very worthwhile and educational show for the attendees who learned about investing from many experts, attended free seminars and had an opportunity to discuss investing ideas with the various financial institutions. There were also some franchise exhibitors in case people wanted to invest in their own business. Fred says that his son did a terrific job in molding these three shows and it was because of his great efforts that they were very successful. They produced these shows for four years, and then they were approached by another major event company which was interested in purchasing the shows. After several months of negotiations Fred sold the shows

It was just before Fred sold the shows that he changed the company name from Canadian Tel-A-Views to National Event Management which, he says, was a far better name describing exactly what they did. Shortly after he sold the Financial Solution Show, they developed another idea and that was the Outdoor Adventure Show which would encompass bringing all the exhibitors in the outdoor industry such as clothing, travel, bikes, tents, etc. together to showcase their products. This show was all under one roof for a crowd that was anxious to get the latest and the greatest products and services in the outdoor industry. They put the show on in three cities: Vancouver, Calgary and Toronto, and to this day, these shows are very successful and still running.

At the same time that they were developing the Outdoor Adventure Show, they also decided to do a Business Opportunity and Franchise Show, which they started in Toronto and managed to expand all across Canada and into the United States. National Event Management, Fred's company, at this time does approximately 20 franchise and business opportunities shows in major cities across Canada and the United States. Their concept is to bring all the major franchises together under one roof and market this show to people who are interested in buying a franchise. Also included are free seminars to assist the people who are interested in going into business for themselves. These shows are very popular and very successful. In 2002 they decided to do a women's show so they started the National Women's Show in Toronto. They contacted and sold space to approximately 500 exhibitors and attracted up to 30,000 people annually. These shows were for women looking for women's products and services whether it was clothing, travel, food, fitness, etc. Today they have expanded these shows and are now doing shows in Ottawa, Montreal and Quebec City. While they were producing the National Women's Show, they were approached by a national newspaper, the Toronto Star, which wanted to buy their Markham Home Show. This was Fred's baby, and he really was hesitant to sell, but the offer they made was just too good to turn down. Fred's company had done the Markham Home Show for about 25 years but he was very happy to sell it to a major conglomerate. He is happy to say the Markham Home Show still continues to run.

Besides running his business, National Event Management, Fred became very active in the community. He coached many hockey teams and was active himself in playing hockey and baseball. Fred has two sons and two daughters and he recognized there was no girl's hockey team in the Markham area so he along with another man started the girl's hockey team in the Thornhill, Arena. His daughter, Deb, played in this league for three years. His children were also very active in the skating, soccer and baseball clubs. When Fred became aware that there was not a hockey team at the local high school, he raised some money from the corporate world and started and coached the high school hockey team. While all this was going on, a couple of friends, Mike Larkin and Art Moad, approached him to start a Board of Trade in the Markham area. For six months, they called on all the businesses and encouraged them to join and come to the networking meeting. They joined and came to the monthly meetings, where they exchanged business cards and got to know all of their business neighbors in the community. Today the Markham Board of Trade is very successful with over 1,000 businesses as members.

Another highlight that Fred really enjoyed in his career was being asked to sit on the initial board of the Toronto Raptors Basketball Foundation. The Toronto Raptors played in the NBA, and when they were initially starting up they hired Isaiah Thomas to be their first general manager. He remembers very well Thomas coming to meet with them one afternoon for lunch right after he was named the new GM. He sat with them for over two hours asking them questions about Toronto, so that when he was recruiting players he could tell them about the great city of Toronto. Thomas asked about the city's diversity, culture, restaurants, theaters, etc. Fred was impressed with the questions that Thomas asked which showed his interest and desire to promote the community to prospective players.

Fred was always very active in various community activities, and eventually he decided to enter the political arena in order to further serve his community and to make it better. Fred was very involved in the community coaching baseball, hockey, playing baseball, involved in the Unionville festival and generally very active in all aspects of the community. In 1988 a good friend, Tony Murphy, suggested that Fred consider running for political office. Fred said it had never crossed his mind and instead encouraged Tony to run for office.After some discussion they decided to flip a coin and the loser would run for office.Fred lost and ran for the office of Ward Three Councilman for the community of Unionville. They gathered a bunch of neighbors together and put on a strong campaign.His campaign staff included his campaign manager, George Shepherd, Tony Bright, John Simpson, Peter Vanderberg, John Homer, Paul Haney and many others. It was an exciting time for all as they put together campaign brochures and literature. Part of the plan was for Fred to knock on every door in Unionville to introduce himself as a candidate. The campaign team organized a parade; Fred's friends and neighbors got together on weekends handing out literature to every home, and they completely dominated the scene for the last month of the campaign. They put up signs on street corners, public meetings were held and coffee parties were held in peoples' homes. The day before the election, Fred turned 40 years old, and that night it was pouring down rain and his staff told him he could not stop knocking on doors. So, that night he went into the neighborhood of his opponent and knocked on every door on his street.

Fred said that going door-to-door introducing himself and having an opportunity to talk to everyone one-on-one was an incredible experience. Some were very receptive and a few slammed the door in his face—fortunately, that didn't happen very often. He says that many people were happy to see him but many didn't care about local politics or didn't vote so they didn't want to speak with him. Fred was thankful that a lot of the mothers and fathers from the hockey and baseball teams he coached were involved in his campaign, and they encouraged other people in the community to vote and give rides to the polls if needed. Fred said he was in awe and it was a heartwarming experience. Fred won the election and was the new councilman for the community of Unionville in the town of Markham.

From that day on his life changed drastically as he was not only representing the community of Unionville, but he was also the father of four active children as well as running his business. He did not want to lose touch with his children. During the next three years, Fred learned the whole political system, met hundreds of new people at the local, regional, provincial and federal levels of government. Markham was a town of 80,000 people, a suburb of Toronto. Development was the key to the future success of Markham, and Fred spent many hours with other staff members and counselors preparing an official plan for the next five to ten years. Fred said it was interesting to share ideas with other counselors, because everyone had different ideas as to what they wanted Markham to look like in the future. Fred praises the mayor, Tony Roman, for being a tremendous individual and a very strong leader. Working under the mayor's guidance and leadership Fred believes they always did what was best for the community. During his first term on the council he sat on many committees and chaired the fire committee, which had one of the biggest budgets in the town of Markham.

One of the subjects that came to mind for Fred was recycling. After many meetings the town decided to purchase a "blue box" for every homeowner to place items for recycling. Subsequently all other municipalities entered into this same program following Markham with the blue box. Looking back, Fred is proud that it was he and three other individuals on the committee who really determined the whole blue box campaign for all municipalities in Ontario. Another highlight that Fred takes great pride in was as chairman of a committee to redo the Main Street of Unionville. The street was very old and had a lot of infrastructure problems. The underground water mains kept bursting, hydro poles were leaning in the wrong direction and wires were leaning over the street. It was a total disaster. For one year the committee worked on burying all the underground cables and water mains, putting in new very historic-looking lampposts and cobblestone sidewalks. When the project was completed, it turned out better than anyone had envisioned. Today, people from all over Ontario visit this magnificent street to shop and just wander. Fred often says it is Canada's most romantic street.

Fred says his three-year term of office went by very quickly and when it was over and it was time to run again he had no opposition. Fred says this was good and bad—it was good that he didn't have to run a campaign and go door-to-door campaigning, but he really enjoyed that. He enjoyed having the campaign team around him give him fresh ideas for the town of Markham. He was sort of envious of all the other counselors knocking on doors in their reelection efforts. However, it was nice to know that he was assured of another term in office.

The next three years he was very busy sitting on many committees far too numerous to mention. However, some of the highlights were building the Markham Theater, the Mountjoy Community Center and the new facilities in Milliken Mills. The Buttonville Airport was another big project that they managed to save. The owners of the airport wanted to close it down and develop the land. The town thought that having an airport right next to the town was very important. Many meetings were held at the federal and provincial levels, and they eventually worked out an agreement to save the airport, which remains open to this day. He also sat on many committees with individuals working to build libraries, a hockey rink, soccer fields, firehouses, theaters and many other facilities to serve the community. They also put in place an official plan to take the town of Markham through the year 2000.

Fred became chairman of the Economic Development Committee, and he says they were fortunate that companies such as IBM, American Express, Allstate Insurance and Philco Ford had corporate offices in Markham. The high-tech community was gaining momentum and they initiated the phrase, "Markham, high tech capital of Canada." In order to promote industry the mayor and Fred agreed to have a business trip to Hong Kong and took along a group of business leaders to promote their companies and to encourage all members of the local Hong Kong Board of Trade to start branch offices or factories in Markham. They also met with all the major banks and Fred says it was a very successful trip as many of those companies did locate businesses in Markham. They also went on trade missions with other business leaders to Dallas, Texas and Raleigh,

North Carolina in order to sell Markham as a place to do business. Markham now has agreements with many cities throughout the world to work in cooperation with and promote business.

After his second term as a councilman Fred decided to run for the office of regional counselor. The region of York is comprised of nine municipalities, and they each send elected representatives to the regional headquarters to discuss issues that affect the entire region. This position also includes a seat on the Markham council. Once Fred decided to throw his hat in the ring, he got his campaign team together to run a campaign over the entire town of Markham. Money had to be raised, signs had to be printed and more literature had to be put together. Also, more people had to get involved because of the much larger area that had to be covered. Fred says it was a great time as many people throughout Markham got involved in his campaign and he won. Since Fred received more votes than the other 10 candidates running, he also became the deputy mayor of Markham in addition to being a councilman.

Fred says that sitting on both councils was a real eye-opener as he was now sitting with nine mayors and 17 regional counselors from across the region of York. The region of York had a population base of 700,000 people. Fred was appointed chairman of the Planning Committee which was a very important and big job. He found his job very challenging, but his staff was excellent and made his job easier. Issues were discussed at the regional council level, and the mayors and councilmen were naturally looking out for their own cities and towns most of the time. It was during his second term as a regional counselor that he realized there was a tremendous waste of money at the regional level with duplication of services.

Fred had an idea and plans to amalgamate all nine mu-

nicipalities into one large city, namely York. Fred conclud-
ed that by this amalgamation they could eliminate nine
city halls, nine planning commissions, nine parks and
recreations commissioners, nine engineering commissioners, nine economic commissioners, etc. Fred figured they
could reduce the number of politicians from 125 down to
only15.There was lots of support for his idea from the taxpayers and the media, but in the end his fellow politicians
voted against this idea as they were fearful of losing their
jobs. Fred said it is interesting that a couple years later the
province of Ontario forced the city of Toronto to amalgamate into a major city including all the suburbs around it.
Fred has had many talks with the province to try to force
the York region and all the other regional municipalities to
amalgamate but these talks led nowhere.

Fred believes strongly in streamlining government to
make it more efficient and less costly. He also believes in
part-time politicians rather than professional politicians.
He was very surprised that, as a counselor for York, he
was the only one of the nine counselors and nine mayors
who had another job—the other 17 people were all professional politicians. Fred believes in term limits of no more
than eight years. There should be fresh ideas coming forth
with new people. He found the waste in government to be
incredible, but he also found politicians unwilling to do
anything about it. They seemed much more interested in
protecting their own job and getting reelected. Fred believes we need more people from the private sector getting
involved in government to make it more efficient and responsible to the taxpayers.

In 1997 a major event happened in Fred's life—Anna
and Fred decided to go their separate ways and divorced.
Fred said this was a very stressful and trying time for both
of them, because they spent a lot of happy times togeth-

er over the previous 33 years and had four great children together. In the year 2000, Fred finally decided to completely retire from public service and concentrate on his personal life and business. He was spending eight hours per day working with his son at National Event Management and was concentrating on building up the business. In that year, he was appointed to the Markham Stouville Hospital Foundation on which he served for seven years. At that time, he became chairman of the annual Markham Stouville Hospital Golf Tournament and for the next 15 years—they hosted a golf tournament and raised money for the hospital. Over the course of 15 years, they raised approximately $3 million.

Five years after his divorce, Fred married Janice Harrison. Janice lived in Thornhill and raised two sons on her own, Braden and Lee. Fred says that both boys turned out to be exceptionally fine young men, as Braden is now a senior executive in Toronto with IBM and Lee is a financial consultant with CIBC Wood Gundy. Over the last 10 years, Janice and Fred have traveled extensively and in 2006 discovered a life of paradise in Heritage Palms Golf and Country Club. The purchased a lovely home here in which to spend their winters socializing and playing golf and tennis. Fred is active in our club and serves on both the Green's Committee and the Men's Golf Association.

Fred has had a very productive and rewarding business and political career and in the process he has achieved financial independence and The American Dream. He has also had a very successful and rewarding personal life and is very proud of his four children—Stacey, Deborah, Fred, Jr. and David. Their first home was an apartment in North York and two years later, in1968, they purchased a home in Unionville, a suburb of Toronto. Their children were very involved in many activities in the community including skating, soccer, baseball, hockey and many other activities. When the children were young, Fred built a hockey rink in the backyard where they all learned to skate with their friends. In the summer, he built a swimming pool which again was the center of activity for all of the neighborhood children, and they had some tremendous times and memories in that backyard swimming pool.

In 1982, Fred thinks they made probably the most important decision a family could make, and that was buying a cottage in the Dorset area on Kawagama Lake. They have spent the last 30 years there and shared many happy times with family and friends. It has been the place where they as a family spent most of their time together. To this day, their four children love going to the cottage with all their children where they swim, boat, ski, fish and play hockey on the outdoor rink at Christmas time. Fred would suggest to anyone who is considering buying a cottage to do so, because it gets the family away from the everyday hubbub and allows them to escape to paradise. Fred says that at the cottage there is only your family and Mother Nature.

Fred is very proud and happy to report that his four children are all college educated and happily married. Stacey married Scott and they have three wonderful boys. Scott works for Colliers Real Estate and is one of their leading sales brokers in all of North America.

Deborah married Roger Hennig who was a star football player with the Hamilton Tigercats and they own a business called Action First Aid. They have three great children.

Fred Jr. graduated from the University of Western Ontario with a business major and married Anne Stevens. They have three children and Fred, Jr. works with Fred, Sr. at his company, National Event Management.

Dave graduated from Dalhousie University and subsequently married Nicole Graves and they have two lovely daughters. Dave is a recruiter with Ventura Recruiters.

Fred is the proud parent of four children and 11 grandchildren, and he is so happy to say that his four children get along extremely well as they all basically live in the same area and they are each other's best friends. Fred says that nothing could be finer as a parent than to see all of your children and grandchildren getting along so well. One of the highlights of their Christmas every year is building a hockey rink on the lake at the cottage. For 30 years they have been scraping the snow off the ice and then flooding it with water. It is not uncommon to see 20 or more family members playing hockey and skating on the rink.Fred says the only downside is that he used to score a goal now and then but now it's the other way around. He is so proud and happy for each of them and almost every day one of them will call and say, "Hi Dad, how are you doing?" He said it is a thrill to hear from them on a daily basis.

William Olson

This is the life story of a man from a very troubled childhood who amazingly grew up to be a great success as an architect. I've known Bill for a few years socially, as well as through playing golf with him here at Heritage Palms. Hel grew up in a bad neighborhood on the south side of Chicago and was involved in mischief and crime at a very young age. As a young adult, he became an alcoholic and overcame it all and became a success.Through desire and determination, he was able to turn his life around and achieve his dreams. I think you will be very surprised that a man with this background was able to pick himself up and become a great success. Through free market capitalism, Bill was able to achieve financial independence and The American Dream.

Bill's parents were Mandis Olson and Frances Lehman. Mandis was born in 1891 and died in 1952 at age 61, while Frances was born in 1900 and died in 1983 at age 83. His parents met in Paw Paw, Illinois in 1925 and after a one year courtship were married in 1926. Bill was born in 1941 and had three older brothers who were from five to fourteen years older and one sister.

Bill's parents owned a two-family apartment building located at 7050 Prairie, Chicago, Illinois in which they rented out the first floor, and they lived in the small two bedroom apartment on the second floor. Bill slept on the living room couch until he was eight years of age which he says was probably the best deal of all. His mother and sister slept together in one bedroom, his two brothers and his father all slept in a bedroom no bigger than Bill's current walk-in closet. His grandmother, who was senile, slept in the dining room on a cot. His oldest brother, when he returned from the War in 1946, slept on a cot in the kitchen with the oven door open to support his feet. All this did not seem abnormal to Bill at the time, because he had nothing with which to compare it.

Bill said he doesn't remember much until age four but his family was very dysfunctional. His father was a stern disciplinarian who was prodded by his wife to punish the kids. Bill remembers one time when his mother told his father that his brother Don had misbehaved, and his father punished him by hanging him by his feet out of a second story window. Don never forgot the punishment inflicted on him and held it against his mother for many years.

Bill's father worked for Chicago Mass Transit on the elevated trains and when Bill was only four years of age his father was diagnosed with Parkinson's Disease. It was soon necessary for his father to retire on disability because the disease had progressed to that extent. This disease was much worse back in the mid-1940s, because there was no medication to really help much. Money was very tight and Bill's mother went back to work as a telephone operator working the 3-11pm shift. As a result the kids rarely saw their mother except on weekends and during school vacation and holidays.

Bill's father was no longer physically able to handle the kids and his mother was rarely there so the kids pretty much raised themselves. So from age five, Bill was left to do as he pleased and was directed down a path of mischief and crime by his brother, Dick. Bill would often stay out until 10 or 11pm until he had nobody with whom to play. He started hanging around with his brother's friends who were about five years older than Bill and learned the things that older delinquent kids had learned. However, Bill was learning these bad things at an earlier age than the others did. One of the things that Bill learned was if he had money then he had so called "friends," especially if they were five years older than him. From the lessons taught to Bill by his brother, Dick, and his friends, Bill became a thief very early in his life and money became an obsession.

At six years of age he was caught stealing money from the St. Columbanus Catholic Church located at 71st Street and Prairie in Chicago. Bill noticed that people put coins in the "poor box" because the coins made a lot of noise. He checked it out and found there was only a thumb screw at the bottom of the box and he could easily empty that box. One day he was lying on the floor under the poor box emptying its contents when he was caught by a priest. He was taken to the Rectory where they notified his father. It was terribly embarrassing for all concerned because his father had just converted to the Catholic faith and became a member of this church only two months prior to this event.

In the neighborhood they were all known as the "wild Olsons." Bill said the only person in his family who had any common sense and was a nice person was his sister who really became his surrogate mother. Bill says, "Thank God for her." Although Bill hung around with his brothers and their friends, he was lucky to not have been caught committing any crimes. Because of the family reputation Bill was often pitted in the neighborhood against other boys in a sandbox at the local park to fight. There was often 15 kids standing around the sandbox to form a ring and Bill would fight with his opponents one by one. Bill was a good fighter and he tried very hard in order to achieve the respect of the older kids with whom he hung around. This lasted for some time until they put him up against twin brothers and he had to fight the two of them. He fought hard and long but in the end he finally lost. Bill said he was very embarrassed, because he had the attitude that he had to be a winner in order to have their respect.

His brother, Dick, was five years older and his crooked role model. He taught Bill how to steal Christmas trees, how to steal wallets on the beach, how to rob the missions in the school by only robbing every third classroom and only emptying part of the can and it went on and on. Dick would take Bill to professional football games where they would sneak in without paying and when the team was practicing field goals Dick would catch one and let the ushers come to him. When they were near him, he would toss the football to Bill who would then run out of the stadium and go home with the football. There were many similar things they did over and over again.

He does remember he didn't have many friends because of their reputation. He can remember calling to a boy to come outside and play and Bill overheard the mother saying, "I don't want you to play with that boy." Bill said he didn't really recognize at the time that he was being shunned by other people in the neighborhood, but now realizes that he was.

Bill doesn't recall the family ever sitting down together for dinner, because his mother was working and his father was too sick. He believes his mother must have prepared something but he remembers eating most of his meals all alone. Because of this, Bill never learned the proper relationship between children and parents. Bill was into everything bad at a young age and at age seven he belonged to a "sex club." Bill became what he describes as "street wise" but he also believes he had common sense. He really had no idea that his family was different than others in the neighborhood.

He came home one day when he had just finished the fourth grade and found his family was packing up and moving. The old neighborhood, he found out later, was changing. Blacks were beginning to move in and his family was one of the first to move out. Bill says his new home at 8049 South Bishop seemed like it was located quite a distance from his old home and when they arrived at the new home it was hard to believe. They pulled up in front of this beautiful home and he was told that his bedroom was upstairs and he would be sharing the room with his brother, Dick. Bill thought he had gone to Heaven. There were several bedrooms and it was quite a change from what they were used to.

That summer, at eight years of age, Bill tried to make friends in his new neighborhood but he was not good at that. After being unsuccessful initially he found himself riding his bicycle to his old neighborhood which was eight miles away. He spent lots of time alone in the park making model airplanes and cars. Eventually he met a boy across the street and a couple other boys that summer and he taught them how to steal and that was how he made friends. When school started in the fall, he started fifth grade and his life began to change. He had to wear a uniform which consisted of a shirt, tie and pants. He felt like he fit in except for his shoes which often didn't even have laces and the pant legs were ragged.

It was a sports-oriented community and Bill was introduced to sports for the first time. The Catholic school was very involved in basketball and Bill was really good at it. One day while diving for a basketball during a game he received a bad cut over his eye which required several stitches. He received praise for continuing to play with blood dripping down his face and he was soon a hero for his tough play and bravery. Bill liked that acclaim. He now had friends and really felt like he belonged. In addition, sometimes the sixth grade boys would pick on the fifth grade boys but on a couple of occasions when they picked on Bill, he beat them up. All of a sudden, Bill became the class protector.

Now that Bill had friends due to his athleticism and bravery, he no longer felt it necessary to steal in order to have money to get friends. Bill says it didn't happen all at once but after about six months he was really fitting in. Bill didn't participate in any school activities or other activities except sports. He only participated in sports, because that was what he was good at and that was how he achieved acclaim. Bill says the next two or three years were great in that he had friends, but now says they were probably more like acquaintances as he really had not learned how to be friends yet. Bill never brought anyone to his home because he was ashamed of his father who by that time was unable to even put on his own pants. He was always drooling from the mouth and everyone in the family pretty much ignored their father.

When Bill was entering eighth grade his father passed away. Bill was walking down the street to catch a bus to go to the circus when one of his brothers came running down the street screaming that their father had died and Bill said he cried. He cried because now he couldn't go to the circus. He had no tears for his father. Bill remembers at the funeral that everyone was crying, but Bill just couldn't bring himself to tears. He was glad his father had finally died. Bill said that feeling would soon change. His mother informed them that now they could no longer afford that beautiful home and had to sell and move back to a "changing neighborhood." That is, a poorer neighborhood which contained both white and black families. Bill said it was like paradise was taken away from him. Bill continued to attend the same Catholic grammar school by riding the bus eight miles each day. It was a good experience because the nuns took pity on Bill and tried to help him. However, Bill did not have good experiences with the priests.

During that eight grade year the school brought in a new basketball coach who was a strict disciplinarian. He was a good coach and Bill became the starting point guard and this team which was one of the best in Chicago. When the school year ended, Bill decided he wanted to attend Mendel Catholic High School because his brother, Dick, went there. It so happened that the entrance and class-level placement exam was the same exam that was given in grammar school. Bill got access to this test which resulted in him scoring very high and not only assured acceptance but he was placed in the most advanced classes. Bill had never studied in school before but now he was attending classes with the smartest kids in school and began to feel that he didn't fit in again.

The first negative response to this placement was when the home-room algebra teacher was a month late arriving at school due to release from the Army. The teacher attempted to make up for lost time by moving quickly through the material. Under ordinary circumstances, Bill would probably have had trouble keeping up but with this accelerated program he was absolutely lost. He said he didn't have the background, study habits or the desire to work hard enough in this class and nearly flunked the course. Bill said this was the beginning of some feelings of inadequacy that stayed with him for many years. He did just okay in his other classes in his freshman year but excelled in his drawing class.

Bill continued to excel at sports. He tried out for the football team but in the end, he simply was not big enough to do well. Because he was rather small he got knocked around a lot and finally decided that he would never excel in that sport so he quit. He then tried out for the basketball team and made the team as a freshman, and eventually after a couple months of play, he was starting at guard on the varsity team. Bill said he was lucky because he had a wonderful coach at Mendel who became his surrogate father. The coach always helped him out by giving him guidance and steering him in the right direction. He was a very spiritual man and Bill respected and admired him.

In his sophomore year, Bill continued starting at guard on the basketball team, but Bill told the coach and his assistants that he didn't think he deserved to be a starter. As a result, the coach put him down on the junior varsity team. Bill continued to practice with the varsity and sat on the bench during their games the rest of the season. It actually turned out well for Bill because the junior varsity team never lost a game the rest of the year and even ended up beating the varsity team at the end of the season. After that, Bill learned his lesson and kept his mouth shut and ended up starting on the varsity team in both his junior and senior years.

Starting his sophomore year, he was still grouped with these advanced students in the classroom. Bill had a geometry teacher who was Scottish and he could hardly understand a word he was saying. Consequently, Bill had to attend summer school after his sophomore year. During summer school, Bill sat next to another boy and together they made a pact that they were never going to summer school again. They decided they were going to cheat their way through school, and that is exactly what they did during their junior and senior years. Bill was even on the honor roll a couple of times simply, because he knew how to cheat. It is interesting to note that after the summer school final exam in geometry the teacher called Bill to tell him that he received the highest grade in his class on the final exam. Bill was astounded and thrilled! However, that didn't change Bill's opinion of himself which was that he was just an average student at best and school continued to be difficult for him.

Bill was not a serious student and never took a book home and skipped all his classes on Fridays because that was game day. Bill got though school by cheating and it resulted in him getting a very poor high school education. This left him behind most of the other students. Through this period, Bill always had plenty of girlfriends and he thinks girls liked him because he was different and perhaps exciting. Going into his junior year, one of his girlfriends told him she had missed her period for two months and she thought she was pregnant. This went on for another two or three months until Bill found out she was just using that to get him to marry her. She was stringing him along to see how he would react. During this time, they did not have sex but when she finally admitted that she wasn't pregnant they went back to having regular sex. This went on until the end of his junior year.

At this point, Bill convinced his mother that he needed to get out of their slum neighborhood and into a new house. Bill said the house as well as the neighborhood was terrible. The house was bug infested and nobody bothered to keep the home clean. Bill convinced his mother that if she would move to a new home that he would take care of it and keep it clean. They moved to a new home and Bill kept his word by cleaning the home from top to bottom each Saturday for four years. He said he made everything shine and never minded doing this work because he was so grateful to get out of the slum.

Bill was one of the best players on the varsity team as a junior and the team had a very good record. The next year,

Bill was the only returning starter on the varsity as the others had graduated. Because this team was new, except for Bill, it was not expected to do well. However, this team fooled a lot of people by getting progressively better, and by mid-season, Bill was recognized as the only legitimate star of the team. The local newspaper did an article on the team in which they praised Bill and said that if the rest of the team doesn't produce way beyond their capability that they looked like fools compared to Bill Olson. This article alienated most of the players on the team against Bill. It did cause some problems for Bill in that the players started not passing the ball to him as a way to show that Bill wasn't the entire team. Then Bill got hurt and was unable to play for three games resulting in the team losing all three games. After that the other players decided it was wrong to blame Bill for what someone else wrote so they started including him again. They continued on and ended up winning the Catholic League championship. The coach, who was such a great role model, helped Bill get two college basketball scholarship offers. He got scholarship offers to both Illinois Institute of Technology and Northern Illinois University.

Next Bill had to take the entrance exam to IIT, and he thought it was hopeless because he was not college material. He had decided he wanted to be an architect even though at that time he couldn't even spell the word and knew little about the field. He thought because he was good at drawing that architecture might be a good choice. About three weeks later his basketball coach called him and said that if he had scored a 70 on the entrance exam they were going to let him in, but he didn't score that high. The coach went on and explained that the only thing Bill got right on the exam was the spelling of his own name. Bill was devastated. The coach said the Dean of Students had agreed to meet with Bill to help give him some future direction. Bill agreed and showed up at the Dean's large office and was apprehensive. The Dean told Bill that he was not college material and that his test results on the entrance exam proved it. The Dean offered to give Bill an exam to determine the best trade for him to pursue. Bill was insulted and became determined to prove the Dean wrong.

Again his basketball coach stepped up and told Bill that he should select a junior college that has mostly minorities as the best chance to get into college and succeed. Bill was one of 320 students who graduated from his high school and all but 20 were going to college. He did find a school like the one the coach had suggested and took the entrance exams. The school was Wilson Junior College, which is now known as Malcolm X. Bill attended this school for one year during which he struggled attending refresher courses. He says the only course he did well at was a design course.After that first year he transferred to the University of Illinois at Chicago (Navy Pier), which Bill is quick to point out is not nearly as difficult as the University of Illinois in Champaign. However, it was a much tougher school than Wilson Junior College. To point out the difference, Bill received a grade of "A" on a design course at Wilson, but when he took the subsequent course at Navy Pier he had to drop out after only two weeks because it was too difficult. He retook the course in design at Navy Pier and got a grade of "C" on the same course he took at Wilson on which he had received an "A."

Bill was 17 years old when he started at Wilson Junior College which was located at 69th Street and Normal on the south side of Chicago. At that time, Bill lived in an area called Mount Greenwood which was located on the southwest side of Chicago—about a 45 minute travel time to school. Bill spent his free time playing basketball and baseball with his former high school friends and drinking every weekend. Drinking didn't seem to be a problem at that time although Bill did notice that when he drank he usually drank too much and suffered the next day.

He says his coach's advice to go to Wilson was "spot on." He says he would never have made it through college had he started his college career at a school such as the University of Illinois. He started his college education in the fall of 1959 and graduated from the University of Illinois in Champaign in January, 1966, with a straight "C" average. Because Bill was unprepared for college there was a lot of back stepping in his college career. On several occasion, he had to retake courses because he failed them the first time.All of this difficulty resulted in him taking three extra semesters to graduate in addition to his five year curriculum of Architecture.He says that starting out his study habits were terrible as he followed his previous way of hardly ever studying or taking a book home. On those occasions when he did study it usually amounted to him staying up all night cramming for an exam. He never cheated in college.

Thinking back, the only books he ever read through the end of his high school career were comic books except one time he read the book entitled "The Red Badge of Courage" which was in his sophomore year of high school. He was astounded as to how interesting it was, but it still didn't encourage him to go to the library to take out other books. He just had no interest. One of the things he struggled with continually was English grammar. When he transferred to the University of Illinois at Champaign to start his junior year he had to take a proficiency exam in English grammar which Bill says he failed miserably. He retook the exam and failed it again. Finally, he was able to pass it in his last semester of college.

In August, 1959, Bill met his future wife, Barbara Zblysk, when she was 16 and he was 18. He met her at a dance on a Sunday evening and was mesmerized by her. She was a fantastic dancer and since Bill was a good dancer they hit it off right away. He asked her for her telephone number which Bill says was a good move because with his problem with English he would never have been able to find her name in the telephone book. They started dating and are still together today.

As Bill transferred to the University of Illinois at Chicago, (Navy Pier) he now recalls the support he received from his family. His mother was committed to working to help Bill get through college while his brothers and sister did not get that help. Even so, his brothers and sister were all encouraging and supportive of the decision to get Bill through college. This was something that Bill really appreciated. Although Bill didn't own a car, his brother and sister would allow him to use their cars on weekends for dates with Barbara and fun with his friends. Travel time to Navy Pier from his home took nearly one and one-half hours each way. Bill would spend this time sleeping rather than studying. He tried out for the basketball team and became a first-string guard. He particularly enjoyed the few times that they played IIT which had refused to allow Bill admittance to its university. He wanted to show the coach at IIT what he had missed. Basketball began taking away time from his academics and he was placed on academic probation during the second semester at Navy Pier.

Bill stayed at Navy Pier for two and one-half years and then transferred to Champaign in January 1962. He had to leave behind his girlfriend, Barbara, which resulted in a lot of lonely weekends. Bill continued to struggle in school earning grades of "B" and sometimes even an "A" in design courses which compensated for the "D" or sometimes even "F" that he got in some of his elective courses. He never knew from semester to semester whether he would flunk out or be able to go on to the next semester. Consequently, he was unable to commit to renting a place for the following semesters until he got his final grades. This resulted in him getting rooms that nobody else wanted and living in slums during his entire time in Champaign.

Every week or two he would hitchhike back to Chicago for the weekend to see Barbara and his friends and drink. While at school he got involved in various activities in order to excuse himself for not studying. He says he became an expert Chess player and became a regular handball player. So, he was constantly creating pressure for himself to cram for exams and papers at the last moment. This pressure resulted in him going to the local bar and drinking beer for hours at a time to relieve the pressure. This resulted in sleeping away many hours which should have been spent studying. He was constantly on and off academic probation and took solace in his drinking and became a bigger loner that he ever had been. He had recurring nightmares that he would never pass the English proficiency exam and therefore not be able to graduate. By the time it appeared he would graduate in January 1966, instead of a feeling of accomplishment or being relieved he had become so discouraged and depressed that he still felt like a loser. However, when he did finally graduate he was euphoric that he had finally achieved his goal.

After he graduated he became eligible for the draft by the Selective Service and thought for sure he would end up in Vietnam. The war was going strong at that time and he thought it was inevitable that he would end up there. He checked with the Selective Service and was told he would be drafted right after graduation. He and Barbara had planned to get married as soon as he graduated so in order to get a 120 day delay he volunteered for the draft in the Army for two years.

Although elated to have finished college, after the marriage Bill was disturbed by his situation. He thought after all the struggles he had been through that it would be for nothing, because he was sure he would be sent to Vietnam and be killed. He and Barbara also struggled with their marriage, because they seemed to be at different polls and at odds on almost everything. Bill thinks he was unprepared to carry on a mature relationship with his new wife. Barbara was mature and outgoing while Bill was immature and introverted.

About a year before they were married they combined their resources, mostly hers, and bought a lot for $4200 in McGinnis Highlands in the southern suburbs of Chicago. They sold that property for $8000 which allowed them to buy another piece of property in Chickesaw Hills. Bill took at job with an engineering company in Marblehead, Ohio. He took this job so he could make some money quickly before he was to report to the Army for active duty. He returned every couple weeks to spend time with Barbara.

The Army encouraged Bill to become an officer so when he took his final physical before entering the Army they found an old injury which they believed would prohibit him from becoming an officer. For eight months he was in limbo while the Army was trying to decide whether the old injury was a problem. Finally in October, 1966, nearly nine months after graduating from college, he received orders to report to Fort Campbell, Kentucky for basic training. Upon arriving at Fort Campbell, after a 14 hour bus ride, they found that Bill's blood pressure was very high, 170/120. He was told that if it stayed high for three days that he would be discharged. It stayed high and after three more weeks of being in limbo he was discharged.

His first real job as an architect began with Bartolomeo and Hanson about one month after he was released from the Army in 1967. He approached that job with a positive attitude and no project scared him that was given to him. He had a good relationship with his bosses and he fit into their type of work. He was assigned to design presentation type projects and with Bill's skills and imagination it worked out well. After two years he was let go at Christmas time and he was told it was because of a slowdown in the economy. It took Bill 30 years to realize that it probably had more to do with his drinking than anything else. Bill says that was a very rude awakening.

In 1969, Bill and Barbara had their first child, Kirsten, who Bill loves very deeply. Kirsten now lives in Ft. Myers and is an attorney for Social Security. Kirsten has a six year old child who is a real joy to both grandparents. Their other daughter, Julie Ann, was born in 1971 and has special needs, but is high function. She lives in a group home in Joliet, Illinois. Bill says she's the best person—innocent and loving and life is a joy to her. She has her own apartment and has worked for Bill the past 12 years. Their son, David, was born in 1972 and has a college degree with a major in communications. Bill says that Dave is everything he never was—a great father, loving husband, freethinker and on and on. Bill could not be more proud of him.

Bill had to serve a three year apprenticeship before he could take the state exam to become an architect. In 1969, while studying for the Architectural State Registration Exam he took a refresher course. The first day they gave a test to determine the general knowledge of the class. While handing back the test results a week later, the instructor noted that nobody had passed the 70% required and most of the scores were in the 30 and 40 percentile range. There was one score in the 50s and one exam had a score of 68. Bill was observing the expressions on the faces of the dozen or so people at his table who looked dismayed and disappointed. Bill was astounded to learn that he was the one with the score of 68. Many of the people who took that exam were friends of Bill with whom he had studied during college and they all got better grades than Bill in college. Bill began to think that maybe he wasn't so dumb after all.

Bill recalls that after college graduation he always had a book in his hand. He studied at every opportunity. He realized how lucky he was that he graduated in spite of his poor attitudes and study habits. His most important goal in life was to pass the State exam. He took the State exam about three months later and passed with a score in the high 80s. The exam lasted four days of which three days were on general knowledge, mechanical, art history, structural design, site design and professional practice and ethics which lasted eight hours per day. The final day was the most important and was on architectural design which lasted 12 hours.

One of the many moonlighting jobs Bill had was for a man named Eric Erickson. He was impressed with Bill's work and one day asked Bill to lunch. He was aware that Bill had recently passed the State exam and was no longer working for Bartolomeo and Hanson. He offered Bill a partnership in his firm. Bill readily accepted. The agreement was that Bill would do all the architectural work and Eric Erickson would take care of the business end.

Eric passed away at age 51 in 1973. Bill had always thought he was doing all the work and didn't realize the contribution that Eric had made to the business. While Bill was doing the architectural drawings, Eric was out calling on clients and prospective clients, bidding on jobs and overseeing construction. When Eric died, Bill was at a loss as to what to do. The business was soon in complete disarray. They had three large projects under construction and there were many problems. It took Bill nearly 18 months to complete these jobs. He was required to visit each job site daily which was a round trip of nearly 150 miles. Bill suddenly realized that Eric Erickson had been doing most of the work and Bill was very unsure of this side of the business. This put extra pressure on him and he relieved this pressure by drinking. This went on for about five years with business declining with each passing year. The drinking continued and both his business and his marriage suffered. He says he was a terrible father.

New work was sparse during the years between 1973 and 1976 and Bill was barely making a living. He was doing contractor work on the side and resented that the construction workers were making more money than he was. He wondered at times why he had bothered to get an education.

He continued to play handball twice a week after leaving college. Racquetball came along in the mid 1970s and racquetball clubs were going up everywhere and all were full of players and making money. Since architectural jobs were scarce, Bill felt with his building experience coupled with his architectural skills he would design, bid out and build racquetball clubs. He paid for a pro forma income statement which showed a tremendous profit was there for the making. Since Bill had very little money he had to go out and look for investors. He approached at least 10 different groups touting his pro forma, drawings and construction of the building as his earned investment in the project. Although the investment was well presented and viable, the investors wanted Bill to have a cash investment in the project.

Eventually Bill got seven investors to invest in a racquetball club in Tinley Park in 1978. The club cost $850,000 with $200,000 cash by the investors ($25,000 each) as a down payment and a mortgage of $650,000. The club opened and was an immediate success and eventually had 4,000 members. The club had 10 courts that were occupied from 6am until 12 midnight. The club was very profitable and they were able to reduce their loan by $200,000 during the first year of operation. They decided to add five additional courts at a cost of $250,000 at a time when interest rates were skyrocketing. They borrowed the $250,000 for expansion and added it to the remaining balance of $450,000. The bank did a new mortgage for $700,000 at an interest rate of 15% which eventually increased to 22%. The economy began to slow down with these high interest rates and membership plummeted to 800 members.

At one point, Bill was offered $50,000 for his original investment in the club which he regrets not taking. Not only did he end up losing his original investment, but he had to agree to pay an additional $50,000 to the bank for a release of his personal guaranty of the loan. The way Bill figures, he lost the $50,000 he was once offered, plus another $50,000 that he had to repay to the bank, for a total loss of $100,000. At that time, in 1982, $100,000 was like a million to Bill.

They sold their home in Chickasaw in 1977 which had doubled in price. They used the proceeds to build a 4,000 square foot home on a ¾ acre wooded lot in 1977. Bill did considerable work on this home including landscaping, painting and other work he could do. He was able to get this home built for a total of $72,000 including the lot.

Unfortunately they didn't have enough money to furnish the home. This was during the period when he was still drinking so it was a difficult time. At this time, Bill blamed his miserable life on Barbara. It was a bad situation.

The architectural business had all but dried up and Bill started selling real estate. With his ability to talk with commercial owners and his credibility as an architect he was able to do enough business to get by. He was instructed by the owner of the real estate firm to do whatever was necessary to get the listings. He often gave optimistic estimates of projected selling prices just to get the listings. As a result, the homes never sold for near the listed price.

In 1977, Bill finally admitted he had a drinking problem and agreed to quit drinking and smoking pot and attend AA meetings. He didn't really think he was an alcoholic, but more or less admitted it to get his wife off his back, after her threats to throw him out if he didn't quit drinking. He attended meetings only sparingly and wasn't truly convinced that he had a serious drinking problem. After about one year of sobriety he was about ready to go crazy and start drinking again when an event happened at AA that changed Bill's life. A lawyer, who Bill had known, asked if he would take him to an AA meeting. Bill obliged and at that meeting people showed up who Bill had not seen before. They had an outlook that made a lot of sense to Bill and he agreed to have coffee with them after the meeting. This resulted in him being invited to join their group to participate in various sports like football, basketball and baseball. This was what Bill enjoyed and because of his athletic ability he was a star in the group. He became active with these people on a daily basis and they are the reason for his continued sobriety which has now lasted for 37 years at this writing in 2014. They are the reason that his life changed.

In spite of this and a deteriorating real estate market Bill was able to supplement his architectural business with income from real estate sales.

He had a space in the real estate office for his architectural business. Barbara contributed heavily at this time by taking a job subbing as a school teacher in addition to being a housewife and single handedly taking care of the three children. She also started selling paintings and with her outgoing personality was very successful. Bill saw dollar signs with the selling of paintings and offered to finance her in a full-time venture. She declined because it was more important to her to raise the children. Her financial contributions during this time kept them out of bankruptcy.

Helping, during those rough times, was Bill spotting a house with high grass, broken windows and no lights on in the evening. With meager funds he was able to buy this house on three acres in a beautiful subdivision for $70,000. After a modest renovation he was able to resell this home for $99,000 and on the same day he had another sale closing which netted them a total profit of $30,000. Bill notes that at this time at the age of 39 they had a net worth of $75,000.

The real estate market crashed in 1982 and Bill applied for a job with an architectural firm in Joliet where a couple of his former classmates from the University of Illinois owned this business. He started to work there in May, 1982 and because Bill was a self starter and motivated they basically left him on his own. Bill enjoyed the work because at this job he had no business responsibilities—all he had to do was draw. He was given a big job and after a couple months he had completed a large part of it and his boss said he would check the work to see how he was doing. A few days later they returned Bill's work with red marks everywhere. They had neglected to tell Bill their office protocol and how they wanted certain things done. Without any instructions, Bill did the job the way he thought it should be done. Bill was devastated to see his drawings all marked up in red. He made the required corrections to the drawings, but he was very disappointed that he did not measure up on that job. He resigned but they asked that he stay until this project was completed. Then he quit.

In 1982, the country was in a recession, interest rates were at an all time high, no construction work was going on and therefore no architects were needed. The only thing going for him at that time was his new found friends. They were always optimistic and it helped Bill to develop a positive state of mind. Bill decided to restart his own architectural business and opened a 600 square foot office in his basement and started making some calls to try to get some business. He realized at this point in his life how fortunate he was to be self employed. He decided that to be successful he would give 110% effort to his clients.He spent days going through his entire Rolodex and was unsuccessful until he got to the W's. At this point a guy he hardly knew suggested he call someone at Hardee's Fast Foods which had been relatively untouched by the recession. Bill made his case at Hardee's and he got in the door by drawing up a simple bathroom and a remodeling of a kitchen. It wasn't much but Bill needed anything he could get and this led to other jobs with Hardees designing other projects. Bill also got work designing some metal buildings. This was enough business for Bill to get by and he now had a very positive mental attitude.

They refinanced their home in 1983 and got an additional $38,000 in cash. Things started to get better and as they did Bill's attitude improved and his optimism grew. In 1985, Hardee's bought Burger Chef and business was booming for Bill's firm. He hired two other architects to help him with all the new work and moved to a new office about one mile from his home. In 1990, a contractor friend asked him to design a couple homes and he did so knowing that there was really no money in designing homes and it was not really his specialty.After that, this contractor asked him to design three model homes for a new subdivision he was developing. It turned out to be an upscale development with many amenities in a great location. It was a win/win situation for both the contractor and Bill. This development attracted buyers that were more interested in buying the property and having the contractor build homes that they desired. Bill designed 150 homes for that subdivision. The surrounding area was also a hotbed of new residential construction and his homes were favored by additional home buyers and contractors. Bill noted that because his fees were fair the customers were happy to pay promptly.

It was now 1995 and Bill was able to keep his home and had paid off his mortgage. He had incorporated the computer into his main stream of revenue which was residential design. He had fired his two architects and had hired two young Cadd specialists. He taught them residential design and now was producing close to 300 homes per year. By 1998, these two computer designers had decided to start their own business and left. They also took with them copies of his computer files. Bill did not panic and was able to hire an architectural college graduate who was competent in residential and computer design. His name was Sean. Some months later, Bill hired Sean's wife, Sue, who had similar qualifications. At this point in his life, now 57 years old, Bill realized he was a winner. He had lived through many setbacks and he was still working hard and really enjoying it. He had done several award winning residential designs that had made his name known. He knew he had to rely on professional people for his important work in his business.

It may seem like a small thing to some but Bill realized how important it was to a contractor to get their first large payment when the roof was installed. Bill asked the contractors to mark up their construction building drawings with the changes they made (always done on buildings) before making a call to the building department for inspection. Bill would make those changes, provide required copies of prints and certify those changes as the architect. This resulted in contractors getting their money as quickly as possible. By the way, he did not charge them for this and it was one of the wisest things he had done. By 2005 he was working with over 265 contractors and had developed a contractor's mentality.

Bill knew from his past building experience what a contractor needed to get his project done, how important it was to collect the money and not just send a bill out for payment. It was important to let the clients and contractors know what he was about. To do this, he developed a working website "Olson Plans" that eventually by 2005 had cost him $450,000 to design and upkeep. He became licensed in the 10 surrounding states. Bill's firm, William K. Olson & Associates, completed 300 homes in 2001, 500 homes in 2002, 600 homes in 2003 and 600 homes in 2004. Then the floor dropped out of the residential market. At the firm's apex in 2005 they designed 1,000 homes at an average price of $550,000 excluding land costs for a total of $550 million in construction cost. Bill and his two associates were making close to a $1 million between them in salary, dividends and perks. "Olson Plans" had become a cash cow for the business. Without doing any work, it constituted 20% of their business income in 2005 or approximately $500,000.

During and after the good years, Bill understood how important it was to receive payment for your work. He knew all too much time was spent chasing owed money. He felt the mentality of a person owing money was that after several months of owing they felt that they didn't have to pay. Bill had learned from his clients, doctors and attorneys that they had a non-collectable rate of upwards of 40% of their fees. Bill's firm in 2005 had an uncollectible rate of 1% on $2.5 million.

The William K. Olson website was making money for his contractor clients. Instead of sitting down with their prospective clients cold—they could send them to "Olson Plans" on the website. They told their clients to pick out a plan and elevation and mark it up with their likes and dislikes. With that information they were able to give the client a reliable estimate of the cost of the home.

Bill also worked this way. Instead of small talking with a prospective client, he went to the most important aspect of their meeting. How much will the architect cost? With a one page simple contract, he was able to educate the client as to cost of architectural service, payment schedule, retainer, payment at midpoint and final payment. He noted to them that the finished drawings would not leave the office until final payment was made. Helping with this painless and smooth procedure was 90% of his clients came in with the marked up drawings from his "Olson Plans" website. Meetings that would normally take two hours now only lasted a fourth of that time. Proper scheduling and protocol allowed each associate to handle upwards to 125 jobs at a time.

In 2005, he was paying a printer upwards of $100,000 a year for "free" prints supplied to the client. He invested in a six roll print machine at a cost of $35,000 and saved the business over $50,000 per year. Bill paid his employees a fair wage, fully paid health insurance, a four and a half day work week, overtime pay and extra incentive money for contract work. He felt a happy employee would work harder and that showing his people respect would pay large dividends in positive attitudes. He allowed his employees five sick days and two personal days per year. At Christmas, a gala party with a 10% bonus was not uncommon.

Because of the Internet, Express Mail and communication links, Bill started to spend considerable time in Florida. So, in 2001, he bought a condo in Fort Myers, Florida. Beginning in 2005, he was able to spend six months a year in Florida living the good life. Projects were sent to him by Express Mail for final check and approval. Bill participated in golf, handball and bike riding. He hired a health coach to improve his eating habits and strength. Barbara played golf and in general maintained a good lifestyle. She was a hard worker, good mother, loving wife and what Bill calls a real keeper. He regrets not always treating her the way she deserved. She is the biggest part of his success story.

The business was downsized in 2008 to a workable level for the work available. He trimmed the number of employees from 18 to 4 but those 4 were the very best employees. William K. Olson & Associates has worked through the last six years at a decent level doing 200 to 300 jobs per year. Bill remembered calling in 2012, the 300 plus names on his 2006 contractor list—only 20 out of 300 still appeared to be in business. Due to their ground breaking design of homes and reasonable prices they are one of the few residential design firms left standing. Bill's part in 2014 is now more of advisor and problem solver.

Bill structured a fair buyout in 2012 that will end in 2020. In the meantime, this business has grown by 20% each of the last two years. In all the years since 2000, this company has gained 95% of their work from referrals from contractors and the "Olson Plans" website.

Bill is basically fully retired in Florida. Two years ago, he decided instead of doing pencil sketches of people and landscapes he would try painting. He had always feared doing this because of the vast knowledge and timing that is required. He took a three hour, once-per-week, water coloring course class in January, 2013. He painted what the teacher called a keeper. He was hooked. He felt like he was back in fifth grade getting the attention he was starved of when he was a child. Today Bill does mostly keepers once a week. It has become expanded enhancement of an already idyllic life. He feels he was fortunate that he never gave up and that he received many helping hands along the way.

Bill's curiosity is greater today than it has ever been. He says it is a fantastic society and country we live in that allows anyone with the will and courage to fail again and again to finally succeed. Thanks to free market capitalism Bill was able to achieve The American Dream.

Dave Storrs, MD

I've known Dr. Storrs for many years playing golf and tennis with him at our club, Heritage Palms Golf and Country Club. During the last year Dave and his wife moved to Pelican Preserve Country Club which is only a couple miles away. Dave has a very interesting story of achievement, from humble beginnings and a learning disability, to graduating near the top in his class in medical school and becoming a noted neurosurgeon. I was surprised at the difficulties he had to overcome and how hard he worked to finally become a physician. He is also one of the nicest men I know. Dave has certainly achieved The American Dream.

Dave was born the only child of Sheldon W. and Mary Evelyn Storrs on August 13, 1937 in Binghamton, New York. Binghamton is a small community located in the southern tier of New York State close to the Pennsylvania border. The city grew along the confluence of the Chenango and Susquehanna rivers. The Susquehanna valley is surrounded by the rolling foothills of the Catskill Mountains. The city of Binghamton along with the villages of Endicott and Johnson City were collectively known as the Triple cities. These three communities were at one time primarily manufacturing communities.

The community was the home of IBM, the Endicott Johnson shoe factories, Ansco film industry, and the Singer Link Corporation, the developer of the first aircraft simulators. These companies were major employers in the area as Dave was growing up, but all have subsequently left New York State and its unfriendly business climate, a problem not unique to the Binghamton area, but one that has destroyed many of the cities of upstate New York. Dave says it's interesting that the healthcare industry is now the major employer in many of the upstate cites in New York and it has become a State of service providers.

Dave's parents were born and raised in two significantly different parts of the country. His father was born and raised in the city of Binghamton. Sheldon was the only child in a long history of one son Storrs' families. He was raised during the depression days of the late 1920s and 1930s with a major part of his adult life occurring in World War II and the Korean era. He was educated in the city school system, graduated from high school and continued with technical training in auto and diesel mechanical engineering. He worked in many positions throughout his life but mainly in the automotive sales and service industry.

Unfortunately his father developed severe diabetes shortly after Dave was born and had a long and difficult battle with the disease. As difficult as his health was, Dave never heard his father complain, he went to work every day, and did his job the best he could. Due to complications of his disease, his father died at the early age of 57.

Although their father and son relationship was tempered by his illness his influence on Dave's early life was significant. Sheldon was very mechanically inclined and they always had a home shop filled with all sorts of tools. Sheldon could repair just about anything that was repairable and he was an accomplished wood worker. He taught Dave how to use most of the tools and spent time with him working on a number of different projects.

Dave says their most memorable project was a soap box racer. Dave later had dreams of building and racing a "real soap box derby car" and going to Akron, Ohio racing for the finals. Unfortunately the time was never right.

The mechanical inclination he inherited from his father along with the skills he taught Dave were invaluable in achieving his lifetime goals including hisoccupation as a surgeon and his avocation, a love of working with wood.

Dave's mother's early life started from a very different background. She was born in Godfrey, Ontario on a farm, the only girl among five older brothers. She learned early to fend for herself. She was a lifelong learner, with her early education in a one room schoolhouse. Her dedication to her education required her to finish high school in a town 30 miles from their farm. The 30 miles in today's time doesn't seem significant however in the early 1900s her only transportation was by horse or horse and buggy. Therefore, her education required her to move to the town of Sydenham, Ontario where the high school was located. She was required to live there in a boarding home, away from her family in order to complete the last three years of her high school education.

From high school she continued her education attending "normal school." Normal school was in preparation for a teaching certificate which she achieved and eventually returned to her one room schoolhouse to teach for approximately two years. She then moved to Toronto to pursue a career in nursing at the Toronto School of Nursing. Unfortunately in her first year, she contracted tuberculosis and required extensive spine surgery. There was no antibiotic treatment for tuberculosis at that time, and her recovery was a slow arduous process which quarantined her in a sanitarium for approximately one year.

When she was considered no longer communicable, she was released to continue her treatment of the time which was "rest in a warm and sunny climate." As part of the treatment she moved to Pasadena, California to live for two years with an older brother and his wife. While in Pasadena, she applied for and received her naturalization papers and became a US citizen. Upon what appeared to be her recovery, (she had a recurrence of her TB at the age of 59), she moved back to the East Coast and went to live with her younger brother who was a young physician, just starting his practice in Binghamton, New York. It was there she met Dave's father and eventually married.

Both his parents were older by the time they married in their 30s and his birth was just a year after they began their lives together. His most early recollection of those the days of the early1940s reflected the times of war. As he looks back to those early years, ages four to seven, the events of the time were all colored by World War II and they still remain vivid in his memory. Gas and food ration stamps were needed for everything and air raids, street sirens, gas masks, street wardens and windows flying gold stars for those families who had lost a loved one in the War were common.

His early schooling was colored as well by the War. His classroom art depicted drawings of swastikas, the rising Japanese sun, airplanes dropping bombs, tanks, jeeps and guns. His play time was filled with war games, carrying guns and playing a game of commandos.

He was taught to be leery of the Germans and Japanese and to be vigilant for attacks from the sky and sea. Going to the movies was not only about cowboy and Indian flicks, but there was the Movie Tone News, graphically documenting the dead and dying, the bombed buildings and the horror of the holocaust. It seemed to Dave that those early life experiences were entirely consumed by the War.

On the more positive side, he recalls helping with the war effort, collecting newspapers, scrap metal, old clothing and flattening tin cans. Each week in school they would prepare Red Cross boxes with toothpaste, pencils, paper and candy for the troops. Everybody was involved in the war effort, everyone was supportive, there were no antiwar or anti-draft demonstrations that he could recall. Throughout those years his family remained intact, as his dad was deferred, as the only surviving member of the family name.

Following World War II, the family moved about thirty miles north from Binghamton, New York to a small town, Whitney Point, New York. Their new home was modest at best, built in the late 1800s, but it did have most of the modern conveniences of the day. It was the first home his parents considered their own as they had always lived with Dave's paternal grandmother. She was a quiet woman who loved to read, play the piano and was a major care-giver in their home while he was growing up. She was there to help, sometimes to his mother's consternation, as both his parents worked full time jobs.

One thing he recalls was his grandmother urging him to take piano lessons, as she had taught piano in her younger years. He has often regretted not taking her advice; however, he did learn to play the trumpet. He started taking lessons with a horn that his father played in fifth grade. He continued to play throughout his high school and early college years. Even though he was fairly accomplished in music, he had to give it up in college because of his study and academic requirements. He says he regrets that decision now, however, at the time, he believes it was the correct one.

In the transition between the move from Binghamton to Whitney Point, he spent approximately one year living with his aunt and uncle, remaining in Binghamton so that he could complete his fifth grade education in the

Binghamton school system. The opportunity to live with his uncle, a medical internist was an experience that introduced him to the life of a physician and opened a new appreciation for good music, the arts and what became a long time passion of his, skiing. His uncle was an avid skier and he often took Dave to the Adirondacks or the Catskills on skiing trips. His uncle became a second dad to him. He had a significant impact on Dave's life with many wonderful memories; many of which influenced his early lifetime decisions.

After moving to Whitney Point, Dave found that his new home was located on the banks of the Tioughnioga River. In his early pre-teen years, he spent much of his spare time after school, as well as his summers, in or around the river. His heroes were Tom Sawyer and Huckleberry Finn of Mark Twain fame. Swimming, fishing and building rafts were memories of those times. Dreams of exploring the rivers and exotic places filled his young teenage fantasies. Little did he know that those early experiences would lead to a lifetime avocation of sailing. His sailing adventures included exploring the waters of the rivers and lakes of New York State, the Great Lakes, the St. Lawrence River and the entire Atlantic coastline. He also sailed the Caribbean and culminating, along with his wife Gretta, in a recent circumnavigation, of the navigable waters of the eastern half of the country, known as the "great loop."

As he approached his teen years his priorities begin to change. There were girls, work, sports and junior high school. Initially, however, academics were not high on his list of priorities. He struggled in his new school, especially with math and English. Spelling was his downfall. He didn't seem to have problems in reading, comprehending or even memorizing but spelling was an enigma and math was truly frustrating. He says he knew how to do the math problems, but he never seemed to get the correct answer. It was especially discouraging when his best friend in high school was a math whiz (he later became an actuary), and Dave felt that he was a real dunce.

Later in his high school years, he found and learned to use a slide rule his father had used in his engineering courses. With the slide rule he was finally able to get some right answers. With practice he taught himself to do some of the more complicated algebraic formulas, log calculations and even simple calculus. This was amazing to him, because without this instrument he could not even do the simplest math by longhand.

It was not until he took a course in educational psychology in college, that he learned a new concept in learning disabilities, namely the dyslexia's. Dave believes he fits the criteria for a form of dyscalculia. Dyscalculia is the dyslexic form of difficulty with calculations. It seems to be a problem with the brains ability to manipulate numerical symbols and not infrequently presents itself with difficulty in numerical sequencing. Sequencing also appears to play a part in individuals who have difficulty with verbal language and especially in spelling. He still has difficulty getting the right sequence of numbers. He has to be especially careful with telephone numbers and credit card numbers, as he frequently copies them out of sequence or backwards.

In today's educational programs, with school psychologists and testing, he thinks his learning disability would have been identified and just maybe have lessened some the frustration of those early years. It's interesting that in today's classroom the use of a calculator is allowed in most math classes and spell-check in writing. With those two gadgets, he says he might have been a genius!

Sports were a major consumption of his time in junior

and senior high school. One of the benefits of the small central school was that they actually needed bodies to be members of the teams. He never considered himself a great athlete but good enough to play and enjoy baseball, basketball and football. He says he never excelled in any one sport, but he was good enough to achieve some All-Star status in baseball and basketball. There were many other memories of the high school years, girlfriends, school dances, parties in the boondocks and running for class office.

There is one experience, however, that stands out as a pivot point in his educational and life choices. This was a simple aptitude test that he took in eighth or ninth grade. He was exploring different career choices and on that aptitude test he scored high in mechanical skills and very low in academic or college required skills. He remembers his teacher suggesting that he consider things such as the building industry, carpentry, plumbing or some mechanical field. There were no recommendations for college and clearly none for medicine.

That summer he worked helping build chicken coops. After that experience, he recalls telling his mother that he wasn't so sure he liked construction because it was too much like "real work." When he returned to school in the fall, he took his first science course and was immediately excited with the study of anatomy and physiology. He remembers dissecting a frog in class and fantasized about being a surgeon. The field of biological science was intriguing to him. With his background of being exposed to the medical field through his uncle and then his mother, who was working at that time with a surgeon in Binghamton, he began to consider medicine as a career choice.

From that point on he excelled in advanced biology, chemistry and physics (as long as he could use his trusty slide rule). His interest in medicine began to seriously take hold. He says he will never forget the response from his parents and especially his mother, when he announced his intention to go to college and become a doctor. She was a bit skeptical to say the least, as she was fully aware of his mediocre grades at that time. Although she was excited with his intent to go to college and pursue a course in premed she remained pragmatic in her encouragement "to find a spot in the medical field than he could achieve."In retrospect, he realizes she was trying to protect him from failure.

Dave was accepted to St. Lawrence University, a small liberal arts school located in the north country of New York State. Besides providing an excellent education, a student faculty ratio of 12:1, St. Lawrence was also known for its winter sports programs. The idea of a small, good quality school that had its own ski area seemed like the right fit for Dave. On the day his parents dropped him off at the freshman dorm at St. Lawrence University, his mother's last words, as they were saying goodbye were "Don't be too disappointed, David, if you don't make it to medical school—there are many other things that you can do besides medicine."

His first semester in college was a struggle. He was placed in special courses for English and math because his high school experience left him far short of the skills needed to compete at the college level. For instance, he had never written a paper and didn't really understand how to use the library. It was clear he had a lot of catching up to do.

He never lost sight of his goal and worked hard. He discovered and conquered probably the most important requirement for achieving his academic goals and that was developing a method of study. Even though he struggled initially, he was able to overcome his weaknesses and use his strengths of memory and communication skills to make major gains in his academic pursuits during that first semester. To his mother's surprise and ecstatic delight, he made the Dean's List the second semester of his freshman year and continued on the Dean's List throughout his college career. He went on to graduate in the top 10% of his class with departmental honors in both biology and chemistry.

During those college years, his dad's diabetes took more and more of a toll on his life. He had difficulty maintaining steady work because of his illness. Dave's mother became the sole breadwinner and they lived on her secretary's salary. His parents had saved for some of his education and provided everything that they could. He was able to get some scholarship help which initially was based on need, but later was based on scholarship. During the last two and a half years of his college education, he supported himself by working for both room and board as well as his books. He worked a number of different jobs—construction in the summer and during the school year he held the position of house manager at his fraternity house which covered the cost of his meals. At the same time, he worked at O'Leary's Funeral Home driving the ambulance or hearse. Dave says it was the same vehicle, but it depended whether the occupant was alive or dead as to what it was called. Dave considered this the final phase of medical care. He also helped with funerals and in the evening he acted as the answering service for the funeral home. He was paid $.25 per hour for babysitting the phone. With the monies he earned from his work in the funeral home and his babysitting the phone, he was able to finance the majority of his last two years at the university. He graduated from St. Laurence University in 1959, in three and a half years and was accepted into the freshman class at Upstate Medical Center in Syracuse. He had met his first goal!

Now it was time to set some new goals. Following his early graduation from St. Lawrence University, he worked at a number of jobs including drug store clerk, substitute teacher, garbage man and during the summer he returned to road construction. He needed to bank as much money as he could for his upcoming medical school tuition. He felt that he was now on his own even though he knew his parents would help as best they could. He felt however, that they had sacrificed enough and it was time for him to be responsible for his own future.

During the six-month period between completing his studies at St. Lawrence University and starting his freshman year at Upstate Medical Center, a romantic relationship with a high school girlfriend, which had been sort of on and off and hit and miss during his college years, blossomed to a point of discussing marriage. Dave says that, in retrospect, it was naïve on their parts to think that they could start a life together under what would become some very difficult conditions. Their parents were less than enthusiastic and his mother voiced her concerns on a number of occasions. A number of her concerns relative to their marriage became very prophetic.

Despite their parent's angst, they were married two weeks before starting his freshman year at Syracuse. With some of the money that he had earned during the summer, they bought a very used mobile home measuring 32 feet long and 8 feet wide. With their trailer in tow and a 1948 Willys car his parents had given them, along with a lot of questions, they started their life together.

His new bride had just finished her nursing degree, graduating at the top of her class. She had no trouble finding an assistant head nurse position at the University

Hospital. She became the primary breadwinner that first year. Dave's time was spent dealing with a huge load of academics that first year. Anatomy, embryology, histology physiology and biochemistry made up the first semester curriculum. Luckily he was well prepared by undergraduate studies at St. Lawrence and academically thrived that first year. He found the key to surviving, however, was to keep up with the work on a day to-day basis. One could not get behind that first year. A case in point was one of the individuals that flunked out that first year was one who entered the class with one of the highest grade point averages of the freshman class. He bragged that he "never had to open a book."

Even though Dave's class work was doing well, their marriage began to struggle. It was clear they spent so much time apart with work and school there was very little time to work on their marriage. There was a clear lack of understanding on each of their parts as to the stresses each faced on a day-to-day basis.

Money was always an issue; the cost of the next semester's tuition, paying the mortgage and bills, purchasing books and materials for school left little to spend on themselves. He found a job his freshman year working for the health department. It helped a bit with the finances but took even more time away from their marriage. Any time they had to spend together was time he felt he should be studying. He soon recognized the wisdom and the reality of some of his mother's prophesy.

He finished his first year of medical school with a straight "A" average. Based on his academic achievement, he was awarded a small scholarship and a fairly significant book allowance.

During the summer he moved back home with his parents to return working construction, leaving his wife in Syracuse working at the University hospital. Being away for a good part of the summer, their marriage took another hit, but somehow they seemed to survive. When the summer break was over and he was about ready to return to the school, Dave and his wife, along with her sister and husband, decided to take a trip to New York City. They wanted to take in a Yankee's game, stay overnight and enjoy a day in the city. This was their first vacation even though it lasted only two days.

Upon their return from their vacation in New York, they were met with devastating news. Their clothes, wedding gifts, the entire contents of the trailer and all of Dave's books were completely destroyed by fire. They were both devastated. They had one week to find a place to live. Luckily they had insurance to cover the loss of their trailer and $500 to replace their clothes, buy some furniture and outfit an apartment. It wasn't much but it was a start. Their family and friends chipped in to help and they finally got settled.

Dave had just started back for the second year of medical school just in time for their 12 year-old car to blow its transmission. Dave said, it seemed like they were living under a black cloud.

The second year of medical school was equally time consuming, although there were more classes that reflected clinically-oriented material, so he hadthe "feeling" that he was on track to finally becoming a physician. He continued to work part-time, now working in the laboratory for a small Catholic hospital in Syracuse. It was a night job that required him to stay overnight four days a week, which along with his study requirements continued to put a major strain on their marriage. He finished his second year and academically he was doing well. He returned that summer to again live with his parents and work construction.

Upon starting his third year of medical school, his wife decided to quit her job at the hospital and eventually went to work as an industrial nurse. She was tired of working swing shift, which was required of her at the hospital, and her new job was a steady single evening shift. With her job and his, they were now apart the majority of the week. Their marriage drifted further apart. There was talk of separation and divorce and "going their own way."They really struggled that year.

Their marriage soon took an abrupt change, with his wife's announcement that she was pregnant. Their first born son, Braden, arrived in October of his senior year. Dave was totally unprepared for parenthood. Even though he now had a family, his study and work schedule didn't change and their marriage remained rocky. Being absent from home so much, he lost out on one of the most significant joys of fatherhood, that time spent bonding with his newborn son. He was an absent father. Despite the trials and tribulations, he finished medical school graduating cum laude with academic honors and second in his class. He was also the recipient of the prestigious Senior Honors Thesis Award for original medical research.

At his graduation in 1963, he was surrounded by all those who supported and encouraged him, his wife and newborn son, who had stuck by his side despite the hardships of those four years, his mother and father, along with his close aunt and physician uncle and many friends who came to honor his achievement. Dave says he will never forget his mother's words after he received his diploma. She said, "I couldn't be more proud and I never thought I would see the day that I raised a Doctor." He had achieved his goal becoming a physician, but not without considerable cost to their marriage.

The euphoria of accomplishment was soon replaced

with the reality of starting a new challenge. He was about to start his internship. Many of his classmates left Syracuse to train at other medical centers around the country. Dave elected to stay in Syracuse, basically because he had a family and lacked the funds to pack up and move. His internship was his first job as a physician. It was not an easy one. He worked every day, except for one day every other weekend. He worked every other night and received a one week vacation. He was paid a salary of $3,000 a year. The year of internship was a chance to learn by doing, but it was also seen as a sort of rite of passage. Dave says the work requirements were arcane and dangerous to patient care. Fortunately those working conditions have been changed in most states to protect not only the interns and residents health but also the patients.

With his work schedule, constant fatigue and the need to continue his studies and even despite having a family, and his wife's personal relationship began to deteriorate even further. They drifted farther apart, separated for a while and most significantly, he lost almost all contact with his new son. In retrospect, those early years of lost time and early bonding with his son continued to haunt the relationship between father and son for a period way too long.

He finished his year of internship in the spring of 1964. It was July, 1964 that the Vietnam conflict began to expand. He was now eligible for the draft, having been deferred for the past eight years of his education. His next decision was to decide his specialty choice. He was pretty certain he wanted to be a surgeon as he was good with his hands and had developed some surgical technique as an intern. However, that decision was abruptly put on hold, because he received his draft notice shortly after he completed his internship.

He reported to San Antonio, Texas in August, 1964 and was sworn into the U.S. Army as a captain in the Army Medical Corps. He was sworn in on the day the Gulf of Tonkin Resolution was proposed. Upon completing his basic training in San Antonio, he received orders to report for duty at Fort Monroe, Virginia. He moved his family and he was now a practicing family physician. He loved it. He had hoped to complete his entire military obligation at Fort Monroe. For the first time in their new army life they were living "high on the hog" with a living wage and really enjoying life together for the first time in their married life. They finally had time together and he had time to start bonding with his son.

Dave thoroughly enjoyed his role as family practice physician. However, their good life lasted only three months. After three months, Dave received new orders to report to Fort Benning, Georgia as a battalion surgeon for the Eighth Air Calvary Division, which was getting ready to deploy to the Far East. This news was devastating for them although not totally unexpected.

As a result of a serendipitous relationship with a Red Cross volunteer nurse who worked with Dave in the hospital, Dave was reassigned to a medical attachment in Fort Gulick in the Panama Canal Zone. It just so happened that the Red Cross nurse volunteer was the wife of a Major General who was also a doctor. He was the commander of the U.S. Army Medical Corps of the United States. With their help, he was spared transfer to a combat unit which did end up in Vietnam and suffered some very significant losses in the early part of the of the Vietnam conflict. His assignment to Panama kept him out of a combat zone, but again separated him from his family for the remainder of his service obligation.

His experience in the military, as a general medical officer, was a positive one. He was not only able to learn and practice the art of medicine, but by virtue of his date of rank was placed in the number of leadership positions. He served as the senior medical officer for the entire Fort and assigned as the public health officer for the Atlantic Command. He became proficient in tropical diseases and served in a support role for the Jungle Warfare Center. As he was completing his tour in Panama, he was lucky enough to be assigned to a search and rescue unit as the chief medical officer covering the Central and South America Emergency Landing Zone for the Gemini Space Program. Their mission was based out of Lima, Peru.

He enjoyed the military despite being separated from his family. As his time was just about up, he was offered a position in the Regular Army, a residency program and a promise for an increase in rank. He gave the proposal a great deal of consideration, as the position was an excellent one and difficult to come by. The pay was good and the support services provided for the military officer were excellent. However, he was uneasy about another overseas assignment and decided to leave the military and return to Syracuse where he also had a position waiting for him in an excellent neurosurgical residency program.

Upon separation from the military and returning to Syracuse, he signed onto a five year program, with a year of general surgery, two years as a research fellow for the National Institutes of Health, doing original neurophysiological research and three years of clinical neurosurgical training. He also signed on for low pay, long hours and the continuing struggle of matching his work with the obligations of a marriage and family.

His first year back as a general surgery resident, allowed him to rotate through a number of subspecialties of surgery. He was assigned three months on orthopedics, plastic surgery, urology and G.I. surgery. That year provided a time to hone some of his general surgical skills, as well as learn the basics about the many complicating problems that he would be required to manage as a function of taking care of complicated neurosurgical cases.

During this first year back, Dave had some time to reconnect with his family. Being away for essentially two years took its toll on their marriage relationship, which was rocky to begin with. It was also tough to return as a father to a son who hardly knew him. As a family they tried to start over. They were able to find a small apartment to live in for the first year. During his next two years in the lab, he was able to do some moonlighting as an examining physician for the local recruiting station. Along with this recruiting income, his salary as a fellow from the National Institutes of Health, his wife's income and considerable help from the G.I. Bill, they were able to buy a small three bedroom home. The G.I. bill with its educational benefits, medical care and G.I. mortgage was a real-life changer for them.

Even though they had a new home they continued to struggle financially, a function of low wages and high student debt. However, the two years in the lab without night call or clinical duties allowed Dave the time to get back to being a husband and father. Both he and his wife wanted to expand their family, as their son was approaching four years old. Dave had grown up as an only child and he felt it was important for his son to have a brother or sister, something that he never had and truly missed. It seemed like there was no problem with his son's conception, but they were unable to conceive again despite an extensive fertility workup. They elected to adopt and were chosen to receive a beautiful newborn baby girl. She was born in the small women's hospital where Dave had worked as a medical student.

With his time in the lab, no night calls, a livable wage, a new daughter and an always busy young son, it seemed for the first time in their lives that they approached some sort of normality. Life outside of their family, however, was hardly normal. It was a time of civil unrest with the Vietnam War protests, civil rights movement, riots in the streets, assassinations of John and Robert Kennedy and Dr. King and the hippie lifestyle of drugs and rock 'n roll.

As Dave looks back at those years, much of it seems just a blur. He missed a lot during those days being cloistered away in the hospital. His two years as a fellow with the National Institutes of Health was interesting but not very productive. He worked on a couple of different projects, wrote papers and presented his work at national meetings. Although the research was stimulating, he was never really very satisfied. One thing he learned about research is that if you try to find the answer to a question using the scientific method, the research always seems to raise more questions than it answers. He found the research to be interesting but frustrating.

With his two years in the lab at an end, he returned to the grind of the clinical residency. He was now 32 years of age, back working 12 to 16 hours per day, with night call every two to three nights and a wage that was below the poverty level. The next three years were difficult, but he was learning the skills of his chosen profession and the realization that he only had three more years to reach his goal. It was enough to make the grind tolerable. He finished his residency in July, 1972, at the age of 35 and16 years after he made his high school decision to enter the field of medicine. He was now a board qualified neurosurgeon but he needed to complete two more years of practice before he could sit for his final board exams. He was finally Board Certified in Neurosurgery in 1974.

Upon completion of his residency, he was faced with another major decision in his career path. He had always thought and planned to stay in an academic position. He enjoyed teaching and he enjoyed the academic environment. The residency program that he had just completed was geared towards producing academic neurosurgeons.

Dave explored several positions across the country, but nothing felt like the right fit.It was not until he had a long talk with one of his mentors and good friend that he began to seriously look at other opportunities in private practice. It was an informal chat over a beer, after a day in the OR, that seemed to put things in perspective for him. His friend candidly told him "David, you will make a much better surgeon than a researcher. You have all the skills of a good surgeon." Dave also felt that he was a better doctor than a laboratory scientist. With his mind made up, he immediately started to look at private practice positions.

Making a decision to enter private practice required some careful planning. To develop a neurosurgical practice, especially one that he envisioned as a university model, had a lot of moving parts. First, he needed to find a compatible partner, one who was established in the community and who was willing to buy into his vision for the future of the practice.

Second, he needed a community large enough to support another neurosurgeon as well as provide the numbers of cases and the types of surgery to allow him to maintain the skill level to deal with complex neurosurgical procedures.

Third, he needed a hospital willing to invest in his vision for a high quality neuroscience program. Neurosciences is not just neurosurgery, but rather it includes a host of support services required to take care of all of the needs of the neurologic injured, such as neurology, rehabilitation medicine, neuro-radiology and neuropathology, to list just a few.

Fourth, he needed an institution that would be willing to provide a dedicated OR staff, ICU and floor nurses. Quality, dedicated nursing care was vital to the success of neurologic patient care. Also required was an institution that would invest in developing neuroradiology staff, the advancing technology including CT, MRI and all of the advanced neuro-diagnostic equipment. A neurosurgical and neuroscience program, as he envisioned it, was a major community investment.

Lastly, he needed a good general medical community with excellence in consultants and support staff. Cardiology, infectious disease, pulmonology, orthopedic, general and vascular surgery was all needed to care and support the neurosurgical patient.

He was also looking to establish a practice tied closely to a major medical center and preferably one that had a teaching or research program. He wanted to maintain his keen interest in teaching. Interestingly enough, he was presented with an offer from a neurosurgeon, Dr. Paul DeLuca, who was in solo practice in Binghamton, New York. Binghamton was his birthplace. After a number of visits with Paul and the medical community leaders, he was surprised to find the community in his own backyard that seemed to meet most of his criteria.

Binghamton and the surrounding villages had four hospitals that serviced a community of approximately 250,000. The primary hospital for the practice, Wilson Memorial, was located in Johnson City, New York, serviced primarily by Dr. DeLuca, and had close to 500 beds. It was an aging, but adequate facility; a teaching hospital with a medical, surgical and primary care residency program. Most significantly it was led by a very enthusiastic hospital administrator who seemed to buy into Dave's vision of a modern university style neurosurgery program. He looked at a number of other practice opportunities that offered more monetarily but he was convinced that he had found the community that best fit his future. Besides it was in located in his own backyard.

He entered into practice on July 1, 1972 joining Dr. DeLuca as a member of Paul DeLuca M.D. PC. His first six months of practice was a rude awakening. As a resident in training you are immune from hospital politics, budgets, community referral patterns and hospital rivalry. One of the most discouraging problems that he faced was a real lack of expertise at all levels of the hospital system as to the needs and requirements for the care of critical neuro-surgical patients. He found the nursing staff enthusiastic, but ill-prepared and literally scared of the complex neu-rosurgery patient. They had not been involved, nor had they seen the serious postoperative neurosurgical patient. Almost all of these cases had been previously referred out of town. He also found the ER staff, the ambulance crews and first responders woefully ill-prepared to take care of neurosurgical trauma and neurosurgical emergencies.

The medical community was divided by four different hospital affiliations and loyalties. Hospital administrators and their physician leaders oftentimes seemed to put pa-tient care secondary to maintaining their hospital loyalty. There was no conceivable way to provide the type of ex-cellence envisioned in neurosurgical care in four separate hospitals. It was abundantly clear that he had a lot of work to do to change the community perspective as to quality neurosurgical care if the was going to make the practice work as he had envisioned. The alternative was not to "rock the boat" and to practice medicine "as we always have," as he was scolded by one of the attending physicians shortly after arriving in Binghamton. It was something that he was not about to do. Although the practice environment was not ideal, he was soon personally overwhelmed with patients as their practice boomed. It was not more than one year into practice that he recognized the need to make some very major changes.

The first was to hire a third man to the group. Dave and his partner interviewed a number of candidates, but it was not until he met with a previous resident colleague of his from Syracuse that he was happy to offer a position. Dr. William Teller was a New York City boy who was his resident equal during his training program at Syracuse. They finished together. He took a position in California at the same time that Dave went to Binghamton. He was unhappy with his relationship amongst the partners and Paul and Dave needed some help. Bill was a bright and accomplished surgeon who shared Dave's dream.

Bill joined their group in1975. With a new member in the group, the three of them started making some very major business decisions. They moved their practice to a hospital site at the Wilson Memorial Hospital, and developed a new physician limited liability corporation, Southern Tier New York Neurosurgical Group. They started planning for their own office building which they eventually built adjacent to Wilson Memorial Hospital in Johnson City, New York. Parallel to the changes that they were making to their personnel practice environment, it was clear they needed to make some major changes in their hospital workplace environment. As their practice grew and their loyalty to the Wilson Memorial Hospital was recognized, the hospital administration soon began to realize the financial gain from neurosurgery to the institution and with that their influence began to grow.

Dave decided early on that it was better to work within

the hospital administration staff rather than use the approach that most of physicians use, which was to demand things of the hospital administration by threatening "to take my patients" to a competing hospital. Working with the hospital administrative staff, they were able to make sizable gains including achieving a full-time dedicated neurosurgical OR and floor nursing staff. This was the first step in developing a neurosurgical center.

The group took on the task of educating the nurses. Their educational program, working with a grant from Binghamton University, took on a life of its own and they were soon enrolling nurses from all over the southern tier of New York State. Their educational programs led to the hospital's ability not only to improve their in house nursing quality, but they also were able to recruit top-notch, highly skilled nurses for the emergency room, ICU and neurosurgical floor care.

At the same time, they were developing their nursing staff they began a push to further upgrade the facility, especially the OR and ICU. Although they saw their needs as a priority, others in the hospital budgetary food chain saw it differently. It was clear that they needed to get involved in the politics of the institution. Dave started out as the chief of neurosurgery and working within the medical staff political structure, worked his way up to president of the medical staff and eventually was appointed to the Board of Directors of the Wilson Memorial Hospital and eventually United Health Services, a position he held for fourteen years.

As his political status grew so did his influence within the institution. They soon had the first-rate facilities at the Wilson Memorial site that Dave had envisioned. The hospital developed a new dedicated neurosurgical intensive care unit and a high-tech OR. Working with the radiology department, they developed a first rate neuroradiology group which included the area's first dedicated neuroradiologist and a working relationship with the radiologists from the Upstate Medical Center in Syracuse.

With the Wilson Hospital's reputation for excellence in neurosurgical care and the dedicated support services, the hospital was designated to receive one of the first CT scanners and MRI machines in upstate New York. Working together, the hospital and Southern Tier Neurosurgery became a Center of Excellence. As it appeared, they were on track to reach their goals of developing the neurosurgical program requirements as an institution; they still recognized there was still a lot of work to do in the general medical community. With the hospitals competing for a shrinking patient population, Dave found out early, just how difficult it was to convince hospital administrators, ambulance crews, ER personnel and referring physicians to buy into his concept. That concept was that to provide the best quality care for the neurosurgical patients they needed a single dedicated institution. This was especially difficult when that institution wasn't theirs.

Early on in his practice it was frustrating for Dave to see ambulance crews decide to take patients in need of neurosurgical care to an institution that had the best coffee and donuts in the emergency room rather than the institution that could offer the best care. He also noted that physicians in the community often times would consult with him as to their family members but avoided referring their patients to him for surgery because he didn't do the operations in "their hospital."

Dave felt it was important to become involved in the countywide medical society; hoping to develop community support for specialty care centers and the hospital consolidation of services. He worked through the ER and trauma committee, gaining enough support for some of his ideas that led to his election as president of the Broome County Medical Society. During his short leadership tenure, he worked to help promote major changes in the healthcare delivery system of the community.

The first change was to lend support to the consolidation efforts of the Wilson Memorial Hospital in Johnson City and the Ideal Hospital in Endicott, New York. These two institutions became the Wilson Memorial Regional Medical Center. They were now down to three hospitals in the community and a start to consolidating neurosurgical services. Consolidation, however, was driven more by finances than it was for consolidating services and improving quality care. The benefits of consolidation, however, soon became evident not only in the financial numbers but also in the improvement in services delivery and the quality of patient care.

The second major project that the County Medical Society contributed to during his tenure was to support the collaboration between the medical community, local hospitals, Binghamton University and the Upstate Medical Center in Syracuse in developing a new concept in medical school education, the Clinical Campus. The Clinical Campus was an experiment in the delivery of the clinical educational experience provided for medical students in their last two years of medical education. Medical students would receive their first two years of basic science at Syracuse, and the Clinical Campus would provide the resources for the clinical years utilizing a community hospital setting rather than the traditional academic hospital. The Clinical Campus would also provide an educational experience with a strong emphasis on family medicine. The concept of the Clinical Campus, although not new to the country was certainly a new and innovative program in New York State.

As the opportunity to become involved in the academic program was one of Dave's criteria for his career, he strongly supported the formation of the Clinical Campus. He worked on the initial board of directors and took on the position of Coordinator of Neuroscience, a position he held for the majority of his practice years. He worked his way up the ranks from Assistant Clinical Professor of Neurosurgery to Clinical Professor of Neurosurgery. He authored a number of publications, made presentations at national meetings and taught not only Neuroscience at the Clinical Campus but was frequently invited to teach Neuro Anatomy and Physiology at Binghamton University and Ithaca College. He enjoyed teaching and lectured frequently for nursing and primary care teaching programs.

Initially the program seemed to lack the enthusiasm and academic stimulus that he had hoped the program would provide to the medical community. There was also a general skepticism by the parent institution in Syracuse, New York that their community-based program could provide the "teaching environment" needed to support the third and fourth year students. This skepticism was reflected in underfunding of the program which led to the medical community, hospitals and physicians teachers to financially support much of the teaching program.

Interestingly, when the two groups of students, one from the main campus in Syracuse and the other from the Clinical Campus were compared regarding test scores, national board exams and residency positions attained there was no significant difference between the academic center and the community based program. Unfortunately, despite these results and even with the commitment of significant personal time invested in teaching, committee work and tutoring, Dave always had the feeling that they were accepted only as second best by the hierarchy of the University.

Over the 30 years of his practice, there were many changes in the delivery of healthcare in the community. There was the introduction of the government—the healthcare programs of Medicare and Medicaid. There was also Sen. Ted Kennedy's experiment in healthcare delivery in which very severe and stringent national and state controls were placed over hospital expansion, program development and equipment acquisitions.

Although many of the Kennedy inspired controls were regressive, there was one component to Kennedy's healthcare delivery system experiment that Dave thought was an important step in the right direction and that was the development of peer review organizations (PSRO's) designed to improve patient care and add quality control to the practice of medicine.

Kennedy's healthcare system controls died a slow but predictable death. The local health system's agency organizations, designed to give local input into the healthcare delivery spending, soon became entangled in bureaucratic regulations and local politics. Although the idea of providing local input in the health planning of the community was a noble idea, the bureaucratic controls applied by the federal and state government regarding the advancement of new medical technology and the expansion of new and innovative services in Dave's mind became an obstruction and detriment to the care of their patients.

The PSRO (peer review) was slow to be endorsed by the medical community; however, as a member of the Board of the organization, he saw the beginnings of real local quality care improvement. Unfortunately, when the initial funding dried up, the program just died.

Dave also lived through the development and decline of the HMO or Health Maintenance Organization. The HMO was an attempt at cost control by emphasizing wellness, primary care medicine and the development hospital systems that could provide a package of health care products. It was the Wal-Mart concept, of one stop shopping for medical care. The HMOs depended upon large groups of patients and physician providers to fund and support their insurance based program.

Many of the larger hospitals saw this as a chance for major expansion. Hospitals began to compete for and acquire smaller hospitals and to developing contract transfer agreements with feeder hospitals so as to expand their system patient base. The hospital systems also began buying medical practices and forming large hospital based group practices. The need for these newly formed hospital systems was to be able to deliver to the insurance company a complete package of services that could be marketed as cradle to grave care. In order for these large hospital systems to compete for the HMO insurance contracts they not only needed to have a large patient and physician base but they had to provide cost effective care.

This led to further consolidation of hospital services in the community with the joining together of the Binghamton General Hospital and the Wilson Regional Medical Center to form a new entity called United HealthServices(UHS). They were now down to two hospitals, the new entity UHS and a well-financed Catholic institution, Our Lady of Lourdes. Further attempts to join the two remaining hospitals into a single institution failed.

With rapidly changing reimbursement imposed by the HMO insurance market, there was a dramatic change in the health care delivery systems. There was a rapid rise in outpatient diagnostics, ambulatory surgery and rehab services. The push to move some of the traditional hospital based services to the outpatient setting was dramatic and led the hospitals to take on a new mission and redesign themselves as high tech acute care institutions. It was recognized by the HMOs that cost control had to be accompanied by quality control. The HMOs attempted to provide a quality control program based on the same principles of the earlier PSRO program.

The peer review, quality control system emphasized best medical practice protocols, case reviews and physician quality profiles, or report cards. Physicians, for the first time were being held to some degree accountable for their patient care based on active and ongoing peer review. It reinforced the concept that quality care was a major factor in cost control. Unfortunately the HMO's came under heavy attack by the public and politicians, as the HMO's were perceived as limiting care and physician choice, in the name of cost control. There was never an enthusiastic acceptance by the patient or physician community, given the HMO's bureaucratic controls over hospital and physician choice, as well as the often delayed authorization for diagnostic procedures and surgery.

The original HMO concept slowly morphed into essentially an insurance company controlled, cost control product. The external peer review and quality care programs were replaced by in-hospital quality care programs. Excluded from any peer review or quality care programs are a large number of physicians, PAs, nurse practitioners who practice outside the hospitals control. Also excluded are the privately owned outpatient diagnostic and surgery centers. Dave says that there needs to be an all-inclusive quality review process. Quality care is not only best practice, but is also cost effective care.

Over the thirty years of his practice, there have been many dramatic and exciting changes in the delivery of health care in their community. With hospital consolidation of services and the development of specialty programs, their hospitals have become centers of excellence. The improvement in the pre-hospital emergency services, emergency room, trauma, acute cardiac and stroke, as well as neurosurgical care, has saved countless lives.

Unfortunately there is also significant unnecessary and poor quality care being delivered by a few poorly educated, minimally trained and unscrupulous practitioners. It is well documented that there is significant over use of diagnostics studies, drugs and unnecessary surgery throughout the medical care spectrum. Dave believes the medical care delivery system still lacks a significant external quality control program that is based first and foremost on a system that emphasizes best practice quality care. If you provide best practice quality care then cost containment will follow.

Our country has now entered a new era in the delivery of medical care with the advent of "Obamacare."It's been clear in his mind, since the beginning of the Obamacare discussions, that the primary emphasis of the federal government's new program is based on cost control not quality control. It is a new insurance plan, not a health delivery plan. As he has watched it unfold, he foresees a plan so expensive that by its very nature it becomes a plan for rationing care not providing care. Who is going to be able to afford the needed care with an insurance plan that requires a $3,000 to $5,000 deductible?

Dave thinks it's too early to tell exactly what's going to happen to Obamacare, but if history tells us anything, it's pretty evident from the failure of the programs in the past that when the government gets involved in the health-care delivery system, the costs become so inflated that the program will follow the plans of all the socialized countries, one that becomes hamstrung by cost control rather than quality control. He hopes that type of system will ultimately be rejected by the American people.

As his career wound down, many of those early ideals and goals he set for himself have been met. Their medical practice, starting with two neurosurgeons and two secretaries, grew to a high of five neurosurgeons and 20 plus secretaries, typists, bookkeepers, form and request managers. The increase in support staff alone tells the story of the modern day practice. Malpractice insurance rates went from $3,000 a year to a high during his practice time of $48,000 per year and that was with only one bogus suit.

And his partners achieved the consolidation of neurosurgery, a university center equivalent neurosurgical program and a high tech training ground for a university-based teaching program. Best of all, his partner, Dr. William Teller, became his best friend, and without his tireless effort and support, many of those initial goals would never have been met. Neurosurgery is a tough demanding business—a young man's profession. At the age of 58, Dave felt it was time for him to retire from active surgical practice. He thinks the concept of "burnout" applies to many of the neurosurgeons he has met across the country, especially those who worked outside the university resident programs and were singularly responsible for night call, covering the emergency room 24 hours a day while still trying to carry out a large surgical practice. Couple working sixty to eighty hours a week with trying to maintain a marriage and family life left little downtime.

Dave was ready for some downtime, but he was not ready to just walk away from his career. After two failed marriages, a couple of years sailing in the Caribbean and the Atlantic seaboard, he was passionate about sailing. He found his present wife and soul mate, Gretta, and was eager to restart his life, reconnect with his family and return to a productive professional career.

He was not ready, however, to return to the rigors of his previous practice. His lifelong interest in quality medical care, coupled with his extensive experience in neurosurgery, neuroscience and pain management led him to form "D.G.S. Consulting" a peer review, quality assurance, second opinion and independent medical evaluation company. D.G.S. Consulting has been very successful, doing work for many independent hospitals, the New York State Professional Office of Conduct and Review, New York State Attorney General's Office, the New York State Medical Liability Insurance Office of Peer Review and numerous second opinions for medical legal cases all over New York State and the country. Although he misses the hands-on surgical experience, he still enjoys the opportunity to evaluate patients, answer some of their questions and hopefully offer some meaningful advice.

As his career came to a close, he received many letters of appreciation, commendation and plaques for service from his peers and professional hospital colleges, but the most rewarding honor came from his old high school, in appreciation for his contributions to the community. He was asked to give a commencement address to the senior graduating class of his old alma mater. He chose the theme of his presentation "You Can Make a Difference."His message was simply, "It's not what you do in life, it's how you do it." He implored them to take that next step because you don't have to be a star to make a difference in people's lives. You don't have to be something special to create new ideas or improve the lives of others. He implored them to take that next step and "Not to just think about it, don't just talk about it, just do it, because you can make a difference!" He took his ideas, his criteria for success and set his goals and just did it. He tried to make a difference. There were many people who contributed to the successful implementation of his dream for a high quality, high tech, community based neuroscience program to the southern tier of New York State. He expresses his gratitude and thanks.

Epilogue

These life stories are the pride and hope of America and were made possible because of free market capitalism.It is people like these entrepreneurs who had the vision, determination and intelligence to succeed and provide products or services to create jobs and make all our lives better. It is freedom that has allowed these people to start a small business and achieve The American Dream.

With all the laws and regulations today, it sometimes seems that almost everything is either mandated or prohibited by law. Many successful entrepreneurs will tell you that their success could not be duplicated today, because of too many laws and regulations. In 2013, the federal government created 3,531 new regulations which resulted in over 77,000 pages of law. For 2014, there are over 4,000 new regulations in the federal pipeline. These laws and regulations make entry into the market very difficult and some simply give up. Many of these regulations are encouraged by existing businesses to keep out competition. Competition forces everyone to be more efficient which keeps prices lower. If existing businesses can keep out competition or make the cost of entry into the market more costly, it allows them to operate less efficiently and increases their profit margins. However, this is not good for consumers.

Bernard Marcus, who started Home Depot in 1978, recently said he could not have achieved the same level of success with the taxes and regulations we have today. Tom Stemberg, who founded Staples in 1985, echoed those comments. For over a decade, *The Wall Street Journal* and

The Heritage Foundation, Washington's preeminent think tank, have tracked the march of economic freedom around the world with the influential Index of Economic Freedom. Ten benchmarks are used to gauge the economic success of 185 countries around the world. The United States ranks 10th on the list for 2013 with Hong Kong and Singapore at numbers one and two, respectively.Nations that rank the highest generally are the richest, and as one proceeds down the list, the nations are progressively poorer.

Many regulations are not to protect the public, but rather to restrict competition. An example of this is in New York City where if someone wants to go into the taxi business they must first purchase a "medallion," a license from the City, at a cost of $1 million. This restricts competition by keeping out small businesses, resulting in higher prices and less service to consumers. Who wants to keep out competition? The people and companies that are already in business want to restrict competition, because this allows them to keep prices high and services low. Government is the problem.

One of our biggest problems is "crony capitalism" where government helps certain businesses at the expense of the others. There was a 12 year-old girl on TV recently who was selling cupcakes for $2 each. The local newspaper wrote a story about how she was doing so well and was saving the money for her college education. This publicity resulted in a visit the next day by the local health department. They put her out of business, because she was baking in her mother's kitchen. They told her this was not allowed.

John Stossel wrote in his book "Give Me a Break" about several examples of government destroying small businesses and killing their American Dream. He tells how government regulators, acting on behalf of existing businesses, made it difficult for others to enter the market. A thriving African hair-braiding business called Cornrows & Company in Washington, D.C., which had 20,000 customers and employed 10 people, braided hair for people as far away as Connecticut, a six hour trip. He thought such a success story of black people creating jobs in the inner city would thrill politicians, but instead the bureaucrats closed them down because they didn't have a license.

The bureaucrats said it was a safety issue because the chemicals they used to dye and perm hair could hurt someone. Stossel continues that hair dye and giving perms is hardly a safety threat, but even if it were Cornrows didn't even do that—they only braided hair. The bureaucrats said that didn't matter and still required the company to get a license. In order to get a license it would be necessary that they spend about $5,000 to get 1,000 hours of training at a beauty school. The strange thing about that is the beauty school didn't even teach hair braiding. It was suspected that other beauticians didn't like the competition so they put pressure on the government to shut Cornrows down enabling them to charge more. The consumers lost.

It is amazing that the bigger our government becomes, the more we are told that just a little more government will solve the problem. More government is a lot like a sink-hole which keeps getting bigger while causing more and more damage. As Ronald Reagan said, "Government isn't the solution; it is the problem." I read recently about bureaucrats closing down a boy's lemonade stand in his own front yard, because he didn't have the proper permit.

We now have a President who says that "If you have a business, you didn't build that—somebody else made that happen." His claim seems to be based on the fact that without a highway system built with taxpayer dollars and other such government projects that a business could not be successful. Don't you believe him; if you have a small business, then you did make it happen. Most businesses are successful in spite of the government, not because of it.

Certainly some regulation of business is needed such as laws that prohibit monopolies and other bad business practices. However, we should do a "cost benefit analysis" to weigh the cost of the regulations in comparison to the benefits or in some cases the harm that they cause. Ronald Reagan said that his opponents have a philosophy of business that "f it moves, tax it; if it keeps moving, regulate it; and if it quits moving, subsidize it." Most regulations were demanded by voters to improve the environment, public safety or fraud. Television reporter John Stossel, once a liberal, became influential because of his consumer reporting and won over 30 Emmy Awards. He was even successful in getting laws and regulations enacted to protect consumers. However, he soon found out that the new laws and regulations often made the situation even worse. He says the laws and regulations always drove up the cost of business resulting in higher prices and government has a way of punishing everyone for the errors of a few. For the most part, free enterprise does a better job of punishing bad businesses than government.

Everyone seems to agree that we need more jobs in this country, yet our government unknowingly does almost everything possible to destroy jobs. Often this results in moving jobs to other countries where the business climate is better and taxes are lower. We keep putting more and more burdens on businesses, which discourage them from creating jobs and actually encourage business to cut jobs. We need to rethink what we are doing to employers. We should make it easier for employers to employ, not harder. Government needs to get off the backs of employers. It appears to me that government bureaucrats look upon business as the enemy and keep strangling business with more and more burdensome regulations. This needs to stop. We are in danger of "killing the goose that lays golden eggs."

Many businesses have reduced their full-time employees so they will not come under Affordable Care Act (ACA) (Obamacare). The Washington Times reported that 7/8 of the jobs created during the first 4.5 years of the Obama Administration are part-time jobs and only 270,000 full-time jobs have been created as of August 31, 2013. The future is so uncertain that they are just trying to maintain their businesses and be ready for growth when this country starts appreciating the free market once again.

Governments at all levels have felt the need to grow when asked by certain citizens to provide more services. Few would disagree that there is a need for government at the local, state and federal levels, but it has gotten out of hand. Politicians found that they could get elected by promising more and more services to their constituents. Certainly building roads, bridges, schools, police and fire protection and national defense are necessary expenditures by government, but governments at all levels have gone way beyond that. The free market can and does police itself and certainly does a better job than government which does nothing efficiently. The free market is the best way to provide the best product and/or service at the lowest possible price.

Ronald Reagan said, "A government big enough to give you everything you want is big enough to take away everything you've got." Traditionally we were a society of self reliance and personal freedom. Our founders knew about the evils of big government and came to this country to escape its tyranny. Today our government tries to protect us from everybody and everything and is smothering free enterprise. Laws and regulations such as the Minimum Wage Law, Americans with Disabilities Act, OSHA, EPA, ObamaCare, Family Leave and others drive up costs and discourage business. In addition, unions drive up wages and demand work rules that, together with the aforementioned laws and regulations, make it very difficult to be competitive internationally.

What makes the government think it knows more than the free market and the law of supply and demand? Our elected government representatives buy votes with taxpayer money and promise more and more unearned benefits. We all know what happens when we subsidize something—we get more of it. When we subsidize people who fail by giving them government money, which was earned as a result of the sweat of taxpayers, we are only encouraging more failure. Instead of subsidizing failure we should discourage it. Giving handouts to people is not big-hearted – it is just plain stupid. Subsidizing the failure of business or government is just as bad as subsidizing the failure of people. When a business fails and files for bankruptcy the stockholders and creditors must pay the consequences. The government must not give preference to one person or group over another. The failure of a business actually gleans the economy of the inefficient and makes the overall economy healthier and more competitive.

Recently we were told by this Administration that we need to extend unemployment benefits for another 90 days. Nancy Peloi tells us that for each $1 we put into unemployment compensation, there is $1.80 increase in economic activity, because of the multiplier effect and that unemployment compensation creates jobs. I actually saw and heard our President say that extending unemployment compensation creates jobs.Of course, this is the same man who told us, "If you like your doctor you can keep your doctor, period. If you like your insurance plan you can keep your insurance plan, period.The average family will save $2,500 with Obamacare, period."My dad used to say, "Figures don't lie, but liars can figure." It just seems like we can't believe much that comes out of this Administration today.

We are heading for financial collapse. Already we have cities as large as Detroit filing for bankruptcy and this is only the tip of the iceberg. Many other cities and counties have also recently filed for bankruptcy and Chicago is in big financial trouble. Many states including California and Illinois are close to insolvency. In Illinois, most of the governors of the last 60 years have ended up serving time in prison, because of graft in their administrations. These giveaway programs by governments at all levels can't be sustained. People must be more responsible for themselves and not depend on government to care for them from cradle to grave.

Government always claims it is working for us, but we know that is not true. If you don't believe me, then just talk to a government employee and you will be convinced. They almost all act like they are the boss and we work for them. Look at the hours they keep. They work from 9-5 Monday through Friday. They should be open on Saturdays and/or Sundays like grocery stores, retail stores and the rest of free enterprise which really does exist to serve us. Even our local library is closed on Sundays.All government offices should be open hours for the convenience of the people who pay their salaries.

Thomas Jefferson said, "When government fears the people there is liberty, but when the people fear government there is tyranny." Before the states would ratify the Constitution they insisted on the Bill of Rights which is the first 10 amendments to the Constitution. Our founders were fearful of the excesses of big government after having lived under the rule of the King of England. The Bill of Rights provided for civil rights and was to protect the people from government. It provided for the rights of free speech, freedom of religion, freedom of the press, the right to keep and bear arms, prohibited unwarranted searches and seizures and demanded fair and speedy trials. Article IX, means that the Federal Government only has those powers specifically enumerated in the Constitution. Our Founders would be very disappointed with the big government we have today.

Margaret Thatcher said, "Socialism works great until you run out of other peoples' money." It has been said that capitalism is the worst economic system ever invented except for all the rest. If we are to save this once great nation then we need to restrict big government and put power in the hands of the people by expanding freedom. Those nations with the greatest economic freedom and least laws and regulations are also the richest and most productive nations creating the greatest standard of living for their people. If we really want to help our citizens improve their standard of living then we need to allow more freedom.

My sisters and I often talk about the "good old days." We are disappointed that the kids today will never experience true freedom. Since they don't know true freedom and are not taught how lucky we are to be native born Americans, they take it for granted.. Schools no longer teach about how the Founders escaped big government to come here for real freedom and fought several wars in order to remain free. We have so many laws and regulations today that we are no longer truly free. The restraints on free enterprise discourage all but the most determined from starting a new business. We are hopeful that cooler heads will prevail and that soon people will once again realize that "government that governs least, governs best."

Ronald Reagan said, "Freedom is a fragile thing and is never more than one generation away from extinction. It is not ours by inheritance; it must be fought for and defended constantly by each generation, for it comes only once to a people. Those who have known freedom and then lost it have never known it again." Daniel Webster said "God grants liberty only to those who love it and are always ready to guard and defend it."

William Nickerson wrote a book entitled, "How I Turned $1000 into $5 Million in Real Estate," which was a very inspirational story about what gave him his plan to succeed. He and his wife were working their way through Fresno State College during the Great Depression when one of his friends told him, "The most you can look forward to is Social Security, and if you're lucky, a small company pension." His economics professor advised the class, "You might as well realize the time for opportunity is past. The best you can hope for is to keep a steady job and stay off welfare. Nobody will ever again be able to build an estate big enough to produce an independent income." Every generation has its pessimists, but our free enterprise system is hard to beat. Although the politicians inadvertently seem to do almost everything to destroy our economy, the free enterprise system just refuses to give up. People will fight for freedom and they can still better themselves and even obtain financial independence through free enterprise, in spite of the government.I've heard it said that "it is always the darkest before the dawn." I believe in America and that cooler heads will eventually prevail and we will become that "shining city on a hill."

About the Author

Bob Russell was born in 1942 and raised on a farm in northern Illinois. He got the idea of being an entrepreneur and retiring early when he had a pig project in 4-H while he was only 10 years old. Forced to keep financial records on his pig project, he was surprised to find he made a profit. He quickly realized that if he had 100 pigs and then 1000 pigs he could make 100 or even 1000 times more. This began his quest of achieving financial independence through free market capitalism. While in college he read a book entitled "How I Turned $1000 into $1 Million in Real Estate" by William Nickerson which helped form his plan to achieve his goal of achieving THE AMERICAN DREAM.

He served in Vietnam as a sergeant in the US Army Artillery. He received an undergraduate degree from North-eastern Illinois University and a graduate degree from the University of Oklahoma. He spent his entire career as a banker in Rockford, Illinois, retiring as VP of commercial loans at AMCORE Bank in 1994 at the age of 51. After retirement, he volunteered as a basketball coach for a few years and also volunteered with an organization called SCORE in which he counseled businesses and helped them write business plans. During his career, he was also an entrepreneur in his spare time, owning apartment buildings and a commercial strip center as well as being part-owner of several waterbed stores in Illinois and Wisconsin.

Of all his accomplishments he is most proud of his daughter, Jill Russell Wheelock, who serves as Marketing Director for a bank in Rockford, Illinois. She is his pride and joy and has made him proud every day of her life. She is married to a great guy named Brad Wheelock who is very successful in the heating and air conditioning industry. They are expecting their first child on October 25, 2014. He is very excited that he will soon have a granddaughter.

Since 1999 he has lived in a gated golf course community in Florida where he plays golf, tennis and bridge six days per week. While pursuing these endeavors he has met and become friends with many entrepreneurs whose inspirational life stories of success were actually the inspiration for this book. These people all achieved financial success and THE AMERICAN DREAM through free market capitalism.

Made in the USA
Lexington, KY
10 November 2014